Redeemed Bodies

Women Martyrs in Early Christianity

Gail P. C. Streete

T0204817

WESTMINSTER
JOHN KNOX PRESS
LOUISVILLE · KENTUCKY

© 2009 Gail P. C. Streete

1st edition
Published by Westminster John Knox Press
Louisville, Kentucky

09 10 11 12 13 14 15 16 17 18—10 9 8 7 6 5 4 3 2 1

Unless otherwise indicated, Scripture quotations are from the New Revised Standard Version of the Bible, are copyright © 1989 by the Division of Christian Education of the National Council of the Churches of Christ in the U.S.A., and are used by permission.

Book design by Drew Stevens
Cover design by Night & Day Design
Cover illustration: Three Lions/Getty Images

Library of Congress Cataloging-in-Publication Data

Streete, Gail Corrington.
    Redeemed bodies : women martyrs in early Christianity / Gail P. C. Streete.
        p. cm.
    Includes bibliographical references (p.   ) and index.
    ISBN 978-0-664-23329-7 (alk. paper)
    1. Christian women martyrs—Rome—History.   2. Passio SS. Perpetuae et Felicitatis.
3. Perpetua, Saint, d. 203.   4. Felicity, Saint, d. 203.   5. Acts of Paul and Thecla.
6. Thecla, Saint.   I. Title.
    BR1604.23.S76 2009
    272'.1082—dc22

                                                                2009001912

PRINTED IN THE UNITED STATES OF AMERICA

♾ The paper used in this publication meets the minimum requirements of the American National Standard for Information Sciences—Permanence of Paper for Printed Library Materials, ANSI Z39.48-1992.

Westminster John Knox Press advocates the responsible use of our natural resources. The text paper of this book is made from 30% postconsumer waste.

To my sister, Wendy, *une femme formidable*

Contents

Preface

In many ways, this has been a difficult book to write. One aspect of the difficulty of writing was the growing abundance of material on Perpetua and Thecla, to which I have contributed in some measure. Consequently, while this book aims at being as inclusive as possible, it does not strive at being comprehensive. Rather, I offer it as a series of reflections on the figures of these early Christian female martyrs, together with a conversation about them with various scholars—some of whom have come to similar conclusions, and others of whom have provoked and challenged me to come to different conclusions.

Another aspect of the difficulty is perhaps contextual and might be more of a fascination: raised in a low-church Protestant tradition, I did not have acquaintance with saints, let alone martyr-saints (with the possible exception of Stephen). I did not encounter the Old Testament Apocrypha until college; the New Testament Apocrypha was only opened to me in graduate school; Perpetua and her like remained likewise unknown until then. Many of the audiences with which I have shared my reflections are similarly unacquainted with either Perpetua or Thecla, and so I have needed to start out by simply telling (or retelling) their stories. This book starts at the same place. I also had to acquire a different language and sensibility to different meanings other than purely intellectual ones, the ones to which I was most accustomed. In my first chapter I try to convey some of the excitement this acquisition presented.

Martyrs, while presenting an interesting phenomenon to the historian or scholar of culture, have another dimension, a visceral one, for those who admire them and find them meaningful. This conclusion leads me to another, perhaps the greatest difficulty in writing this book. Reading extensively about the torture, death, and dismemberment of female bodies has been a task that I believed to be necessary but one that has taken more of an emotional and even a physical toll than I had expected. At times I felt myself struggling to say things that would not surface for a long time; at other times, I felt connections that others had also made, and I feared I would never have enough time or space to acknowledge adequately the many serious studies that have been made of martyr literature, let alone literature that is as closely confined in topic as the subjects of this book. I invite the reader to consult the bibliography for readings that I have found instructive. Still more problematic to me was the feeling that what I had to say and believed was necessary to say, particularly in the last chapter, comparing the Columbine martyrs and female suicide attackers, would wound or offend readers and friends. But these are my impressions and conclusions, and I must own them.

As always, there are many people, not only other members of the profession, who have contributed to my thoughts and reflections that have found their way into this book. First among these are my students at Rhodes College, particularly in my first-year Humanities classes, in which we have read, discussed, and reacted to *The Martyrdom of Perpetua and Felicitas* and *The Acts of Paul and Thecla*, in encounters that for them are always new and for me instructive. I thank my classes in Apocryphal New Testament for letting me try out my "divine woman" theories with them and, I think, convincing some of them. I also would like to thank my classes in "Sex and Gender in the New Testament" and my two sections of "The Redeemed Body: Martyrdom and Asceticism in Early Christianity" for their serious attention, consideration, and advancement of my thoughts about how religious ideas are so often written on bodies, particularly those of women. I thank them also for their own thoughtful contributions. The adult education class at Calvary Episcopal Church in Memphis was a wonderful immediate venue for sharing some of the ideas that appear in this book, and I thank Adam de Nobriga and George Yandell for inviting me.

As I write these words, I have just returned from a few days at the beach with some members of my extended family, grateful for those moments of companionship, peace, and relative tranquility, and especially grateful that neither of my two oldest stepgranddaughters, accomplished as they are, have heard of or know the martyrs of whom I write. There is time for that disturbing word later on. I hope that neither they nor any of my grandchildren will ever be on the front lines of an ongoing war in which women's bodies—even with their own apparent consent—are used by others to make political and religious statements.

I thank my husband, Jack, and my Memphis family and friends for understanding that writing is working and that I would not be available for many activities while I was doing it. And finally, thanks to Laika and Sonya for understanding about limits on their walkies.

Memphis, Tennessee, 2008

Abbreviations

AJA	*American Journal of Archaeology*
ANF	*Ante-Nicene Fathers*
AThR	*Anglican Theological Review*
BibInt	*Biblical Interpretation*
BMCR	*Bryn Mawr Classical Review*
CBQ	*Catholic Biblical Quarterly*
CH	*Church History*
Cont	*Continuum*
DOP	*Dumbarton Oaks Papers*
DRev	*Downside Review*
ET	English translation
HDR	Harvard Dissertations in Religion
HTR	*Harvard Theological Review*
JAAR	*Journal of the American Academy of Religion*
JECS	*Journal of Early Christian Studies*
JFSR	*Journal of Feminist Studies in Religion*
JR	*Journal of Religion*
JRelS	*Journal of Religious Studies*
JTS	*Journal of Theological Studies*
LCL	Loeb Classical Library
LSJ	Liddell, H. G., R. Scott, and H. S. Jones. *A Greek-English Lexicon*. 9th ed. with revised supplement. Oxford, 1996.
LTQ	*Lexington Theological Quarterly*
Musurillo	Musurillo, Herbert, ed. and trans. *The Acts of the Christian Martyrs*. Oxford, 1972.
NPNF[1]	*Nicene and Post-Nicene Fathers*. Series 1
NPNF[2]	*Nicene and Post-Nicene Fathers*. Series 2
OCT	Oxford Classical Texts
PG	Patrologia graeca [= Patrologiae cursus completus: Series graeca]. Edited by J.-P. Migne. 162 vols. Paris, 1857–1886.

PL   Patrologia latina [= Patrologiae cursus completus:
              Series latina]. Edited by J.-P. Migne. 217 vols. Paris,
              1844–1864.
PRSt   *Perspectives in Religious Studies*
RBL   *Review of Biblical Literature*
SBL   Society of Biblical Literature
SBLDS   Society of Biblical Literature Dissertation Series
SBLEJL   Society of Biblical Literature Early Judaism and Its
              Literature
SBLSCS   Society of Biblical Literature Septuagint and Cognate
              Studies
SC   Sources chrétiennes. Paris: Cerf, 1943–
StPatr   Studia Patristica
VC   *Vigiliae christianae*
WLGR   Mary R. Lefkowitz and Maureen B. Fant, eds. *Women's
              Life in Greece and Rome*. 2nd ed. Baltimore: Johns
              Hopkins University Press, 1992.

1

The Power of Bodies

> We are . . . always carrying in the body the death of Jesus, so that the life
> of Jesus may also be made visible in our bodies.
>   —2 Corinthians 4:8, 10

WHY PERPETUA AND THECLA?

The stories of the early Christian martyrs Perpetua and Thecla represent two modes of women's spiritual empowerment: the first through martyrdom, the second through asceticism described in the language of martyrdom. Both are ways of constructing an identity through the body as an element in space and time, but not as a purely physical being. They each also demonstrate the ambiguous value of these routes to authority and their relationship to definitions of "maleness" and "femaleness," sexuality, spirit, and the body in Christian life. The shaping of their stories responded to specific needs within developing Christianity, functioning as models of and for female authority, spiritual and institutional, in ways that still have resonance for us as inheritors of that developed identity. Even now we "read" these stories in the ways we need to read them. Some, for example, have read them as struggles about gender and authority that reflect ongoing struggles in the leadership of Christian churches; others, as ways to interpret their own spiritual or historical identities. My aim is to discover, first and primarily, how their earliest "readers" read them or audiences heard them. Scholars certainly know enough now about historical criticism to neglect it at our peril. Yet we must also be aware that few people read and interpret stories like this in a historical-critical manner. In fact, the first question of scholarship must

1

always be Why does this matter? The second question should always be To whom?

I know why Perpetua and Thecla have mattered to me, for more than twenty years now. I see their great luminous eyes, depicted in Byzantine mosaics and icons, looking calmly and preternaturally beyond "this slight momentary affliction" (2 Cor. 4:17), having become the saints required by the memory and the need of emerging Christianity. But for them, and for their more shadowy sisters like Felicitas, Maximilla, Blandina, Agnes, and the many other heroines of early Christian lore, legend, and literature, what was that "affliction"? Certainly it was not merely the torture through which their bodies became inscribed as "witnesses" to the steadfastness of their conviction, their *pistis*, or faith. Taken in the Pauline sense, their affliction was no less than their physical existence and its constraints. Ironically, in the very act of transcending physical and social limits, their bodies are caught, reembodied in and by texts, through their own writing (in Perpetua's probable case) and through writing about them, and in artifacts that are material commemorations of their physical bodies and deeds—thus in the rewitnessing of those who lived and died. As the writer of the Epistle to the Hebrews put it, the early Christians were surrounded by a growing "cloud of witnesses" (*martyres*, 12:1), which they in turn constantly beheld, as the image of the cloud implies, in shifting images that suited the growth and evolution of the faith. Perpetua (*The Martyrdom of Perpetua and Felicitas*) and Thecla (*The Acts of Paul and Thecla*; *The Life and Miracles of the Blessed Thecla*) are preeminently symbols of the ways in which early Christian bodies that are both a "sight" (spectacle) and a "site" (a location with which to be in touch as a symbol and a referent).

I remember when I first encountered each of these women, and what discovering these stories meant and still means to me and many others in the understanding of scholarly and personal identity. They had an impact on me so strong that no one who has ever been a student of mine will be able to avoid reading *The Martyrdom of Perpetua and Felicitas* or the *Acts of Paul and Thecla* at least once or possibly two or three times before he or she graduates. When I was writing my dissertation[1] in the early 1980s, my adviser suggested that I look beyond the canon for important information on emerging Christianity, and I thus became acquainted with the strange and colorful world of the apocryphal acts of the apostles. At the time, since I was only looking for models of Jesus and his (male) disciples, I initially glossed over the presence and meaning of the female characters.

Yet I was amazed and continued to be fascinated by this material, which I had never encountered before. These Christian popular novels of the second to fourth centuries contained tales of miracle-working holy men *and* women, both of whose power was derived from their celibate Christianity. Their bodies, sealed off symbolically but powerfully by the "seal" of baptism (*APTh* 6.14, e.g.) from all assaults of the brutal pagan society in which they found themselves, had essentially become replicas of the resurrected body of Christ himself, transcending their constraining flesh, centers of divine authority that superseded that of the dominant political and social realms. Although the male apostles, as heirs of Jesus' authority, and "divine men" themselves[2] served as the initiating figures and focus for these apocryphal acts, it soon became apparent to me, as well as to other readers, that their female converts frequently achieved a status equal to, if not on occasion superseding, that of the male apostles. Such was the case in the *Acts of John* with the converted and chaste Drusiana being able to raise the scheming slave Fortunatus from the dead; in the *Acts of Peter* (*Actus Vercellenses*) with the concubines Agrippina, Nicaria, Euphemia, and Doris, who "survive every injury" inflicted by their erstwhile master Agrippa; in the *Acts of Andrew*, where Maximilla steadfastly resists her husband Aegeates's sexual advances and becomes the leader of a new community after the death of the apostle Andrew and Aegeates's subsequent suicide; and in the *Acts of Thomas*, where the noble Mygdonia flees from her husband, Charisius, and survives prison, later anointing and baptizing women in the name of Christ.

But the power of the celibate female convert was clearest in the *Acts of Paul and Thecla*. There the heroic protagonist and focus of the story most definitely is not the apostle Paul (who ironically and often cravenly keeps avoiding his new female convert, despite her constant peril) but "the noble virgin of Iconium," Thecla, who renounces marriage and family in order to live a resolutely ascetic life that she deems "pure." She survives burning at the stake, attempted rape, spurning and testing by her teacher Paul, and nearly being annihilated by a number of beasts in Antioch, until she not only baptizes herself but also prays her benefactress Tryphaena's dead daughter into a better place and finally achieves commissioning as an apostle by the reluctant Paul to die peacefully back in Iconium. In a later, longer version of the story, Pseudo-Basil's *The Life and Miracles of St. Thecla*, she travels to Seleucia, teaching and performing miracles until the last assault on her chastity by men jealous of her healing and consulting powers causes God to enclose the doughty virgin in a rock, where her presence ensures the performance of still more miracles.[3] An anonymous writer, frequently identified as Tertullian, later observed of an equally impressive woman, Perpetua, "What a woman! [*Tanta femina*]" (*Martyrdom of Perpetua and Felicitas* 21.10). Thecla and her apocryphal sisters, as might be imagined, gave me a lot of ammunition, and like many others, I later attempted to reconstruct, if not a "usable past"[4] in the sense of a provably accurate history, at least an inspiring model.

DIVINE WOMEN

Criticism of feminist interpretations of such stories, particularly that of Thecla, have emerged in recent years, often counterbalancing the continued feminist interest in them. Jan Bremmer has provided a brief description of this interest, which began about the time of my interest in the apocryphal acts, in the 1980s. He also points out that by the "end of the decade, a reaction set in."[5] We should be appropriately cautious, heeding Elizabeth A. Clark's carefully reasoned suggestion about laudatory tales of early Christian ascetic women, that as literary "traces" of holy women and their words they are "embedded" (one might also say "embodied") in "a larger social-linguistic framework and reflected through male eyes." Yet it is also true that these stories do appear to construct a type of "holy woman" that is not the exact equivalent of the holy man but a potent and interesting parallel.[6]

Reading these stories, I developed a theory about the characteristics of these women with holy power, calling them "divine women" (*theai gynaikes*), a feminine version of the *theoi andres*, or divine men, the constructed ideal woman of second century and later Christian encratite circles that depicted celibate women as having miraculous power equal to that of the apostolic celibate "divine men."[7] Peter Brown's study *Society and the Holy in Late Antiquity* (1981), to which Clark refers, noted that the miracle-working powers of the ascetic holy man, living on the fringes of settled society, were often (to his mind, wrongly) associated with those of "divine men," among them the apostles, because of their ability to dedicate themselves to God wholly, mind and body, in sexually abstinent devotion, exercising their powers *outside* of society.[8] Originally, I cataloged the miracles associated with these women as the result of divine power given to them because of their conversion to celibate Christianity of the type that the male apostles had modeled, textually demonstrating divine approval of their choice of this way of living (*bios*).[9] Interestingly, unlike the martyrs, these apocryphal women did not die violently, although they frequently found themselves in threatened circumstances, where, if these had not been tales for the sake of edifying propaganda, they would have died—nobly—but died nevertheless. (The chaste Drusiana, in the *Acts of John*, actually does die and then is raised from the dead; 79–80.) Nevertheless, their bodily dedication to God through Christ was total, in the sense that like the ascetic holy men, they literally enacted Paul's maxim that those who did not marry could concentrate their attention totally on "the things of the Lord" and his imminent coming (1 Cor. 7:32–35). I also was convinced by Virginia Burrus's argument that these "Christian chastity stories" created the model for women's "triumphant attainment of singleness" that meant female autonomy on a par with that of men and escape from male control.[10]

Because of my giddy excitement about these women's power, however, I neglected to notice its source and how it was transmitted. Instead of the power to work miracles coming *through* the women, as through the men, miraculous power was used to *rescue* women from situations that threatened assault on their bodily integrity and therefore their resolve for Christian chastity. My analysis of the roles of women and their relationship to authority in the apocryphal acts showed me that their authoritative behavior resulted in the *direct* working of miracles by women only twice: Drusiana in the *Acts of John* raises Fortunatus from the dead; the unnamed "virgin" of the *Acts of Andrew* I (Pap. Copt. Utrecht) is able to cast a demon out of her brother through prayer. Authoritative ecclesiastical behavior by these divinely empowered women was exercised in terms of Christian leadership roles only twice: Thecla preaches and teaches, but with the sanction of the apostle Paul, although she does baptize herself, an important act not lost on other Christian women who knew her story; the sexually abstinent Mygdonia in the *Acts of Thomas* anoints and baptizes *other women*, but only with the sanction of the apostle Andrew. Only in the fifth-century extended version of Thecla's story, *The Life and Miracles of the Blessed Thecla*, does Thecla as apostle, martyr, and saint perform miracles solo, and only because she is alive in spirit but invisible in flesh. The women portrayed in the apocryphal acts did not so much reject "the roles imposed on them by [the] social order" as to adopt "an ideal that men had originally chosen and promoted for themselves."[11] In other words, they are portrayed as "becoming men."

It was also in the ebullient days of emerging feminist scholarship in the 1980s that I became acquainted with the story of Perpetua, via Patricia Wilson-Kastner's *A Lost Tradition: Women Writers of the Early Church* (1981). Vibia Perpetua, a twenty-two-year-old Roman noblewoman with a nursing son, is arrested with a number of other Christians, including the slave woman Felicitas, who is eight months pregnant. Tried before the Roman proconsul, Perpetua refuses to renounce her Christianity, even when her father continually tries to persuade her on familial and social grounds to do so. She is condemned with the others *ad bestias*, to fight and be killed by the beasts in the arena, as part of a "show" for the future emperor Geta's birthday. Imprisoned, she at first fears for her son's health, but later when he is taken away by her father, she is quite serene, believing it is God's will. While in prison, she experiences four visions, one in response to a request by a Christian brother, in which she climbs a ladder into heaven and sees God as a kindly old shepherd; one in which she sees a dead brother suffering; one in which she sees him relieved from that suffering by her prayers; and the final one, before she goes into the arena, in which she becomes a male gladiator and symbolically defeats the devil. Her sister martyr Felicitas, in answer to prayer, gives birth prematurely to a baby girl, who is taken to be raised by another Christian. Both women bravely face their deaths in the arena with their fellow Christians, Perpetua especially nobly, guiding the sword of the trembling soldier sent to kill her—to her own throat.

Here I found myself initially on less contested ground than that of the apocryphal acts:[12] the martyrdom itself could be fairly reliably dated to the early third century (203 CE), and there was every reason to believe that the section of *The Martyrdom of Perpetua and Felicitas* attributed to its heroine, Vibia Perpetua, the so-called "prison diary" recording her arrest, trial, and imprisonment along with her remarkable "visions" or dreams, up until the point when she is going to be led into the arena to die, was in fact written by her.[13] In addition, she is a major character in a vision or dream by a male fellow prisoner, Saturus (*MPF* 11–13). Sometimes, however, it seemed as though Perpetua's story became lost in the growing interest in what was perhaps the more feminist story of Thecla. Thecla, after all, does not die; she gets to be an apostle. Perpetua, on the other hand, gets to be a figure of importance literally in her dreams and has to die in order to have her story told.

Yet one might wonder whether there is any continued relevance in these stories of women whose bodies perished, if not their significance, before Christianity became first a legal religion and then *the* religion of the Roman Empire in the fourth century. In 2002, European authors Jan Willem van Henten and Friedrich Avemarie published a book called *Martyrdom and Noble Death*, in which they claimed, "Ostentatious forms of violent death hardly fit in with modern views of life."[14] They mentioned the self-cremation of members of Falun-Gong in Beijing, of Jan Palach in Prague during the Russian domination of Czechoslovakia, of Buddhist monks in Vietnam during the war there. But it seems as though they were ignoring events that had occurred before the publication of their book and that were occurring at the same time and after it was published. One might wonder why Chechen, Tamil, Iraqi, and Palestinian suicide attackers, all of whom demonstrate in the present time "ostentatious forms of violent death," are not mentioned. Significantly, Bremmer, who has frequently published on ancient religion and particularly on Perpetua, has seen a connection between the Palestinian women who are regarded as martyr-heroines and Perpetua.[15] On the other hand, J. K. Elliott's review of the *Feminist Companion to the New Testament Apocrypha* (2006) asserted that many of the articles, including my "Buying the Stairway to Heaven," that found resonances of the tales of Perpetua and Thecla within the stories of the "martyrs" of Columbine High School, which he called "references to an event in Colorado in 1999," had a limited appeal, perhaps to North American audiences only.[16] Nonetheless, the interpretation of that event, particularly of the death of two victims of the Columbine shooting, Cassie Bernall and Rachel Scott, who both supposedly confessed to their faith in God and were subsequently shot, has become so enshrined in evangelical American Christian legend that it inspired Elizabeth Castelli to write her intriguing study *Martyrdom and Memory* (2005), a study that made the "unexpected move, connecting early Christian culture making in relation to martyrdom with contemporary Christian commemorative practices organized around the figure of 'the martyr.'"[17] These stories, as will be seen, are less concerned with historical accuracy than in representing the church as embattled and persecuted, through new martyrologies and new relics that once again include female heroines as confessing Christians, anti-Christian opponents, and a significant emphasis on the women's sexual purity as a marker of dedication to God and marriage to Christ.[18]

The recasting of the Columbine tragedy of 1999 as a martyrdom with deliberate reference to the early Christian martyrs has some unexpected common threads with the stories of Palestinian female suicide attackers, who are spoken of and who saw themselves as martyrs, the product of a culture of martyrdom that also sees itself embattled, and that envisions women's bodies, like women themselves, as private entities that are uncharacteristically and spectacularly annihilated for a potent cause. Castelli notes that Americans resist understanding suicide attackers, particularly after 9/11, as they portray themselves: that is, as "martyrs." The reluctance to interpret self-immolation in the cause of killing others as "martyrdom" is the end product of seeing one kind of self-sacrifice as noble while another as reprehensible, even though the rhetoric of martyrdom comes from similar roots. In short, we allow ourselves to interpret a "martyr" only in terms of our own cultural understanding. And we often do not see the "embedded danger" in the idealization of "pain with achievement."[19] I think this observation provides one explanation of why—for the last ten years, as long as *The Martyrdom of Perpetua and Felicitas* has been, largely at my urging, in the "canon" of readings for Rhodes College's first-year humanities course—my students, especially the women, have never found the figure of Perpetua admirable. They find repugnant her willingness to sacrifice not only her own life but also her eventual indifference to the fate of her living family, especially her infant and dependent son. They have seen her as different in degree, but not in kind, from female suicide attackers, and sometimes, ironically, less understandable, because they read her story as that of one who has a real choice *not* to die.

In fact, it might be said that in recent years the revived interest in the figures of Perpetua and Thecla, manifested in a spate of literature on both,[20] serves to contradict Van Henten and Avemarie's assertion about violent death not fitting modern life, suggesting that there may be ways of understanding what seems anomalous in the present, by linking the present to a past, admittedly idealized, in a way that continues to give meaning to both. All of these works indicate growing interest in these figures as intriguing and highly debated parts of a neglected but potentially retrievable past for women, especially as leaders in the Christian churches. Continuing to find meaning in the stories of Perpetua and Thecla has taken interpreters on some very different and often contested paths and reflects the difference in the very first interpretations of their stories, which, as Francine Cardman notes, were manipulated "to serve new interests."[21] Particularly important in this respect is the suggestion of and resistance to the question of gender. On the one hand, the suggestion of a "gendered" reading of texts whose major figures are female in a time when women were not usually portrayed as protagonists is irresistible, as is asking why there appears to be an emphasis on the gendered bodies of these women. On the other, when reviewer Linda Honey asserts that Scott Fitzgerald Johnson's literary study of Pseudo-Basil's *The Life and Miracles of Thekla* "makes the welcome observation that the *LM* [*Life and Miracles*] is not a gendered text," we must ask why this is "welcome."[22] Is it problematic for us to read of this text as gendered? Do our present notions of gender assume something quite different from what the ancients supposed—always a possibility, if not a probability? And why, ultimately, and to whom do such distinctions matter?

And yet a certain amount of caution is necessary, in order to avoid the besetting sin of what Carol Meyers has called "present-mindedness" or "presentism."[23] When I first discovered Thecla and the other women of the apocryphal acts of the apostles, as an excited feminist scholar, I did have an inclination to overemphasize their asexual independence and power. For example, even after several readings of the standard text of the *Acts of Paul and Thecla*,[24] I had totally failed to note the fairly erotic scene in which Thecla rolls on the ground of the prison in the place where the absent Paul had sat (20) and skipped over the implications of her "kissing his chains" (18). Although it would be difficult to romanticize the martyrdom of Perpetua or that of her companion Felicitas, it nevertheless took my own students to shock me into a realization of how *The Martyrdom of Perpetua and Felicitas*—especially the "prison diary" of Perpetua—could be read as repellent rather than inspiring, even by those who were touched by contemporary versions of martyrdom such as those of Columbine High School. It must be noted, however, that this current year's students (2007–8) presented a total reversal of what had been a near-universal opinion for over a decade: when given a choice of which early to medieval characters to represent from the literature we had read, I had eight "Perpetuas" out of a class of seventeen. Perpetua was at last an admired character, if admittedly not to be imitated. Another section of this same class, however, had no Perpetuas.

These often contentious and diametrically opposed interpretations reflect the serious ambiguity present in these stories and others like them, and in their interpretations, from the time they first emerged. It is therefore necessary to examine the early interpretations of these stories, insofar as is possible, without using our contemporary cultural presuppositions, although naturally the stories we choose and the way we choose to read them will be those that most address our interests. As a martyr, Perpetua was and remains an ambiguous model for female heroic behavior. The Latin *Martyrdom of Saints Perpetua and Felicitas* (early third century) has long been considered remarkable because a great part of it consists of what is assumed and represented to be Perpetua's own account of her visions, actions, and reflections through her imprisonment for Christ: the "I" narrative or prison diary. In one of these visions, her last, Perpetua sees herself symbolically transformed from female roles of daughter, wife, and mother to one of a male, an athlete who is victorious in the arena. Nevertheless both the introduction to the martyrology and the account of the martyrdom itself are written by another, presumably male hand, often alleged to be that of the Carthaginian theologian Tertullian, her contemporary, who praised Perpetua as one who could enter again the paradise closed to the first woman, Eve, and to provide a way for others—men and women—to enter (*The Soul* 55). This framework emphasizes Perpetua's "masculine" courage in willing her death with the simultaneous "feminine" concern for her modest appearance in public and for appropriate behavior as a Roman matron. The woman with a man's courage, a male in her dreams, was used as a tool to promote bravery in martyrdom for both men and women, while at the same time preserving feminine decorum.

As portrayed in the Greek text of the apocryphal *Acts of Paul and Thecla*, written at approximately the same time period as Perpetua's martyrdom, the "noble virgin of Iconium" Thecla rejects all familial and other social ties in favor of a celibate lifestyle as promoted by Paul. She transforms herself from a young woman who appears to fall in love with Paul's exotic words and lifestyle into a person who crosses the border between accepted definitions of maleness and femaleness, risking death to become an apostle like Paul. At the same time, however, Paul keeps his distance from her because he fears her "feminine" frailty and also his own potential for temptation, thus anticipating the antifemale stance of later male desert fathers and ascetics within the church.

In both stories, the "virilization" of the martyr-visionary Perpetua and the martyr-apostle Thecla served for some as a vision of "female power and autonomy" and even an actual possibility for imitation.[25] Bremmer suggests that it is even possible that Perpetua was inspired by reading the story of Thecla in the *Acts*, as other Carthaginian women had been.[26] There were difficulties with and contests over these claims, as will be seen. Certainly what may have been a powerful story for Perpetua and her female contemporaries was in the mind of Tertullian a dangerous fabrication to be attacked precisely because it provided a precedent for female authority (*Baptism* 17.5). But by the fifth century, Thecla's supposed tomb in Seleucia was the site of miracles, a destination for pilgrimages, and the center for a double monastic order of men and women, eagerly visited by the Spanish pilgrim Egeria in the fourth century.

Both Perpetua and Thecla functioned in ambiguous and potentially contradictory ways. In the formative period in the second to fifth centuries, Christian writers spoke of them as models of "masculine" virtues of courage and self-control, at a time when the virtues of women were usually characterized as those of modesty and chastity, private or domestic rather than public or civic virtues. Nonetheless, when women laid claim to institutional rather than spiritual or moral authority in the church in accord with these same virtues, they were censured for appropriating "male" roles. Ironically, these pioneering women often made such claims with reference to heroines like Perpetua and Thecla, seeing their stories as more evidence of the power and divine sanction of their antisocial behavior. In Perpetua's case, her power as imprisoned confessor and later as martyr gave her the authority to intercede for the living and the dead: a safe power for the church to incorporate after her death. Later, the "translated," apparently dead-but-still-living Thecla is given that same church-sanctioned power in Pseudo-Basil's *Life and Miracles*. Women wishing to adopt the sort of authority often reserved for men in a church that was still developing leadership roles used Thecla's story as authorization, as Tertullian's rant about their audacity in *Baptism* shows. But men and women alike could also use Thecla, in a way different from Perpetua, as a model for the piety of the ascetic virgin life that was equally ambiguous as the public virtue of martyrdom. At one and the same time, the ascetic as celibate was passive (the normally "feminine" connotation of virgin as receptive and in need of direction) and active (the normally "masculine" virtue of self-control, control of the passions). Thecla, like Perpetua, is portrayed as a martyr in a very public way, but she survives death because her "witness" is to the miraculous power of her resolute celibacy, not simply chastity as in the Greco-Roman womanly idea. In both cases the stories of martyrs are "witnesses" or models for appropriate behavior—and for its opposite—for men and women, but because the model is ambiguous, so is its appropriation.

For these purposes, gender and its portrayal definitely matter, not merely in the texts themselves but more importantly in the way they have been read over time, beginning with the ancient contemporary audiences and their own ideas about bodies and gender, some that may be consonant with ours and some that may be different from ours. There are some interesting common threads in reading these narratives, apart from the obvious facts that they have to do with developing Christian identity, with martyrs (in Thecla's case, a would-be martyr, but not for lack of trying), and with women. In both, the main characters are women. In both, the women martyrs (Thecla, Perpetua, and Felicitas) are literally "exposed" to the public gaze: they all appear naked at least once, and attention is deliberately drawn to that nakedness.[27] In the case of Perpetua and Felicitas, this nakedness is pointedly emphasized as being *female*. In all three cases, this emphasis is a characteristic of the third-person narrative, rather than the woman herself, as in Perpetua's diary. In both narratives, contrasting with the pointed emphasis on the female bodies of the characters, are scenes in which they "become male." Thecla offers to cut her hair and wear men's clothing in order to follow Paul, a gesture he refuses but that she later undertakes on her own initiative. Perpetua's final vision, from which she realizes that "there was no more hope in this world," is one in which she actually "becomes a man," a male gladiator. When Felicitas, who undergoes a difficult childbirth in prison, is being taunted by a soldier who questions her ability to bear the pain of martyrdom, she replies that in the arena, another will be "inside" her, and "he" (Christ) will help her bear the pain. Even within the most obvious physical fact of motherhood, giving birth, Felicitas's body is the container for the risen and victorious male Christ.

INSCRIBING BODIES

This book is thus, ultimately, a book about bodies, or rather a book of *stories* about bodies, bodies as spectacle and symbol. These stories are also about bodies and power, how power is "embodied" through power of the body and power over the body, specifically through the twin ideals so important to the early Christians, martyrdom (*martyria*), the public offering of the body as witness (*martys*), and asceticism, the discipline (*askēsis*) of the body for the sake of its spiritually directed transformation. In both, the body serves as a visible symbol of the power of God as it was imagined to exist over earthly opposing powers, political, social, and personal, working through the limits of fragile mortal flesh, so that it becomes transparent, as a "wholly convincing spectacle of power."[28] Even more, however, these stories are "stories about women and their bodies," as Maureen Tilley has observed of *The Martyrdom of Perpetua and Felicitas*, one of the most resonant of these narratives, but by no means the only one.[29]

The stories of these women occur in arenas, often quite literally so, in which debated or contested cultural issues and norms, including and especially those of bodily existence and gender, are challenged, rejected, or reinscribed. Women are placed in threshold situations, in which standing on the border of a cultural norm may result in its purposeful transgression only in order to serve as its symbolic reinforcement, marking it as unusual and therefore "outsider" behavior to be rejected except in crisis situations; or as a call for rejection or transformation of the norm. This type of outsider behavior critiques those within who have assumed illegitimate dominance. Martyrs, for example, suffer and usually die[30] as outsiders to dominant cultural or political hierarchies that cannot tolerate them, but also serve as upholders of new, different, or resistant cultural norms, which in turn enshrine them as cultural ideals. As Daniel Boyarin has aptly noted, the stories of martyrs in both formative Judaism and emerging Christianity, which develop at approximately the same time in the period from the late first to late fourth centuries, are shaped by and help to shape "modes of cultural resistance" that often raise "issues of sexuality and gender."[31] Martyrs, especially female martyrs, not only provided excellent vehicles "to think with" but exemplary "spectacles" for the writers, disseminators, and hearers of their stories.[32] In martyr stories, women become men through spectacular acts of endurance and courage; and men become women through submitting their bodies passively to humiliation and exposure. Elizabeth Castelli argues that "this spectacle [i.e., "display" of martyr's bodies] borrows from the broader culture's repertoire of ideas about gender, honor, shame, and the power of the gaze."[33] The spectacle, either of the martyr's death or of the ascetic's singular self-abnegation, involves not only the actual audience that is watching but also the one that is *intended* to "watch," not only actually but in terms of future generations as the *martyria*, the "witness," a term that necessarily involves both demonstrating and watching, continues in oral, written, and even visual form. It is, moreover, the *audience* that identifies the martyr as martyr. As Carlin A. Barton puts it, "Those who call the Christians 'martyrs' are the martyrs of the martyrs."[34] This is also true of the companion and other side of martyrdom, itself a bodily form of witness to transforming power, the ascetic life, which Teresa M. Shaw has called "a way of life that requires . . . intentionality in bodily behaviors."[35] Despite their sometimes elusive retreat to deserts or caves, ascetic men and women served as icons and magnets for those who came out to see, visit, and talk to them and models for those who were inspired by their superior bodily self-mastery (*enkrateia*).

EMBODYING POWER

But what do the bodies being displayed and watched signify? How were they interpreted, and how should they be interpreted? Why "speak" a martyrdom, as in the Latin term for martyrdom, *martyriam dicere*,[36] not merely (and sometimes not at all) with one's voice, but with one's body? What does a martyr *embody*? To understand the significance of the bodily witness in a *martyria*, we would need to know something about how those enacting and reading martyrdom understand their bodies, and what differences there might be between bodies, not always having to do only with gender, but certainly having to do with the fact that notions of body, like those of gender, are always embedded in culture. As Elaine Scarry observes in *The Body in Pain*,

> At particular moments when there is within a society a crisis of belief—that is, when some central idea or ideology or cultural construct has ceased to elicit a population's belief either because it is manifestly fictitious or because it has for some reason been divested of ordinary forms of substantiation—the sheer material factualness of the human body will be borrowed to lend that cultural construct the aura of "realness" and "certainty."[37]

In the case of emerging Christianity, of course, the execution of Christians as criminals by the Roman imperial government was an attempt in a literal and immediate way to exercise power over the bodies of Christians as an inherently rebel group, subversive of the ideals of the Pax Romana, the Roman peace enforced by the military and civil rule of Rome under its gods. Over and over, as portrayed through letters and trial narratives, the Roman notion of *pietas*, a citizen's loyalty to the gods of Rome, to Rome itself as divine, and to one's family and sanctified ancestors, clashed with the "new" religion that challenged this foundational ideal. Christians in turn rendered attempts against them futile in the face of their belief in the triumph of the Kingdom of God, their rhetoric powerfully describing martyrs as "victors" and "conquerors" in the battle between the good heavenly empire, soon to be instantiated, and the evil earthly empire, already being defeated. As that great apocalyptic apology for martyrdom, the New Testament book of Revelation, has it:

They have conquered [the accuser] by the blood of the Lamb
     and by the word of their testimony [*martyria*],
for they did not cling to life
     even in the face of death.

(12:11)

The body thus is not only an immediate visual device but also, through narratives about bodies, a "textual device," one that is put to use in the service of the writer's rhetoric.[38] Thus the body of the martyr is doubly witness: once as literally visible and often speaking, hence as continually "seen" or "speaking" through the text, the written witness. This rhetoric is surely contingent upon the historical culture in which it is embedded, or it would lose its force. As Averil Cameron observes of the evolution of Roman imperial culture in the second century in the Greek East (the putative site of composition of Revelation in the late first century), it "had become in political terms a spectator culture. . . . Showing, performance, and affirmation became as important as argument."[39] The continued effectiveness of the rhetoric in turn depends upon its validity in subsequent cultural configurations.

But what *did* people in late antiquity, when Christianity began to emerge as an offshoot of apocalyptic Judaism and classical culture, think about bodies? Did they understand their bodies in the same ways that moderns (or postmoderns) do? What significance and difference did they attach to their bodies? One of the most compelling narratives from the period of early Christianity is that of a body—a slave woman's body—naked, mangled with torture, "small, weak and despised," transformed by those watching into the powerful body of Christ: "For they looked on her in her conflict, and beheld with their outward eyes, in the form of their sister, him who was crucified for them."[40] Through one body we are actually "seeing" another in the text, the body of Christ, whose own suffering and death the martyrs are reenacting, as begun with the first written Christian "martyrology," the death of Stephen as described in Luke's book of Acts (7:54–8:1). But we are seeing something else about bodies as well: a slave's body and that of a woman—both disempowered—being transformed symbolically into a powerful male body, the body of the Savior become divine. It is not simply that Blandina is a slave and so would be systematically subjected to torture, either as interrogation or punishment, but she is also a female slave and thus even more "despised" and "weak." Yet she is described as "filled with power" and "like a noble athlete (*gennaios athlētēs*),"[41] at the same time as her torturers are weakened.

The transmitter of this narrative of the martyrs of the Gallic cities
Lyons and Vienne is Eusebius of Caesarea, a bishop comfortable in his
role as biographer and chronicler of the triumph of Christianity with
its acceptance by Constantine in the fourth century CE. He follows an
already-established yet paradoxical tradition: envisioning the victims of
the pagan state as their conquerors, as symbolic incarnations of the suffering yet triumphant Christ, with Christ as heavenly judge depicted
in the vision of the dying martyr Stephen in Acts 7:56 and as world
conqueror in Revelation 19:11–21. In fact, Blandina's transformation
into the paradoxically crucified yet powerful Christ in the martyrology
is in order "*that s/he might persuade those who believe on him*, that every
one who suffers for the glory of Christ has fellowship always with the
living God" (Eusebius, *Hist. eccl.* 5.1.41). According to Elizabeth Goodine and Matthew Mitchell, the subject of the Greek verb *peisē*—"might
persuade"—is ambiguous: it could be either "he" (referring to Christ) or
"she" (referring to Blandina). Goodine and Mitchell argue that in this
context, where Eusebius, like many other narrators of women's martyrdoms, concentrates specifically on the transformation of Blandina's deval-
ued, virtually dismembered slave woman's body into the powerful one of
Christ, the ambiguous grammar deliberately reflects the persuasiveness
of *Blandina*. Her *body* is the effective rhetoric. The fact that Blandina is
called a "noble" or "wellborn" (*gennaios*) athlete, in the grammatically
masculine gender,[42] further signifies her elevation from the "weak and
despised" slave girl to a noble male, who would be expected to exhibit
admirable courage in the face of extremity.[43] The fact that a woman in
the arena was an unusual sight is borne out by the decree of Septimius
Severus banning women gladiators in 200 CE, just three years before the
death of Perpetua and Felicitas in the arena at Carthage.[44] He apparently
had no trouble with so exposing women criminals.

In the early second-century *Letter of Pliny to Trajan* (*Letters* 10.96),
we possess valuable insight into the way that Roman men of power perceived Christian bodies.[45] The letter of a Roman provincial governor to
his political and spiritual overlord, the emperor, questions whether he
ought to proceed in the same fashion against those guilty of Christian
crimes without regard to their age or bodily condition, whether "delicate [*teneri*]" or "more robust [*robustiores*]." Interestingly, in his quest
for the "truth" about this "depraved and immoderate superstition,"
Pliny neither questions nor shows regard for differences in gendered
bodies. He examines under torture two "serving girls" (*ancillae*) who
he says are called *ministrae* (apparently deacons), while acknowledging

that this dangerous "superstition" (the Roman term for nonrecognized religion) has attracted persons "of both sexes [*utriusque sexus*]." These brief descriptions signal the kinds of persons and interactions in religious movements of which Roman authorities had always been wary: mixed genders and mixed classes.[46] In order to be exempt from the capital punishment both he and his emperor consider appropriate for persons belonging to this cult, those charged and examined would have to change from worshiping Christ "as a god" and offer worship to the image of the more "powerful" deity, Trajan himself. Without going into the ways in which this episode is only one of many documented clashes between the Kingdom of God as understood by the Christians and the Kingdom of God understood as the Roman imperium, beginning with the original martyr executed by the Roman authorities, Jesus himself, we can see that the subject is one of power: who truly has it, how it is embodied, how it is exerted, and who asserts it rhetorically.

We also possess a letter from a Christian authority (a bishop) who himself envisions what will and even what he hopes should happen to his own body as he prepares himself and his fellow Christians for his martyrdom. Ignatius, the bishop of Antioch in Syria, who became a martyr in Rome somewhere between 107 and 115, during the reign of the same emperor (Trajan, 98–117 CE) mentioned above, wrote an extraordinary letter to the Roman Christians, warning them not to hinder his martyrdom "under the pretence of carnal affection":[47]

> Suffer me to become food for the wild beasts, through whose instrumentality it will be granted me to attain to God. I am the wheat of God, and am ground by the teeth of the wild beasts, that I may be found the pure bread of God. Rather entice the wild beasts that they may become my tomb, and may leave nothing of my body; so that when I have fallen asleep [in death], I may not be found troublesome to any one. Then shall I be a true disciple of Jesus Christ, when the world shall not see so much as my body.
>
> (*To the Romans* 4)

In a frankly macho vision of bodily endurance in the arena, Ignatius goes on to describe the breaking apart and even annihilation of his body: "Let fire and the cross; let the crowds of wild beasts; let tearings, breakings, and dislocations of bones; let cutting off of members; let shatterings of the whole body; and let all the dreadful torments of the devil come upon me: only let me attain to Jesus Christ" (5). Ignatius's description of his own coming martyrdom is remarkable in that he wants his body to become transformed, first into food (the "pure bread" of God, which is a metaphor for transformation into the Eucharist, and hence into the sacrificed body of Christ; cf. 7) and then into invisibility. His body is to be the vehicle by which he becomes "a true disciple," but more importantly, it is for him something to be overcome, in order for him to become a true "man of God."[48] Indeed, it appears only to be overcome through its being marked first *as* body, something that physically is set on fire, crucified, eaten, shattered, torn, with bones dislocated and limbs cut off, so that it may no longer *be* body.

This desire to make the body disappear, to be invisible to the world, and yet control the means of its disappearance, echoes the Platonic heritage of literate Eastern Christians like Ignatius, an inheritance that tended to view the body and its desires and necessities, if not as an enemy, at least as an unruly and burdensome "other" or simply as a container in which the soul (*psychē*, a term that seems to have embraced what we would also call mind and spirit, as in Plato's *Republic* 442c) resides. It could also be viewed in Platonic thought as a tomb (*Phaedrus* 250c; *Cratylus* 400b; *Gorgias* 493a) or a guardhouse or prison (*Phaedo* 62b). In his *Phaedrus* and *Republic*, Plato also envisioned a tripartite psyche in which godlike reason needed to control the passions and appetites associated with the body. Nevertheless, the same Greek word for tomb, *sēma*, also meant "sign" or "marker" (originally, perhaps, the grave marker for a dead body) and in Plato's *Cratylus* 400c, Socrates also offers that interpretation of the body, the body as a "signifier," or something to which the soul gives "signs." He also gives the etymology of the word "body" (*sōma*) as something that is "saved" (*sōzetai*) by the soul.[49] Hence, a "body" could be either a receptacle or restrainer of the soul, a "signifier" of the soul's actions, and the recipient of salvation by the soul, all ideas that are to figure largely in later Christian discourse about the relative importance of body and soul and their relationship to each other.

Plato's views, those of aristocratic Greek males for whom philosophizing was an extension of their *scholē*, or leisure time that was not spent in the business of governing the *polis* or in the lawcourts, came into early Christian thought as filtered through discussion, dissension, or refinement by Aristotle and the later Roman Stoics and Cynics until they simply became background for the way in which literate male Christians envisioned themselves and their own bodies. For Plato's famous pupil, Aristotle, who sometimes disagreed with or refined his teacher's views, "The soul does not exist without a body and yet itself is not a body" (*The Soul* 414a19).[50] He also posited that all living organisms had "souls," which made them living or animate. Plants, for example, had the basic function of growth (and reproduction), animals of motion and sense perception, and humans of rationality (*The Soul* 413a23). Humans as living beings possessed all three kinds of "soul."

Nevertheless, when it came to bodies, especially with regard to what was an essentially vegetative function (reproduction), there was an essential and eventually fateful distinction that Aristotle made between the bodies (and functions) of men and the bodies (and functions) of women. He saw human females like other female animals as weaker, having an "inability" and a "deficiency," in that they could not formulate semen but only receive it, supplying the material element on which the formulating and developing principle of the male ejaculate, endowed with "soul," acted (*The Generation of Animals* 737a25).[51] For Aristotle, this distinction was merely a rational deduction from what he believed to be a fact of nature, just as he observed the "natural" ruling of certain groups (women, children, slaves, barbarians) by others (men, fathers, masters, Greeks) in his work on *Politics*, especially in 1.1–2. In the *Politics* he also considered the idea that while women had moral virtues, they were unlike those of men, and these included obeying and keeping silent. Among the chief moral virtues for men were courage, in Greek *andreia* (lit., "manliness," a term that translates into Latin as *virtus*, from which we derive the English "virtue") and *sōphrosynē*, or self-control (e.g., *Nicomachean Ethics*, bk. 3).

In this respect Aristotle was formulating nothing new or outrageous, only what men of his time and place, and for a considerable time to come, believed about the human body.[52] Nor would it have been necessary to have read either Aristotle or Plato in order to have these ideas about the body, although educated Christian elites, many of whom would become bishops, would have. Women, the most visible "other" to male writers, became a symbol, even of these writers' own male bodies, as a physical aggregate of desires and needs that needed to be carefully watched, guarded, and controlled. A male body could even become "feminized" if it was not under the control of ruling reason, or was subject to the control of another, like the passive male partner in homosexual intercourse.[53] The male anxiety over loss of bodily control became politicized, especially with Roman Stoicism, adapted from its origins in the Greek philosophy of Zeno and Chrysippus, during the tumultuous days of the late Republic (with Cicero) and the collapse of the Julio-Claudian dynasty (with Epictetus, Seneca, Musonius Rufus) and the exclusion from power of those accustomed to rule others.

Epictetus, one of the most influential of the Roman Stoics, who like the Greek Stoics believed in living according to "nature," which was sovereign reason, was himself a slave and so had occasion to analyze the "natural" limits of power and control. In his *Enchiridion*, or *Handbook*, he observed that the physical body was not "in our control" (1),[54] and therefore "things relating to the body" should be "done incidentally," whereas the "whole attention" should be given to the care of the mind (41). Like most other Stoics and philosophical writers in general (with the possible exception of the Epicureans), Epictetus addresses his comments to men. On women and their bodies, he tells men that they should make women "sensible," not adorning themselves to please men physically, except in "decent, modest, and discreet behavior" (40).

Once again, women's bodies are objects of speculation and molding by men into qualities perceived to be admired by men. Nonetheless, women on occasion were perceived by Stoic philosophers as being capable of "manliness" that equaled or surpassed that of men. Not surprisingly, this courage was reflected in the willingness to die in the style that Stoic circles admired: the "noble death," the self-execution of the body when an honorable life could not longer be supported. In one of his *Moral Epistles* (24.16–17), for example, Seneca speaks of the "clogging burden" and the "fetters" of the body.[55] According to Roman Stoic teaching, Seneca's enforced suicide when he was indicted for conspiracy against Nero was accompanied by the attempted suicide of his wife, Paulina. Tacitus, the early second-century chronicler of this event, relates that Seneca supposedly told his wife, "I will not grudge you such a noble example. Let the fortitude of so courageous an end be alike in both of us, but let there be more in your decease to win fame."[56] The anticipated death of Paulina (which was forcibly prevented by others present) would be more "famous" because it was that of a woman, who was not expected to take the courageous step of annihilating herself. Pliny the Younger, in a letter to Cornelius Nepos, speaks admiringly of Arria, the wife of Caecina Paetus, whose courage was greater than that of her husband on a number of counts: she pretended that their dying son was living when her husband himself was ill; she resolutely attended her husband in his imprisonment as his servant; she criticized wives of conspirators against the emperor Claudius for remaining alive when their spouses died; and she herself took the sword before Paetus' suicide, encouraging his death by uttering the immortal words "*Paete, non dolet*. Paetus, it does not hurt."[57]

These examples serve to reinforce the widely held ancient pagan idea, amply reinforced in early Christian literature, that women, in imitating men—particularly in rational choices and the extraordinary exercise of control over what were regarded as weak, passive bodies, especially subject to irrational passions—attained "a higher state of moral and spiritual perfection."[58] This idea was to be dominant in the rhetoric of developing Christianity and its understanding of bodily existence in the world. Perhaps its most remarkable phrasing comes via gnostic Christianity, a trajectory that emphasized, as did Greco-Roman philosophy, the tension between body and soul, in what is probably an addition to the second-century Coptic *Gospel of Thomas*, Saying 114. In it, Peter, representative of the emerging orthodox and patriarchal church, tells Jesus to get rid of the female disciple Mary Magdalene because as a female she does not "deserve [the] life" of the males. Jesus replies that he will "make her male," a "living spirit" that will then enter the spiritual perfection of the kingdom of heaven.[59]

The rage of the Carthaginian presbyter Tertullian over the influence Greek philosophy had on Christian thought (especially on the thought of those he deemed heretics, including the Gnostics; *Prescription against Heretics* 7.9), reflects the extent to which, even after the five centuries that intervened between Aristotle's *The Generation of Animals* and Tertullian's own writings, this view of male and female prevailed. Indeed, Tertullian himself, despite his protests to the contrary, initially shared the views that differentiated male and female bodies, including the idea that women ought to be, as far as possible, "invisible" in public places in the sense that they have their heads covered and be dressed in a way so as not to attract male attention (*The Veiling of Virgins; The Apparel of Women*). He could, however, extol the public spectacle of women's bodies like Perpetua's as exemplars of virtue in martyrdom (*The Soul*, 55) and at the same time deplore the audacious immodesty (*impudicitia*) of women who dared to use the impudent example of the apostle Thecla to make declarations on the public right of women to make pronouncements on baptism (*Baptism* 17.4–5).

In this writing, Tertullian looked to the authority of the "true" Paul rather than the "construction" he alleged the narrative of Paul and a female apostle was. The authentic Paul for Tertullian, as for later orthodox authorities in general, was the same as the writer of the epistle 1 Timothy, in which "the apostle" forbade women to speak or have authority over men (1 Tim. 2:12). Yet despite the contested status of the authorship of this and the other Pastoral Epistles (2 Timothy and Titus), to which we will return, Tertullian, writing at the cusp of the third century, was well aware of the attitude of the apostle toward bodies as signifier and significant. Indeed, in his own use of athletic metaphors for martyrdom in his exhortation *To the Martyrs* (3.5), he refers to "the Apostle's" use of the same metaphor: that athletes (runners in particular), who "exercise self-control in all things," do it "in order to receive a perishable wreath," the athlete's "crown" (Lat. *corona corruptibilis*), whereas the martyrs achieve an "imperishable" one (cf. 1 Cor. 9:25). The athletic imagery conveys the ideal behavior of one who disciplines the body's physical needs, desires, and appetites, allowing the body to be taken over by the controlling spirit.

Paul—a thoroughly Hellenized Jew who more often seems to understand "the body" as an entity in the Jewish sense of *nephesh*, a being endowed with life, as in his famous reference to "physical" and "spiritual" bodies in 1 Corinthians 15:35–55—did not downplay the conflict between flesh and spirit: he recognized the struggle of the physical nature of the body with the cool dominance of intellect and reason that made men in particular in the image of the divine (cf. 1 Cor. 11:7). Even Paul at times, despite his insistence on the "body" as an entity that could be either physical or spiritual—more like a personality—expresses the longing "to be away from the body and at home with the Lord" (2 Cor. 5:8). The physical body (often called "the flesh," *sarx*, by Paul) thus was for him the same deadly burden needing the constant vigilance of a controlling authority as it was in Greco-Roman philosophy: for example, he asks rhetorically for a deliverer "from this body of death," which could also mean, "from the body of this death," but in any event he connects the body with mortal existence (Rom. 7:24). Paul also differentiated, and also wished to have publicly differentiated, the bodies of men and women, at least of men and married women. In 1 Corinthians 11, for example, he creates a hierarchical list: God is at the head of Christ, who is at the head of the man, who is at the head of his wife (who presumably signifies the body, 1 Cor. 11:3). In the Deutero-Pauline letter Ephesians (5:23–24), the author (long assumed to be Paul and still assumed to have his authority) returns to the metaphor of the wife as body, comparing her to the feminine "body" of the church, which is saved by the male Savior, Christ, just as the husband/head "saves" the body/wife.[60]

Christianity as an offshoot of Greco-Roman culture thus preserves both a positive and a negative attitude toward the body: positive in that the body is a script for being transformed by its temporary resident, the soul, mind, or spirit; negative in that its appetites and passions are viewed as at war against their spiritual transformation. Women's bodies in particular need both to be restrained, as Plato envisioned the soul restrained by the gods in the "guardroom" of the body, and governed by the sovereign reason of the "head," the governing male spirit, or *psychē*. Women who would transform themselves thus had to overcome the distinct "disadvantages of the female gender,"[61] usually by modeling themselves after male behavior, in itself a risky business. They could not become men (and remain approved by evolving Christian culture) in the sense of being sexually aggressive[62] or, if married, assuming positions of leadership that were public and often exclusively male prerogatives, except for the widely accepted one of benefaction.[63] In short, if the gnostic Jesus in *The Gospel of Thomas* is any indication, they are "led" to the masculine role, largely in texts that are written by men for men *and* women. As Sebastian Brock and Susan Ashbrook Harvey observe of the hagiographies of Syrian holy women, "Men are telling these stories to women as their audience and to men about women."[64]

Early Christian writers and their audiences thus tended to define the "feminine" as substantially identical with female embodiment and female sexuality, and as such an obstacle to spiritual progress and in need of redemption. Through death by martyrdom and by means of its companion and successor, ascetic restraint, women could not merely deny but also "overcome" the obstacle of femaleness, effectively erasing their bodies and their gender. Martyrs, especially female martyrs, provided excellent vehicles "to think with" but exemplary "spectacles" for the writers, disseminators, and hearers of their stories.[65] Virginity, usually depicted as the symbolic erasure of the feminine sexual self, a kind of death of the gendered being, was more problematic. The female virgin's body was essentially "male" because it was intact, unpenetrated, but the virgin herself was still present as an embodied female being, and thus a potential source of suspicion and trouble, depending on whose control she was under. If her own, the volatility of feminine desire might subvert her resolve, as expressed in the *Acts of Paul and Thecla*, where Paul seems to be more concerned with Thecla's potential lapses than he is about the dangers of his own masculine desire, or that of other males. In a later version of the tale, the "solution" is for another act of God to enclose her in a rock (11.12). Lustful males cannot penetrate it, but this text also "fixes" Thecla in one place, at the service of orthodox clerical interest. She is said to have appeared in a vision to the emperor Zeno, assuring him of the restoration of his rule (Eusebius, *Hist. eccl.* 2b.3.8). Nevertheless, as Kate Cooper claims, Thecla's story is the source of some "rich paradoxes . . . in the imagination of the early church."[66] Just one of these appears in a variant of her story, in which Thecla appears "still alive" after her enclosure in the rock in Rome, still in pursuit of Paul, who is already dead. There she dies and is buried in the catacomb that still bears the name of St. Thecla.[67] Such is the power of the martyr's bodily presence. Martyrs (and would-be martyrs, the spectacular ascetics) are malleable. How malleable is the subject of the following chapters.

2

Body Talk: The Martyr's "Voice"

Neither the melodies of sirens nor the songs of swans attract the attention of their hearers as did the voices of the children in torture calling to their mother.

—4 Maccabees 15:21

SPEAKING THE MARTYRDOM

The Greek term *martys*, as previously noted, means "witness" in several senses: to watch, to make a spectacle (for watching or reading), and to speak.[1] Most commonly, however, these meanings of martyrdom are subsumed under the accepted meaning of dying for one's faith or cause. Jan Willem van Henten and Friedrich Avemarie observe that "definitions of martyrdom often mention the aspects of witness or confession as a central characteristic of the martyr's action, taking a semantic development of the Greek noun *martys* ('witness') and the related verb *martyrein* into the early Christian title 'martyr.'"[2] They also point out that this heroic witness is "older than the Christian or Jewish terminology that indicates it": Greek and Roman pagan traditions of "glorious" yet violent sacrificial death or noble suicide actually precede and provide models for Jewish and Christian martyrologies, with the important exception that the latter reject the choice of inflicting violent death out of fidelity to God and accept "the decision to die violently rather than give up [their] conviction, or to die for the benefit of others."[3] In *Dying for God*, Daniel Boyarin similarly points to the development of the "novelty of late antique martyrdom as a practice of both rabbinic Jews and Christians" and proposes that "we think of martyrdom as a 'discourse,' as a practice of dying for God and of talking about it."[4]

Death spotlights the "witness," inviting a participation in the witness by seeing, and, as Allison Goddard Elliott has pointed out, hearing the martyr "speak the martyrdom."[5] Martyrdom thus needs to be public, so that the witness can be "published" effectively. Speech is as important as spectacle. Both Boyarin and Elliott point to the "central act" of the martyrdom as the "verbal *agōn*," the "ritualized and performative speech act."[6] The verbal and the physical actions of the martyrdom focus upon the challenge to and potential subversion of the values and norms of the dominant culture. In fact, the martyrs undergo their trials because they present a challenge to the value system of the dominant culture. One of the purposes of the written martyrdom is thus symbolically to overcome or subvert this value system. By their very definition, then, martyrs behave "inappropriately" according to the dominant norms of late antique society. In the same way, as Richard Valantasis has argued, ascetic behavior is also "a system of performances designed to inaugurate an alternative culture, to enable different social relations, and to create a new identity."[7] The creation of a new identity, however, is still a social one: not all of the values and norms of the dominant society will be cast off as the new emerges. In particular, what makes a female martyr less of a problem as a tool for cultural opposition is that she dies (like Perpetua). When the "witness" lives (like Thecla), she continues to hold open the oppositional mode, even to the emerging alternative society.

THE MAKING OF MARTYRIA

When we are speaking of Christian witnesses, we need to speak of the figure they consciously construct their behavior to imitate: Jesus. And in speaking of Jesus, particularly of his death, we must also speak of it within the framework of Judaism, particularly in its opposition first to enforced Hellenism and then to Rome, both prime situations for the making of martyrs. As van Henten and Avemarie have informed us, Jewish and Christian martyrdoms have a good deal in common, not least the motivating factor of fidelity to religious conviction.[8] Jesus and his first followers were all Jews. Their Scripture was that held authoritative by Jews, whether in the learned language of Hebrew, in Aramaic versions, or in the Greek form common in Mediterranean Diaspora Judaism, the Septuagint. By these means, Jesus' followers interpreted his life and death. For emerging Christianity, then, the inexplicable death of Jesus the Messiah (Christ) was interpreted in two main ways: first, in terms of the Suffering Servant of God (*'ebed YHWH*) motif, especially by reference to Isaiah 52:13–53:12, which became so ingrained in Christian consciousness that the average Christian today firmly believes that the prophet was foretelling the passion of Jesus; and through the motif of the righteous martyr, found in 2 and 4 Maccabees particularly, which could be seen as an extension of the righteous Servant. As Amy-Jill Levine relates of her childhood study of the New Testament: "Nor was the cross [of Jesus] strange. The story resembled that of the deaths of the Maccabean martyrs, the mother and her seven sons, whom we recall at Hanukkah. Making the connection even closer, these Jewish martyrs also anticipated vindication and resurrection."[9]

Yet 2 Maccabees, probably written in the first century BCE, as an excerpt from the longer work by the historian Jason of Cyrene, and 4 Maccabees, written perhaps in the first century CE, although Jewish, are not only Greek in language but also reflect Hellenistic Greek ideas: in the case of 2 Maccabees, the style of Hellenistic historiography, which included set speeches as part of the story, and in the case of 4 Maccabees, a thoroughgoing apologetic adaptation of Stoicism, including the triumph of reason, identified as the true philosophy embedded in Judaism, over passion, identified with the irrational and idolatrous Gentile tyrant Antiochus. In both books the action consists of graphic descriptions of gruesome bodily tortures, but interspersed are speeches in which each side, but particularly the martyred Jews, expounds its philosophy. Particularly in 4 Maccabees, torture is paradoxically the occasion for speaking against the dominant regime. In both texts speech is therefore a significant part of the narrative, perhaps reflecting the belief of the Stoics and their philosophical relatives, the Cynics, that *parrhēsia*, free or open speech, was the mark of a free *man*. This type of speech, which came to be identified by the Cynic philosophers with the address "to a social superior by someone powerless," part of the Cynic subversion of the usual public "sense of shame," could be but was not often used by women, who were regarded as signifiers of public honor or shame for their men.[10] The female Cynic philosopher Hipparchia is an example of a notable exception, quoted both in Diogenes Laertius's *Lives of the Philosophers* (6.96–98) and in an epigram by Antipater of Thessalonica (*Greek Anthology* 7.413), speaking in the first person of her choice of the Cynics' "virile life," another case of a woman adopting "male" behavior.[11] The Cynics, like the Epicureans, "allowed women to be partners in *parrhēsia*," but even this partnership implies that women did not act alone.[12]

Given the importance of speech, especially oppositional speech, it is all the more curious that the New Testament evangelists do not portray Jesus, either at his trial before Pilate or at his death, as saying much of anything, let alone giving the speech that the conventions of *martyria* seem to demand. Only in the last-written canonical Gospel, the Gospel according to John, does Jesus have a response of any length to Pilate, a discourse that is typical of the lengthy dialogues Jesus utters throughout the Gospel, on the nature of truth. It is also in John's Gospel that Jesus says three of the traditional "seven last words" or utterances on the cross. During Passion Week in Christian churches, especially on the day Christ is believed to have been crucified, Good Friday, there are services that commemorate the "seven last words," ironically highlighting these brief sayings with sermons that last much longer. Some of these last words refer directly to Scripture: for example, Mark 15:34 and its parallel in Matthew 27:46 refer (in Aramaic) to Psalm 22, a psalm of lament; John 19:28 ("I am thirsty") may refer to Psalm 69:21. Since Jesus dies for a political crime, it is perfectly understandable for the evangelists to portray him in an apologetic vein as not resisting or opposing the Roman authorities, even in word; but it seems odd that these writers, especially Matthew, who refers more than any other to Jesus' words and actions fulfilling scriptural prophecy, would have Jesus say so little at his death. Luke, who gives us three more of Jesus' last "words," one of which, granting the repentant "bandit" entry into paradise because of his confession that Jesus is indeed the Messiah or Lord, also provides us with a means of interpreting Jesus' silence, again through an interpretation of a passage in the last Servant Song of Isaiah.

In Luke's book of Acts, following the initiation of a "severe persecution" (8:1) that begins with the death of the first martyr for Jesus, Stephen, and impels Jesus' followers away from Jerusalem, the apostle Philip is on the road "from Jerusalem to Gaza," when he hears a court official of the Candace of Ethiopia reading aloud from Isaiah 53:7–8, a passage that focuses particularly on the *silence* of the humiliated Servant: "Like a lamb silent before / its shearer, / so he does not open his mouth." The official's puzzlement over the passage ("About whom . . . does the prophet say this?") provides a teachable moment for Philip, who explains to him that it refers to Jesus (Acts 8:30–35). Thus, for Luke, as perhaps for the other evangelists, Jesus' silence is a necessary component of his fulfillment of a prophecy that is already being applied in many particulars to his otherwise inexplicable death. In a gnostic version of Jesus' crucifixion, the Valentinian *Gospel of Truth*, it is because of worldly ignorance or error that God, the "Father of Truth," causes the Jesus to be nailed to the cross, in order that the immortal Word of truth be "published" to the world (10). Yet, as Elaine Scarry contends, it is the bodiliness of Jesus, even after the resurrection, which is the "central premise" of the New Testament narratives, in that the "boundary between body and voice" is dissolved.[13] Jesus' embodiment as Word of God makes that body into a form of authoritative speech.

Embodied voice is an important part of the subsequent portrayal of Christian martyrs. Luke's book of Acts also probably contains the first Christian martyrology, the death of Stephen, in 7:54–60, preceded by his lengthy verbal "witness" in 7:1–53. The death of Stephen, whose name ironically means "crown" (*stephanos*), the crown that later in Revelation deliberately marks the victor-martyr, and who is the best and brightest of those designated by the original "inner group" of the apostles to receive Jesus' spirit (Acts 6:1–8), provides for Luke a deliberate parallel to Jesus that is distinctly different from the parallel to the other miracle-working "divine men" apostles, none of whom (including Paul, who is dramatically chosen later) are actually shown dying in the book. Like Jesus, Stephen is accused of blasphemy, particularly against the Temple, by false witnesses (6:11–15). Like Jesus, Stephen is brought before the Sanhedrin. Unlike Jesus, however, Stephen is actually executed on the charge of *blasphemy*, and unlike Jesus, he makes a lengthy, historical defense that is more in the Lukan apologetic vein of an indictment of his persecutors (7:1–53). Much as Jesus had prophesied during his own brief testimony before the Sanhedrin in Luke 22:69, Stephen sees "the heavens opened and the Son of Man standing at the right hand of God" (Acts 7:56), and like Jesus he asks forgiveness of his executioners (Acts 7:60//Luke 23:34) and commends his spirit to the Lord (Acts 7:59//Luke 23:46). The only part of Jesus' own death to which Luke does not draw a deliberate parallel by Stephen's death is Jesus' "word" to the confessing criminal: "Today you will be with me in Paradise" (Luke 23:43), but there is no need to do so: the confessing Stephen's *martyria* has already opened paradise for him (Acts 7:56).

The description of Jesus' death as a righteous martyr, following the Maccabean tradition, the understanding of his death as purposeful, and the following of that righteous martyr model as portrayed in Christian literature of the late first-century book of Luke—all reveal certain constant characteristics that van Henten and Avemarie have noted about the development of Jewish and Christian martyrologies: the element of fidelity to religious convictions makes them different in the main from pagan models of noble death. They find that the elements of these martyr tales include transgression of rule, law, or decree, by dominant authority (usually pagan) that cannot be obeyed without violating a prior religious commitment; the choice of death rather than violating that commitment in obedience to illegitimate worldly authority; the martyr's decision made public by examination (in which the martyr often makes a defense, or apologia, against wrongdoing), torture, and execution, the latter of which is an important element in the testimony (or there may be a miraculous rescue that proves the decision was right).[14] Add to this the faith by believing "witnesses to the witness" that suffering and death will be vindicated through some form of life with God and the hope that other believers will be encouraged to imitate the martyr's example. This written witness becomes propaganda that for its purposes tends to obscure the cost of defying social norms and worldly expectations, a cost that is death. Death becomes transformed through the martyrology into a goal, a praiseworthy conclusion to and redemption of earthly life, an entrance into the realm of memory and fame for those who otherwise might not gain such glory on earth. An existence that might have been meaningless now is given meaning by a new generation of interpreters.

EMBODIED "VOICES": VIRILE SPEECH
AND FEMININE SILENCE

Yet the "inappropriateness" of the martyr's behavior—and the extent of the subversion of values and reassertion of others—proves to be different in the accounts of women martyrs than in those of men. As Brock and Harvey have pointed out in their account of Syrian women martyrs, the leadership roles and public speech of the women are actions that "disconcert the popular sensibilities." Since their behavior is "called forth by divine authority," it is indeed extraordinary: it provides no mandate for changing women's roles "in either the religious or the social sphere."[15] The departed martyr may thus be used to project whatever ideals the emerging propaganda wishes to promote, without substantial change in the lot of those who are still living.

Moreover, in the late antique world, as in the ancient Greco-Roman world in general, if one may hazard such a generalization, the virtues of men, particularly the definitively "manly" virtue of courage (*andreia*, *virtus*) contributed to public and civic life, as Karen Jo Torjesen has observed.[16] In the Funeral Oration of Pericles, one of the set speeches constructed by Thucydides that commemorates the fallen at the end of the first year of the Peloponnesian War in the fifth century BCE, the leader of the Athenian government speaks at length about the city's civic virtues. At the end of the speech, as almost an afterthought, he cautions the noble women who are now widows to act appropriately for their "nature" and "not to be spoken of" at all by men (*Peloponnesian War* 2.6). Hence the definitively "womanly" virtue for such highborn women—and we must remember that both Perpetua and Thecla are noble—was keeping chastity safe by not venturing into the public sphere. Moral teachings from a variety of contexts—from a Pythagorean treatise of the third to second centuries BCE that cautions respectable women not to leave their homes unaccompanied and only at midday to sacrifice to the chief deities on behalf of their families (*WLGR* 107, 208), to the Christian Pastoral Epistles of the early second century CE—almost universally reinforce the necessity of avoiding feminine "display," whether of inappropriate clothing or inappropriate venue.

Male martyrs could also behave "inappropriately" with respect to their dominant cultures, not by being "unmanly," but by using their courage to defy the political and social order.[17] The male martyr takes on the role of the hero in combat, a role culturally appropriate to men. Female martyrs, the accounts of whose martyrdoms usually function as parts of "conversations that men are having," as Shelley Matthews notes,[18] are thus doubly transgressive. The female martyr is in a sphere not appropriate to her (public) and thrust into combat that requires a male virtue (courage). For the purposes of the physical combat in the arena, the female martyr is temporarily "virilized," but typically the martyrology refeminizes her through emphasizing—and sometimes overemphasizing—her physical attributes, feminine gender roles, and above all her feminine "modesty," showing what is "appropriately female," defined through chastity, circumspection in public, and silence. Her being thrust into a public situation is in a sense at her choosing, as it is for any martyr, but the choice for a woman is problematized in a narrative that never lets the readers forget that they are looking at a woman and that the sight is doubly unusual because she is acting like a man, particularly with regard to open and defiant speech. In her study of the deaths of women in Greek tragedy, Nicole Loraux observes that what is *seen* on stage is secondary to what is *spoken* about these women. Since "silence is the adornment of women," a sentence found in Sophocles and later in

Aristotle, women who become involved in the public sphere, "the men's world of action, . . . have suffered for it."[19]

These points may be illustrated through a comparison of women as martyrs in the Hellenistic Jewish 4 Maccabees (and to some extent in 2 Maccabees) with *The Martyrdom of Perpetua and Felicitas* and the Thecla cycle contained in part in the *Acts of Paul and Thecla*. These present the female "witness" as saying little or nothing (the mother of seven; Felicitas; Thecla in the first part of the narrative that takes place in Iconium) or offer a "translation" of what she does say (the "private speeches" of the mother of the seven; the difference between Perpetua's own "prison diary" and the account of her death in the arena). In these narratives one is invited to watch the spectacle of a woman's body enacting a drama usually scripted by another, one that ironically employs contemporary social constructions of "femaleness" (or femininity) to promote a male ideal, courage or virtue (*andreia, virtus*). The heroine is praised because she transcends the perceived limits of her gender and its social values and both embodies and promotes the "perfect" masculinity of martyrdom. Nevertheless, this imitation of men is an imitation that is possible only in death. It incites memorial, but on the whole it does not promote a paradigm for lived social behavior (the story of Thecla is a complicated exception). The martyr may speak, yet she is not supposed to continue speaking in her own voice, but through appropriate (usually male) authorities.

The martyrology of the Maccabean "mother of seven" occurs in two different versions, in 2 Maccabees 6:1–7:42, written perhaps in the first century BCE, and in 4 Maccabees, written "perhaps a century later," in a more elaborate and extended account.[20] Both versions relate the martyrdoms of an aged priest, Eleazar, and of seven sons and their mother, none of whom are named.[21] Thus they all (including perhaps the named Eleazar) may be employed the more readily as symbols or types, especially the mother who, as Robin Darling Young points out, is included with other unnamed "pious, observant Jewish mothers" who are martyred with their offspring in 2 Maccabees (6:10; cf. 1 Macc. 1:60–61).[22]

In the account as contained in 2 Maccabees, all of the martyrs, beginning with Eleazar, exhibit the virtue of *andreia*, manliness or courage.[23] Eleazar has refused even the pretense of eating pork, offered out of sympathy for his age, to escape torture and death, welcoming death instead with *eukleia* ("good fame"; honor, 6:19). In his spoken *martyria* (6:24–28, 30), he emphasizes his age as setting an example for the young men to follow: "Therefore, by bravely [Gk. *andreiōs*, lit., 'like a man'] giving up my life now, I will show myself worthy of my old age and leave to the young a noble [*gennaion*] example of how to die a good death willingly and nobly [*gennaiōs*] for the revered and holy laws" (6:27–28). He dies, racked and beaten, confessing that he gladly receives in his soul the blows to his body because he obeys God (6:30). The narrative concludes of him, "So in this way he died, leaving in his death an example of nobility [*hypodeigma gennaiotētos*] and a memorial of courage [*mnēmosunon aretēs*]" (6:31).[24] Another Jewish leader, Razis the elder, also prefers to die nobly (*eugenōs*), rather than to "suffer outrages unworthy of his noble birth [*eugenia*]" (14:42), acting in a noble manner (*gennaiōs*). His story, related in 14:37–46, is much more active and less verbal than that of Eleazar, in the mold of the Greco-Roman "noble death." According to van Henten and Avemarie, even his "unparalleled name" may be symbolic.[25] Certainly both Razis and Eleazar express different dimensions of manly fortitude: Eleazar preferring to endure torture heroically, Razis also "like a man [*androdōs*]" (14:43) falling on his sword and, being unsuccessful in dying instantly, throwing himself off a wall and taking out his own entrails to throw at the mob, "calling on the Lord of life" (14:46) as he does so. A short speech, but graphically illustrated. Both behave in a manner worthy of men of their social station: they resist the Greeks, but in a recognizably Greek manner, showing the courage that universally defines noble manhood.

Immediately after the aged priest Eleazar's death, seven young men, brothers, are arrested and do follow his example, individually speaking their martyrdoms as they undergo varied graphic tortures. We thus are witnesses to spoken as well as physical martyrdom. But their mother, who is standing by during the persecutions, encourages them individually and privately in "*tē patriō phonē*," a phrase whose gender-inclusive translation in the NRSV of the Apocrypha unfortunately obscures the emphasis of the Greek, "in their *paternal* tongue": probably the Hebrew tongue whose utterance itself defies the ruling Greeks (2 Macc. 7:21, 27). She encourages them thus because she has "reinforced her woman's [*thēlun*, female] reasoning with a man's [*arseni*] courage," even to the extent of denying giving them life and breath while in her womb, attributing this to God, the Creator of the universe (7:22, 28). When asked to use her maternal persuasion to convince her remaining youngest son to submit, again she speaks privately, "leaning close to him." With heavy irony, we "overhear" the kind of speech that one might expect a woman and a mother to give: she urges him to pity her because she has carried him in her womb, nursed him, and nurtured him to his present age. Instead of urging him to recant, however, she essentially urges him to remember God and "be a man": that is, not to "fear" the tyrant and to prove "worthy" of his brothers (7:26–29). Encouraged, the youngest son "speaks his martyrdom" at some length (7:30–38) and dies nobly or "pure" (*katharos*, 7:40).

"Last of all, the mother died, after her sons" (7:41) is the short description of her own martyrdom, prelude to the brief, dry ending of the martyrology in 2 Maccabees: "Let this be enough, then, about the eating of sacrifices and extreme tortures" (7:42). Without giving the mother's death much coverage, let alone relating any public utterance, the narrative nonetheless emphasizes how "amazing [*thaumastē*]" (7:20) a woman she is because, while appearing to become "masculine," she performs the mother's role of instilling the appropriate "manhood" in her sons, not as Eleazar did, by example, but by using her motherhood as an appropriate albeit ironic persuasive tactic. Even here, she emphasizes for her sons the belief "that not she but the Lord had brought about their conception and birth."[26] She remains "womanly," refusing any speech or spectacle in public. Thus she is denied both of the features of what Elliott calls the "hagiographic epic" style of martyrdom: the verbal and physical contest in which the hero triumphs "in word and deed."[27] She is thereby defined in contrast to Eleazar, her sons, or Razis.

The mother's story in 4 Maccabees, much more developed than in 2 Maccabees, becomes the "climax" of this latter Stoic tract that uses martyrology as a way of demonstrating the triumph of reason over the passions.[28] In 4 Maccabees, as in 2 Maccabees, the mother is also a symbol, this time embodying the triumph of one of the cardinal Stoic virtues, *andreia* (courage, manliness) over "temporary love of children," that mothers are expected to have.[29] In 4 Maccabees the author's encomia of the martyrs do not allow the reader to miss the point of their witness. Eleazar's speech under torture (4 Macc. 6:16–23, 27–28), in a classic apologia, or defense, the model for which in the ancient world is Plato's *Apology of Socrates*, refutes the charge of irrationality with a countercharge: it would be truly irrational to act *malakopsychēsantas*, "in a soft [often understood as 'effeminate'] spirit" (6:17). The encomium of Eleazar after his death reinforces this view that reason overcomes passion: "For only the wise [*sophos*] and courageous [*andreios*] man is the master [*kyrios*] of the passions" (7:23, my trans.).

When the seven "lads [*meirakiskoi*; *neaniai*]" are brought in, their youth emphasized in contrast to Eleazar's age, they appear even to the tyrant Antiochus as "modest [*aidēmones*]" (i.e., "knowing what is shameful" in action), and as with Eleazar and Razis, "noble" or wellborn (*gennaioi*, 8:3–4). As is expected of such noble young men, they do not speak as "*deilopsychoi* [base-souled]" and "*anandroi* [unmanly]," whose speech the author parodies, but they speak "with one voice" and with "one mind," although each speaks separately—and at length—as he undergoes tortures. Their encomium praises the triumph of reason mastering even the positive emotion of "brotherly love" (*philadelphia*, 14:1).

The highest and the longest praise is reserved, however, for the martyrs' mother, who is also a martyr-mother, precisely because she has both the "woman's mind [*gynaikos nous*]," and "natural" maternal feeling (*sympatheia*, 14:11–17:6), but these debilities are overcome by her manly fortitude. The Roman Stoic Seneca, in *Providence* 2, also emphasized this maternal sympathy, only in order to criticize it because the father, like the omnibenevolent divine Reason, has enough fortitude of mind to discipline his children for their own good. All expected femininity, however, the mother overcomes through "reverent reason [*eusebēs logismos*]" (15:23) that shapes her not only for courageous female roles such as "daughter of Abraham" and "mother of the nation" (15:28–29), but that also makes her manly and courageous (*andreiōsas*) in the midst of her sufferings (15:23), "more noble [*gennaiotera*] than males in steadfastness" and "more manly [*andreiotera*] than men in endurance" (15:30–31). Throughout his (assuming the author is male, which is probable) encomium of the mother, the author constantly balances supposed "feminine" and "maternal" qualities with those that are "masculine." The 4 Maccabees version of the story deletes the persuasive "maternal" speech in 2 Maccabees spoken privately by the mother to the youngest son to encourage his martyrdom: instead, the author imagines this speech as one she "might" have given but does not because she is both a "mother" and a "soldier of God" at the same time (16:14). Instead, the mother again encourages her sons "in the Hebrew language" (not called "the father's tongue" here), and we overhear her more detailed exhortation, reminding her sons of the examples of Jewish heroes like Abraham, Isaac, Daniel and the Three, and Eleazar (16:16–25). Although it is not clear whether the encouragement is private, there is no direct indication that it is any more public than that in 2 Maccabees: it is an address to her sons to fight in the "*gennaios agōn* [noble contest]" and thus to contend through witnessing (*diamartyria*) on behalf of the ancestral ("father's") laws (16:16).

The mother's end in 4 Maccabees does emphasize her modesty more than the brief reference in 2 Maccabees, however. We do not even get to see her death; we only hear about it: "Some of the guards said that when she was about to be seized and put to death she threw herself into the flames so that no one might touch her body" (17:1). In this way, a woman who is addressed in the male athletic imagery so important in these martyrologies as "*agōnos athlophore*" (15:29), the victor or "bearer of the prize [*athlophoros*]" in the athletic contest (*agōn*), combatant in a very public arena indeed, is at the end prevented from the womanly shame of exposure and immodesty, having her body violated by being touched by alien hands. In an apparent addendum or afterthought to the book in 18:6–19,[30] the mother is given a lengthy speech, again directed to her children, but one that emphasizes more typically "feminine" virtues (virginity, chastity, "guarding the rib from which woman was made") while it mentions for the first time in either account, 2 or 4 Maccabees, the young men's father. It is he who has given them the solid grounding in the Law, the Prophets, the Psalms, and it is he, not she, who has taught the sons the examples of the Jewish heroes (18:6–19). As Young notes, the father "replaces" the mother "in a pious, domestic setting."[31] The mother is thus refeminized, a process only hinted at in the narrative ending, which emphasizes her feminine modesty, the guarding of her body, even in death.

A rabbinic retelling of the story of the sons and their mother, now named as Miriam bat Tanhum, appears in its longest version in the fifth-century *Lamentations Rabbah*, a midrash on the book of Lamentations.[32] The tale, now set in the Roman persecutions of Jews, probably in connection with the Second Jewish War (132–135), largely serves to exegete the quote from that text with which it ends: "For these I [the Holy Spirit] weep" (Lam. 1:16). Van Henten and Avemarie note that one of the most obvious points of comparison between the later story and its earlier version in 2 and 4 Maccabees is the centrality of the character of the mother: "The fact that a woman plays the central role is exceptional, since the heroes of rabbinic martyr traditions are normally men."[33] In this version, the old priest Eleazar is absent, as is any mention of a husband or father. The focus is on the Miriam the mother and her sons. Each of the sons is given the option of prostrating himself before an image; each refuses, quoting Scripture as a reason, and each is summarily executed.

The youngest son, whose age is variously given as "six and a half years and two hours" or "two years and six months and six and a half hours,"[34] has the longest (and one might add most precocious) dialogue with "Caesar." When he is about to be executed for his defiance, his mother encourages him in a short speech that connects her, like the mother in 4 Maccabees, with Abraham. She tells him that he is soon to join his brothers in the "bosom of Abraham," and when he is there, he should give the patriarch the message that while he built an altar for one son, she has built seven and also actually sacrificed seven sons. But before this, when the order to execute her son is given, Miriam begs to "kiss him and hug him," and when he is given into her embrace, on the spot she "took out her breasts and nursed him with milk." This rather startling action is inexplicable, even in connection with the fulfillment of Scripture, from of all things the erotic Song of Solomon 4:11 ("Honey and milk are under your tongue"), but in the body rhetoric of martyrology, it makes sense in that it reinforces both the pathos and the courage of the mother (without using any of the descriptive terms in 4 Maccabees) while at the same time it effectively signals, more than in the Maccabean versions of the story, that she has a woman's body.

In the end, Miriam's suicide is not shown as an act of courage, but the result of madness, another touch of pathos. As Robert Doran suggests, "Perhaps the editors of the Babylonian Talmud did not want to show such prominence to a woman, and so they opted for the alternative death of the mother": by suicide rather than martyrdom.[35] Boyarin, who connects her story to another rare female martyr story, the execution of the (unnamed) wife of Rabbi Hanina ben Teradion, points out that for both of these "martyred mothers," the martyrdom is "simply an appendix to the martyrdom of the men in their lives."[36] It is not what the mother of the seven *says* or does, but what she *endures* as a woman that is important to the narratives, which see her role as that of encouraging the men to be active in the *agōn* rather than acting herself, except for taking charge of her own end: that encouragement is a mother's *martyria*. An interesting observation by Corinna Hasofferett in her blog, "Time in Tel-Aviv," provides a contemporary view of Miriam bat Tanhum's story: "Our tradition notes and appreciates deeply the passive heroism of the Israeli woman."[37] Perhaps the term "passive heroism" is the transformation that the transmitters of the story of Miriam bat Tanhum had in mind, although Galit Hasan-Rokem finds a strong resemblance between the rabbinic story of Miriam bat Tanhum and the Christian martyrdom of Perpetua. While denying influence either way, Hasan-Rokem suggests a "shared narrative tradition" between the two, a sharing that according to Boyarin would not be impossible, but even probable.[38]

In the early third-century CE *Martyrdom of Perpetua and Felicitas* we have other "martyred mothers," of whom Perpetua is the more prominent, a woman whose role is not merely encouragement of others but also a model for their behavior. The *Martyrdom* is another exercise in the complex process of verbal "virilization" and "refeminization." On the one hand, we have a rare first-person narrative of an upper-class female Christian convert whose social station ("*honeste nata, liberaliter instituta*," meaning "wellborn, brought up as a free person," 2.1) as well as her spiritual prominence ensures that her commands will be obeyed by others, even by men: for example, she is so imperious with the power of her choice that both her own father and her brother call her by the title "*domina*" (4.1; 5.5). Maureen A. Tilley observes, "In Perpetua's own self-portrait, the reader sees a young woman who moved from dependence on men to virtuous victory of her own virile image over the devil. In each encounter she took control of her bodily self."[39] Yet despite these images of control over men and Perpetua's own imaginary "virilization," the story at the end remains, as previously noted, "a story about women and their bodies."[40]As the introductory material to the Latin *passio* notes, there is among confessing Christians a prophetic unity of *virtus* (1.3), a *virtus* that the soldier Pudens perceives among them universally, even in prison (9.1); yet while this "manliness" is shared among the martyrs, it appears spiritual rather than physical, since they are still confined under judgment as criminals and their bodies are at the disposal of the Roman state.

At first the martyrdom of Perpetua seems a perfect illustration of Elliott's description of the *passio* as "hagiographic epic," whose "climactic center" is the "interrogation scene in which the tyrant and martyr face each other in the public courtroom."[41] Arrested for the crime of being Christian, tried before the public tribunal of the Roman governor Hilarianus, Perpetua asserts herself twice: she responds, "I will not" when encouraged to make sacrifice, and she affirms that she is a Christian. In the inverse of the way in which the mother of the Maccabean martyrs privately encourages her sons, her father publicly (and under pressure of the Roman official) attempts to discourage his daughter from persisting. Perpetua thus does "speak her *martyria*" in public, defying family and government authority, as Thecla is also to do.

Gradually also, again according to her own account, Perpetua sheds her female family ties rather than remaining connected to them, as in the martyrdom of the seven sons and their mother. Her father, whom she at first describes as using the "arguments of the devil [*diaboli*]" (3.3), fails to dissuade her, even by appeal to those very familial relationships that are most valued in the Roman world as part of the definition of *pietas*, devotion, which keeps that world alive (5.3) and that should be Perpetua's responsibility as a Roman matron.[42] Here she is described in much the same way as the unnamed women martyrs in 2 Maccabees and Miriam bat Tanhum (and later the lactating Felicitas) as having an "infant son at the breast [*ad uberam*] (2.2), and at first the fortunes of her infant preoccupy her. When he is taken away, however, her breast milk dries up and she no longer worries about him or the pain in her breasts. For Perpetua, her breasts, like her infant son, are no longer part of her concerns. One brother, Dinocrates, is dead: her prayer "delivers him" from after-death torment, so he too no longer concerns her. Another brother is with her in prison, but he addresses her as "*domina* [lady]" and asks the favor of a prophetic vision (4.1).

Perpetua asks for and is given better treatment for herself and others on two occasions: first, in her own account, to be allowed to have her baby with her (3.9); and again, in the martyrologist's account, in protest against the foolish severity of the tribune who suspects the Christians of using magic to get themselves out of the prison (16.3). Later, in the arena, she "fights back [*repugnavit*]," reminding her executioners of the agreement that she has made with them not to wear the garments of Roman pagan deities (18.5). On the day before the prisoners are to fight with the beasts, Perpetua has her last vision, that of fighting an "Egyptian," symbolic of the devil. Attended by young men, she describes herself as having her clothes stripped off and becoming herself a man: "*Et expoliata sum et facta sum masculus*" (10.7). Her nakedness is appropriate to a male combatant, where it would be disgraceful (as it later is, when she briefly appears naked in the arena) for a woman. As a man, "she" defeats the Egyptian. Nevertheless, the *lanista*, or trainer, from whom she receives the palm of victory, becoming an *athlophoros*, like the mother in 4 Maccabees, does not acknowledge her transformation: he calls her "daughter [*filia*]."

In her fellow martyr Saturus's vision, which is also recounted in the *passio*, however, both he and she have "gone out of the flesh" (11:2), and according to Saturus, Perpetua says she is happier than in the flesh (12.7). Thus far it seems as though in Perpetua's own visionary descriptions, she conquers as a man; in the male Saturus's vision, the "fleshly" gender does not matter. Perpetua also has a mission to accomplish: she and Saturus, already released from worldly concerns, must reconcile the quarreling bishop Optatus and the presbyter and teacher Aspasius, Perpetua speaking to them in Greek (13:4), apparently more learned than Saturus in the language of the higher clergy.

Of Felicitas, the other martyred mother, we do not have her own account, only the description of her imprisonment and martyrdom, both of which emphasize her female embodiment and neither of which describes her as overtly "masculine," except when the endurance of Christ is "within" her. Her pregnancy (lit., her "belly [*ventrem*]," 15.2) is emphasized because it might prevent her from being executed with the rest of the martyrs. Felicitas speaks only when, in response to her prayer, she is in the midst of a painful, difficult premature delivery and is taunted for her pain by the soldier. In the arena, she responds, "Another will be in me who will suffer for me, because I also will have suffered for him" (15.6). This is the extent of her testimony, and as if to emphasize what is physically "inside" her, a baby daughter is born, who is immediately taken from her to be brought up by "one of the sisters, as her daughter" (15.7). Felicitas, like Perpetua, no longer has family ties, and the only tie mentioned is female, not male. As with Perpetua, Felicitas's husband is not mentioned: since she is a slave woman, a usable "body," subject to the sexual predilections of a master, she may have no husband and hence no blood family ties. The favor of her "master" given to Felicitas is that of "the Lord [*Dominus*]," presumably Christ, and it allows her to give birth so that she can die with her comrades, her substitute *familia*, one of whom is the wellborn Perpetua (15.1).

From this point, as the martyrology moves with Felicitas and Perpetua toward the "spectacle," their female bodies and feminine behavior are emphasized and underlined, balancing if not undercutting their manly courage in the public eye. Moreover, in the arena, the women martyrs are emphatically *women*. Although graphic sexual mutilation, a persistent feature of many later accounts of women martyrs like those described by Brock and Harvey, is absent, exposure of their bodies, especially their breasts, is definitely present.[43] Instead of sexual mutilation or annihilation of these women's bodies, which both underlines them as female and then erases them, in the martyrdoms of Perpetua and Felicitas we have an overemphasis on them *as women and as women who have bodies.* As she walks toward her death, Perpetua is described as "*matrona Christi, Dei delicata* [the wife of Christ, the darling of God]."[44] Felicitas, who is glad because she has "safely given birth," is going "from the midwife to the *retiarius*, about to be washed after birth in a second [bloody] baptism" (18.3). Felicitas, like Miriam bat Tanhum and Perpetua earlier in prison, is also a nursing mother, a fact that may lead to her sometimes being conflated with the mother of the seven, as Felicitas of Rome.

Clothing and the lack of it is also emphasized, and it serves further to feminize the women. After Perpetua's imperious request for nonpagan clothing is granted, she sings (*psallebat*) as if she is "already treading on the Egyptian's head" as in her vision (18.7). Mentioning of the vision reminds us that she conquered the Egyptian in her *male* guise, thus linking her demand and its fulfillment to her masculine identity, and preparing us for the next event, in which her clothing is stripped off—but here she does *not* become a man. Instead, Perpetua and Felicitas are called "*puellae* [girls]," whose gender is to be matched with that of a "most ferocious heifer," the "beast" chosen as fitting for their female bodies (20.1). Stripped of their clothing (*dispoliatae*), the women stand exposed as a "delicate girl" (playing on the "*delicata Dei*" of Perpetua's entrance into the arena) and one "who had recently given birth, with dripping breasts." Even the public recoils at this shameful spectacle. Suitably reclothed, Perpetua seems to put on feminine modesty with her dress. When she is tossed by the heifer and her tunic is ripped, exposing her thigh, the Latin martyrologist rhymingly suggests that she is "*pudoris potius memor quam doloris* [more mindful of shame than of pain]" (20.4). She puts up her hair since it would be "unfitting for a female martyr to suffer with loosened locks [*non enim decebat martyram sparsis capillis pati*]" (20.5). While Felicitas says nothing further after the premature birth of her daughter, Perpetua's final words are to encourage her brother and the rest: "Do not let our sufferings cause you to stumble [*scandelizemini*, the Latin nearly identical with the Greek]" (20.10). Unlike the mother of the seven or her later incarnation, Miriam bat Tanhum, Perpetua's verbal encouragement is not private and only occurs after she has spoken a very public *martyria* at the tribunal and taken part in the *agōn* in the arena. Although her final words are encouragement of her brother, a related male, they are not her only words and do not constitute her only *martyria*. Her last utterance, however, is a scream as the trembling young gladiator strikes her on the bone, but she nonetheless guides his wavering hand to her throat, in the classical gesture of feminine death. As Loraux notes of women's death in Greek tragedies, women's glory—and mastery of themselves—is achieved in violent death, thereby crossing the boundaries between masculine and feminine.[45] Yet these boundaries can only be sustained on the stage or in the arena: crossing them is indeed death.

The final description of her by the narrator, however, is to call her "*tanta femina* [so great a woman!]." It is true that, as Lisa M. Sullivan observes with regard to this *passio*, Perpetua's visionary sex change "is at the very least indicative of what she perceives as her ultimate victory through resistance," that is, "of the submissive group (female) appropriating the imagery of the dominant (a powerful male body) in order to converse on the dominant's terms."[46] But the narrative ultimately also robs her of this victory by emphatically refeminizing her as physically female and thereby silencing her continuing challenge to those who live. Although in this case the dominant male body was a trembling Roman soldier, and although Perpetua may have willed her own death, as the narrator strongly suggests (my students see her as suicidal throughout), Perpetua does die in the Roman arena for the crime of being a Christian. Although she may converse with the dominant in the dominant's language (masculinity), she dies as a woman. Defiance cannot continue.

In the *Acts of Paul and Thecla* from the apocryphal New Testament, which Jan Bremmer suggests Perpetua may have read and in which she found her inspiration,[47] we have some very mixed messages indeed about appropriate behavior. Margaret P. Aymer has cogently suggested that the *Acts* as we now have it, with the virgin Thecla appearing overall as the ideal of Christian continence, represents a redaction of two separately originated folktales: one centered in Iconium, in which most of the women, including Thecla, "are silent, yet passionate actors"; and the other centered in Antioch, in which the women all oppose the male authorities and "have most of the speaking roles."[48] A further complication is offered by Elliott, who sees the *Acts of Paul and Thecla* as an alternative to the "hagiographic epic," the martyrology: the "hagiographic romance," with elements borrowed from the Greek romance novel, in which lovers vow chastity and fidelity to each other, despite parting and tribulations, only to be reunited in a happy ending.[49]

Given all of these observations, we must also remember the fact that, strictly speaking, the *Acts of Paul and Thecla* is not really a martyrdom at all in the sense of a *passio*, but a series of near misses. Thecla does not die in the several arenas where she is exposed; she is always miraculously saved; she is said to "give her witness [*martyria*]" only at the end of the story, to her murderous mother, Theocleia; after that, "having illumined many with the word of God," she "falls asleep with a beautiful sleep" (43).[50] Nevertheless, we might note two important things about Thecla: first, in both parts of the story, her physical beauty, along with her virginity and nobility, is emphasized, and in both parts also, as Gilbert Dagron has observed, she "is depicted naked more often than usual."[51] Accompanying this nakedness, which is part of her exposure in the arenas of Iconium and Antioch, and perhaps in contrast to it, is Thecla's appearance in male guise: she vows to cut her hair short in order to follow the recalcitrant Paul (25) en route from Iconium, and she finally adopts "*schēmati andrikō* [man's clothing]" when she searches for and runs him down finally in Myra (40). Both this "nakedness" and this "transvestite motif," as Brock and Harvey have termed it,[52] call for further exploration. Thecla's nakedness (her shameful public "exposure") emphasizes her female body and identity as a vulnerable woman; yet according to Stephen J. Davis, her male clothing not only disguises but "undoes" her status as a woman, enabling her to become a traveling apostle, her first attempt in Antioch being unsuccessful because she is dressed like a woman.[53]

In the Iconian narrative, Thecla, like Perpetua, "loses" her relationships to her household, when she becomes virtually enchanted (*thaumazein*) by Paul. Her mother, Theocleia, operating within the marriage paradigm of her Greco-Roman social world and the narrative traditions of the Greek "romance," cannot imagine anything other than that Thecla has fallen (unsuitably) in love. She suggests that Thecla's maiden modesty (8) has been "mastered" by "a new desire and a terrible passion [*kainē epithymia kai pathei deinō*]" (9) and calls her fiancé, Thamyris, who urges Thecla to "have some shame" and tell him about it. She is silent, not responding, whereupon Thamyris, Theocleia, and the maids of the household all weep "for the loss of a wife, a daughter, and a mistress" (10), as if Thecla is dead to all of these social roles. Indeed, on the level of expected behavior for a respectable Greek virgin, it appears as though Thecla is enamored with Paul and has lost all shame, immodestly leaving her household, visiting him in prison, kissing his chains. How debased can a noble girl become than to kiss the fetters of an unrelated man of a different ethnicity and social class? Her mother, anxious to be a good citizen at whatever cost, orders her—as a "lawless one [*anomon*]" and thus a threat to the civil order, an "unbride [*anymphon*]" and thus a threat to the familial order on which the civil order is based—to be burned in the "*theatron* [theater, but lit., 'place for seeing']" as a spectacle and an object lesson to terrify women who have listened to Paul. Thus, Thecla's "martyrdom" is intended for Paul, not for herself, although he ironically is not present. Thecla is brought in naked (*gymnē*, 22), a publicly shamed symbol of her immodest behavior (think of the crowd's gasps at Perpetua's and Felicitas's nakedness; here they are silent) and exposed to the crowd, including the young men and virgins who cooperate in bringing the wood (they all appear to be against her). Yet the governor "is astonished [*ethaumasen*]" at the "power in her." Thecla, as throughout the narrative so far, is silent, looking around for Paul "like a lamb in the wilderness for the shepherd," and has a vision that she thinks is Paul but is actually the Lord Jesus, who vanishes into the heavens (21). Still mute, she makes the sign of the cross, at which signal God causes a hailstorm to put out the fire, and Thecla is saved (only later does she find out this is not in response to the sign of the cross but from Paul's prayer at a distance, 24). In none of this action is Thecla other than silent and passive. Although her maidenly modesty appears to her family and city to have been lost, she has merely transferred her allegiance to a purer object of affection, "the word of the celibate life" as spoken by Paul.

Once she meets Paul, however, he will not allow her to follow him, even when she suggests that she cut her hair, because "the time is *aischros* [ugly, disgraceful] but you are comely" (25). Ironically, he fears *she* will be tempted. He says that he fears *she* will act "like a cowardly man [*deilandrēsēs*]," recalling the praise of the masculine courage of the Maccabean mother. When she persists, "Only give me the seal [baptism] in Christ, and no temptation will touch me," Paul demurs, again urging her to be courageous: "You shall take the water." With the male/female roles already switching, the scene shifts to Antioch, where Paul betrays Thecla in terms reminiscent of the betrayal of Jesus by Judas, claiming he does not know her, "nor is she mine" (26), and thus exposes her to sexual attack by the Syriarch Alexander, "a very powerful man," who tries to embrace this "loose" woman on the open street. Thecla boldly stands up to him, speaking in public for the first time: "Do not force the stranger [woman, *xenē*], do not force the slave girl (*doulē*) of (the) God." Imperiously, she makes a quasi-epic boast: "I am the first woman [*prōtē*] of the Iconians, and because I was unwilling to marry Thamyris, I was expelled from the city." After making her short *apologia*, Thecla in turn exposes Alexander to public shame by pulling the wreath, symbol of his office (and its power), off his head and ripping his cloak.

Brought before the governor of Antioch by the insulted Alexander, Thecla is again bold. She speaks out, confessing to her deeds, and is sentenced "to the beasts," the typical Roman condemnation of criminals *ad bestias*. Here is the speech act that makes the heroic *martyria*, the main element in hagiographic epic. The women of the city all cry out against the "evil" and "unholy" judgment, and one of the prominent women, Tryphaena, offers to keep Thecla "pure" (sexually unmolested) until her death. When Thecla is led to the beasts, once more the women all cry out against the "bitter spectacle [*theama*]" (32). This time the spectacle, not Thecla, is "lawlessness [*anomia*]." Like Perpetua, Thecla is once more stripped and thrown into the stadium. Once more, one of the beasts is matched with the martyr's sex, but the "fierce lioness" does not harm her: instead, she defends Thecla to the death.

As Thecla prays before she faces the next lot of beasts, she sees a "ditch full of water" and decides, "Now it is the time [*kairos*] for me to be washed." Not only does Thecla herself decide that it is time to baptize herself (without waiting for Paul); she also actively seeks what might be her death in the manner of the mother of seven, Miriam bat Tanhum, and perhaps even Perpetua, by leaping into the pit of seals, saying, "In the name of Jesus Christ, I baptize myself on the last day!" (34).[54] God not only destroys the seals with a lightning bolt, but also surrounds Thecla with a "cloud of fire," so that none can see her naked, preserving her maidenly modesty in this very public setting. Various other attempts to kill Thecla fail, including setting loose on her ferocious bulls whose testicles are prodded with red-hot irons (Thecla's male enemies have no shame; the symbolism is quite obvious). She is finally released after her patroness Tryphaena appears to die, whereupon Alexander asks for the combat to stop lest the whole city be destroyed. When the governor asks, "Who are you?" Thecla gives her testimony, beginning with Pauline rhetoric, "I am the slave girl of the living God." When he offers to put her clothing back on, Thecla, above shame, retorts, "He who clothed me when naked among the beasts will clothe me with salvation on day of judgment" (38). All the women cry out "with a loud voice [*phonē megalē*]" when Thecla is released, "*so that the whole city was shaken by their voice*" (38). Thecla's bold speech and testimony, in contrast to her silent meekness in Iconium, gives the women of Antioch, already vocal, a literally earthshaking "voice." Tryphaena, Thecla's substitute mother, and the maids of her household are converted by Thecla's preaching "the word of God," thus reversing the situation in Iconium (39). Thecla's triumph over the powerful men in Antioch is complete, made possible by the women, from the "queen" Tryphaena to the maids.

Although there is "great joy," this story does not make it the happy ending. Thecla finally does adopt male garb to go in search of Paul (perhaps having learned her lesson in Antioch about lone women appearing on the streets), upon whom the tables are turned when *he* is "amazed" to see *her*, as she was at first at his preaching. Once more trying to avoid her in case of "some other temptation" in her (this time it is clear *he* is tempted, not she), she retorts, "I have taken the bath, Paul" (40). The use of the term *loutron*, "washing," gives us ironic resonances with Felicitas's "going to wash [*mellousa lousasthai*, in the Greek version of the *Martyrdom*]" (18.3), and the "well-washed [*kalōs elousō*]" of Saturus (Gk. *Martyrdom* 21.1) of the second "baptism" of martyrdom. Finally emboldened to touch her at last (he takes her hand), Paul sends Thecla away immediately, back to Iconium, but with the words, "Go, teach the word of God" (41). For the last time, Thecla has to submit to Paul's authority, even such a feeble one. She gives her witness in Iconium (*diamartyramenē*, 43) and finishes her ministry in Seleucia, "having illumined [*phōtisasa*] many."

What does all this switching of male-female roles, silent physical witness, and bold speech in the *Acts of Paul and Thecla* indicate about constructions and subversions of social ideals of "femininity" and "masculinity"? Aymer's view—that two separate folktales about Paul and Thecla, the male and female apostles, were put together and "harmonized" by an early Christian redactor—is confirmed in part by Boyarin, who claims that earlier Christian texts like the *Acts of Paul and Thecla* that depicted the "virilization" of women were transformed in later centuries to those that "feminized" men by exalting the "passive female virtue" of withdrawal, silence, and virginity.[55] If this is indeed the case, we would expect to see, as I think we do, the *Acts of Paul and Thecla* as a "transitional" text, in which a single female character appears to embody both genders and a male character is "feminized," although in my opinion, the most that one can say for Paul here is that he is on his way to being demasculinized. Nevertheless, I do not think that the ideal of virginity is necessarily that of a male following a female model, but more of the reappropriation of a variant male model: that of the self-controlled, continent male who will not succumb to fleshly temptation. In this sense, Thecla is defeminized. It remains to be seen whether this is a good thing or not. As Brock and Harvey note of Syrian Christianity, accounts[56] of female martyrs are stunning for the regularity with which they depict either "sexual mutilation" or "sexual violence" against women or the "transvestite motif," in which women "destroy their identity as women" and take on that of men. This motif certainly emerges in the story of Thecla and to a lesser degree in that of Perpetua. About these phenomena, they observe:

The sexual mutilation of women by torture and the sexual annihilation of women by the taking on of a male identity are both about the same issue—namely, power and dominance in the relationship between men and women. And these events are found in hagiography about women, both legendary and historical. The events described in each given instance may or may not be true. But men are telling these stories to women as their audience and to men about women, and they tell them as if they were true. What are we to hear?[57]

Inevitably, modern readers, at least judging from the many contested "readings" of these stories, especially that of Thecla, which is the most ambiguous, perhaps deliberately, perhaps thanks to Aymer's putative "reconciliation" of the oppositional Iconian and Antiochene versions of the story, will "hear" different things. But what did those who first formulated, listened to, interpreted, and were inspired by these stories "hear" or "see"? The next chapters will examine the early Christian spectrum of responses.

3

Tough Mothers and Female Contenders: Perpetua and Felicitas

> So she got up and when she saw that Felicitas had fallen, she went to her and extended her hand and lifted her up. And the two stood together.
> —*Martyrdom of Perpetua and Felicitas* 20.6–7[1]

MAKING MARTYRS MEN

If we are to discover how the stories of women martyrs like Perpetua and Thecla were interpreted in emerging Christian circles, we need look no farther than the composition of their martyrologies,[2] which are conscious constructions, for the purposes not only of pious propaganda but also of communal identity making. As Gillian Clark asserts with regard to the Christian church's exaltation of martyrdom, "Martyrdom supplied . . . a dominant image of what it is to be Christian."[3] Martyrs and holy people might appear in narratives to construct their own identities, challenging and resisting the society around them, but they do not serve in isolation as examples of conduct and self-formation: rather, they serve as an example of the collective reconfiguration of a community's understanding of itself.[4] When, according to the *Martyrdom of Perpetua and Felicitas*, Perpetua finishes her own prison diary and invites the continuation of the narrative to describe the action in the amphitheater—"*Si quis uoluerit, scribat* [Let whoever wants to, write it]" (10.15)—this is a clue to the careful reader that someone indeed was already willing to write the account and to mold it into the propaganda for conversion and edification that it became. As Herbert Musurillo also observes of the *Martyrdom*, "This *passio* is, in a sense, the archetype of all later *Acts* of the Christian martyrs," and so we might expect its interpretations and variations to be part of the unfolding of the Christian story as it emerged from persecution to eventual recognition and as it later faced challenges from within during the second to the fourth centuries CE.[5]

The one who was willing to write the rest of the narrative, including the account of Perpetua's fellow martyr Saturus's vision, "which he himself wrote," as well as the scene of the martyrdoms, was long assumed to be Tertullian, the acerbic churchman of Carthage. His dates of activity during the late second and perhaps the early third century might just coincide with the deaths of Perpetua and Felicitas. Certainly reverence for martyrs was an important part of North African Christian worship and continued to be so long after the persecutions by the Roman imperial government ceased. Women were also included in the tally of North African martyrs. Even before Perpetua and Felicitas, the *Acts of the Scillitan Martyrs*, a brief account of the testimony of Christians who were sentenced to be beheaded at Carthage in 180, included five women, Donata, Vestia, Secunda, Januaria, and Generosa. Three of them (Donata, Vestia, and Secunda) have brief, one-line speaking parts before the Roman proconsul, in which they confess to being Christian, very much like Perpetua's own trial and answer before the proconsular tribunal (*Martyrdom of Perpetua and Felicitas* 6.3–6).[6] In *To Scapula* 3.4 Tertullian mentions the proconsul named in the *Acts of the Scillitan Martyrs*, Vigellius Saturninus, as the first to bring executions "here [*hic*]," for which he was stricken with blindness. Tertullian also mentions Hilarianus, the Roman proconsul who tried Perpetua and her companions (3.1), although he does not mention Perpetua here. He does mention Perpetua's passion in *The Soul* 55.4, in that she sees only other martyrs in paradise in a vision on the day of her death (a vision actually received by Saturus), supporting his argument that the only way to paradise is through martyrdom.

One more consideration to add in deciding for or against Tertullian's composition of the preface to the *Martyrdom of Perpetua and Felicitas* and the account of the *passio* itself is whether the whole of the account, including Perpetua's visions, is "Montanist" or not. Montanism, named after the only prominent male of the group, is also called the "New Prophecy." It was a form of prophetic eschatological Christianity that arose in Asia Minor in the second century and soon spread throughout Christian congregations, especially in North Africa. The New Prophecy placed a premium on ascetic sexual abstinence accompanying ecstatic visionary experiences, especially those of women, and its most prominent prophets were three women, Maximilla, Quintilla, and Priscilla.[7] The movement did not shy away from martyrdom, either, since its members believed that Christ would soon return (according to the vision of Priscilla, as a woman), and therefore the resurrection of the dead would soon take place. Tertullian, who became a convert to Montanist Christianity, mentions a Carthaginian ecstatic Christian woman in *The Soul* 9.4 who can converse with angels and occasionally even with God. Timothy Barnes claims that the *Martyrdom of Perpetua and Felicitas* is thoroughly Montanist, beginning with a polemical preface defending visionary experiences that are not past, but continue into the present as signs of the coming of the end.[8] Nevertheless, Barnes does not wholeheartedly endorse the belief that Tertullian was the "author," or at least the author of the preface and *passio*, of the *Martyrdom of Perpetua and Felicitas*, although he certainly knew of a version of it.[9]

None of these arguments support the authorship of Tertullian or even possibly the Montanist character of the *Martyrdom*,[10] but what they do indicate is the lively interest in martyrdom, particularly of women, in North African Latin literature by the beginning of the third century CE. Tertullian, one of the first great Latin church fathers, refers both to the Scillitan martyrs (although perhaps not to the written *Acts*) and to some version of the martyrdom of Perpetua that also included the visions of Saturus. Tertullian is thus the terminus a quo for knowledge of Perpetua's story, presumably in some written form. (Ironically, he is also the terminus a quo for the *Acts of Paul and Thecla*, as we shall see.) What version of this story existed at the time (since according to the *Martyrdom*, it took place in 203 CE)? According to Jacqueline Amat and Åke Fridh, two early versions of the story existed, a Latin and a Greek; in Amat's opinion the Latin seems to be derived from an earlier Latin "archetype" that in turn may have passed through an oral phase, while the Greek is a translation of yet another Latin original.[11] In addition, there are two *Acta*, containing only an abbreviated trial and arena scene, with only one third-person account of Perpetua's first vision of the ladder, from the fourth or possibly the fifth century, that date the martyrdoms from at least fifty years later. Interestingly, these *Acta* supply Felicitas with a brother (Revocatus, her "fellow slave" in the earlier Latin *Martyrdom*) and a husband, whom she despises; and Perpetua with a husband as well, who appears with her family to implore her recantation.

In both versions of these *Acta*, the Roman judge seems more sympathetic, Perpetua more adamant (she rejects—lit., "throws off"—her infant son), and Saturus has a leading role, responding for all of the Christians at the initial trial.[12] Although Amat does not accept the argument of P. Monceaux that the epitomes of the *Martyrdom* were edited to remove all "Montanist" references, she does concede that they contain written and oral elements that attest to an ongoing tradition and perhaps a revision of the story of the martyrs. In the same fashion the inscription found by Père Delattre at the site of the Basilica Maiorum in Mcidfa, a suburb of Carthage, where Perpetua and Felicitas were supposedly entombed, recites the names of all of the martyrs, beginning with Saturus, and then ending with Perpetua.[13] This list essentially follows that of the first version of the *Acta*, in which Saturus and Saturninus ("*uenerabiles uiri*, [worthy men]" head the list, followed by Revocatus and Felicitas, brother and sister, and finally Perpetua (*Acta* I.1). The popular thirteenth-century catalog of martyrs' stories, Jacopo da Voragine's *Golden Legend*, perhaps following the second version of these *Acta*, lists Saturninus as the principal saint, with Satyra (rather than Saturus), Revocata (male), Felicitas, and Perpetua (7.17).[14]

The evolution of the story of Perpetua and her companions, and the way in which subsequent audiences "heard" or "saw" them, does not actually begin with the writing down of their martyrdoms, or with their commemoration in tombs and inscriptions, but with what is said *about* the martyrs and their significance for the fledgling church. Not surprisingly, this "witness," like the written martyrologies, is gendered. Francine Cardman notes that of the martyr stories from the second to fourth centuries, the time when most martyrdoms occurred until the "peace" of Constantine, most that contained narratives about women also included stories of men, and only two are "solely about women," but that in accounts of women, "the inherent ambiguity of martyrdom is dramatically displayed in women's bodies with a directness unmatched in the case of men."[15] In the writings of Tertullian, who is the first to mention Perpetua and Felicitas; the later North African Augustine, who preached three sermons for the martyrs' feast day; and Quodvultdeus, the mid-fifth-century bishop of Carthage, who also preached on the subject, seemingly more reluctantly—gender and its value are important factors in understanding the martyrs' significance, just as they are in the *Martyrdom*.[16]

TERTULLIAN AND THE KEY TO PARADISE

To begin with Tertullian, we might expect that his post-Montanist writings (if we can identify these with any confidence) would be less polemical against women's authority than his pre-Montanist writings, simply because women's leadership with regard to prophetic and ascetic behavior was more prominent and revered in the New Prophecy than in Catholic Christianity. He does refer to woman as the "*ianua diaboli* [gate of the devil]" in *The Apparel of Women* 1.1, a quote famous for its apparent misogyny, and castigates with considerable vitriol the female "viper" who dares to make pronouncements on baptism, claiming the example of Thecla from a work Tertullian declares "made up" (*Baptism* 17.4–5); both works date from his pre-Montanist (or rather his Catholic) phase. He also quotes from Montanist women prophets in what seem to be post-Montanist works, referring to an "oracle" of Prisca (Priscilla) in his *Exhortation to Chastity* (10.5). Nonetheless, as the work of Marie Turcan has shown, it is not the "Montanist" dividing line that changes Tertullian's attitude toward women, nor is that attitude ever entirely negative: what seems to concern him is the welfare of the soul, which can be hampered by a female body that is too subject to the vanity, norms, and customs of society when persecution is on the horizon.[17] He gives his praise to Christian women who are able to dress modestly, but he characterizes this modesty in masculine terms: luxuries, particularly in adornment, through their softness (*mollitia*) are capable of "making the manliness of the faith effeminate [*fidei virtus effeminari*]" (*The Apparel of Women* 2. 13.3). Tertullian advocates casting off such *retinacula* (fetters) for an ascetic type of training that focuses on hardships and aims at persecution, ready to assume the *stolae* (female garments) that are prepared for martyrs (2.13.5).[18]

That he fully expects women to be capable of such effort as they aim at martyrdom is clear from his address *To the Martyrs*, in which he again uses athletic and military training as models for Christian bodily preparation, adding that "holy women" should be worthy of their sex, using the pagan examples of Lucretia's suicide to "gain glory for her chastity" (*Martyrs* 4.4), along with those of philosophers, among whom Dido queen of Carthage is included, who in Tertullian's view killed herself honorably to avoid a second marriage (4.5); and the wife of Hasdrubal, who threw herself with her sons into the fire lest they see their husband and father dishonored before the victorious Scipio (4.5). Along with examples like that of the noble Roman Regulus is oddly included that of Cleopatra, a woman submitting herself "freely [*libens*]" to the "beasts [*bestias*]," alluding to the condemnation of the martyrs *ad bestias* (4.6). As an example of one who feared neither death nor torture, he includes "the Athenian prostitute," who being tortured by the tyrant Hippias in connection with a conspiracy, defiantly bit off her own tongue and spat it into the tyrant's face rather than give him information (4.7).[19] (Interestingly, Augustine also uses Lucretia's suicide as an example, but to show what Christian women, even when raped, should *not* do, because it is taking a life; cf. *City of God* 1.19.) For Tertullian, martyrdom is an expression of true manliness. In *The Soul* 55.5 he urges Christians not to die "of gentle fevers and on [soft] couches," but as martyrs, following the example of their Lord.[20] This exhortation follows his use of the example of Perpetua, whom he calls "*fortissima martyra*," the "bravest (female) martyr," who in a "revelation on the day of her passion" sees only martyrs in paradise, a proof that only those who die in Christ can enter the place closed to those who die "in Adam" and not "in Christ"—meaning not as martyrs (*The Soul* 55.4).

It is tempting to find connections between Tertullian's preaching about the necessity of martyrdom and the glory it confers on the martyrs and the composition of the *Martyrdom of Perpetua and Felicitas*. Although by now many scholars are skeptical of the assertion that Tertullian, in his Montanist period, was responsible for writing the preface and the actual martyrdom, Dom G. D. Schlegel asserts "striking parallelism" between Tertullian's *To the Martyrs* and the *Martyrdom of Perpetua and Felicitas*. In his view, the language of training Christians in "preparation for the fight" in *To the Martyrs*, including the comparison to gladiatorial training and combat, "is very suggestive of the description by Perpetua of her wrestling match with the Egyptian."[21] Although it is likely that Tertullian either himself had witnessed a martyrdom in the arena at Carthage (and he certainly was well aware of the "spectacles" in that city, warning Christians against attending them as spectators, in *Spectacles*), it is not necessary to assume that he is the person who took up Perpetua's challenge to write of the coming contest, still less that he himself wrote the whole of the *Martyrdom*. Nonetheless, it might be said that this statement looks suspiciously like an editorial comment, an endorsement by the chief martyr herself to write an eyewitness account, which though quite different in language and emphasis than Perpetua's own prison diary, shares some of the assumptions about men and women, their bodies, and gendered behavior with it. Primarily, these assumptions are that strength in combat is an attribute of men, particularly men whose training as soldiers and athletes includes "hard" exercise and indifference to pain (e.g., Tertullian, *To the Martyrs* 3.1–5), and that women's bodies, with those of "softer" and more effeminate men, are less capable of bearing pain, more susceptible to public shame when exposed.

The scene in the *Martyrdom* (15) that portrays Felicitas's childbirth is quite instructive in this regard. As she experiences the "natural difficulty" of premature childbirth and a painful labor, one of the servants in the prison taunts her: "What you are suffering now, what will you do when you are thrown to the beasts [*bestias*], that you had so little regard for when you refused to sacrifice?" (15.5). While the obvious focus in this encounter is on Felicitas's reply, that Christ will be suffering for her in the arena (15.6), there is an underlying assumption that relates women's endurance in childbirth to that of men in combat. Although several Greek tragedies make this comparison, its most notable example is that of Euripides's Medea (in *Medea*), who says she would rather be a soldier in the line of battle three times than bear one child.[22] When first in prison, Perpetua likewise describes herself as "tormented" with care for her nursing infant (3.6), but in her combat with the "Egyptian" in her final vision (10), she fights naked, a shameful condition for a woman and a matron-mother at that (20.2–3), and actually becomes a man (10:7), oiled by her male assistants, unafraid to fight all-out, battering her opponent in the head with her heels. This vision foreshadows her paradoxical victory through death in the arena and demonstrates the "endurance of the flesh [*sufferentia carnis*]" promised her at her baptism through the same vision-granting Spirit (3.5).

Saturus's vision (11–13) repeats some of the imagery of Perpetua's visions: the ascent (but up a gentle hill, not up a dangerous ladder); the garden with the old man (white-haired here rather than gray-haired as in Perpetua's vision; 4); the presence of previous martyrs (which may account for the conflation of visions in Tertullian's *The Soul*); the sense of childlike happiness (they are told to "go play" by the heavenly elders) and freedom from the flesh. There is no sense of combat here; there is only peace. Saturus and Perpetua even intervene to settle a quarrel between bishop Optatus and Aspasius the presbyter, clergy they respected in earthly life (13). Unlike her first vision (4), Perpetua does not have to come behind Saturus, who has already reached paradise; they ascend together, side by side, and work together to reconcile the ecclesiastical quarrel. In this vision both are happy: Saturus when he wakes up; Perpetua because she has had her wish granted, no longer to be "in the flesh" (12.7), however enduring. The account of Saturus's martyrdom, however, implies rather than strongly emphasizes valiant behavior appropriate to a male combatant: he exhorts the convert soldier Pudens (21.1); he is dispatched, as he wanted to be, by a leopard rather than a bear, being "well-washed" in his bloody baptism (compared to Felicitas, who is also "washed" in the blood of martyrdom after childbirth); and at the point of death he dips his ring into his own blood as a memorial for Pudens, urging him to have no fear but to stand firm (21.4). In short, he behaves like a soldier facing a noble death. There is no need to emphasize his courageous masculinity any further. Saturus is the leader: first to ascend the celestial ladder, first to die, the one who voluntarily gave himself up and who "edified" the rest (4.5). He dies, as he lived, like a noble man.

THE MANLY WOMEN OF CYPRIAN AND AUGUSTINE

According to Amat, some of the strong resemblances between the writings of Tertullian and others to the *Martyrdom of Perpetua and Felicitas* can be explained because of the latter's virtually immediate wide diffusion among Christians in the province of Africa, its popularity contributing to the shorter editions in the *Acta* and their similar widespread distribution.[23] This group was already known for its emphasis on martyrdom and its valuing of visionary experiences that often preceded and sometimes (in the case of visions of the martyrs) followed martyrdoms. Cyprian, the first bishop of Carthage to be martyred (258), after going into hiding under the persecution of Decius (249–250), refers to martyrdom in two texts, *Exhortation to Martyrdom* and *The Glory of Martyrdom*. In the former, rallying the "soldiers of Christ for the heavenly and spiritual contest" of martyrdom, he cites the "admirable" mother of the seven in 2 Maccabees, who "was neither broken down by the weakness of her sex, nor moved by her manifold bereavement" (11).[24] In his own Tertullianesque *The Dress of Virgins* 6, Cyprian urges virgins to "glory in the flesh" only when it is "crucified for confession of the name [of Christ]," in which case he finds "a woman is found stronger than men in tortures, when she endures fire or crosses or iron or beasts, to obtain the crown [of victory]" (PL 4:173). In *The Glory of Martyrdom*, Cyprian urged (presumably male) Christians to abandon spouses, children, and grandchildren for the sake of a heavenly victory (17) and portrayed Christ as "rejoicing in his soldier" (26). Cyprian is extremely concerned about the possibility of men becoming women in "spectacles," particularly in the theater, which portrays "emasculated men," the sexual vigor of whom has been "softened" by the disgrace of an "enervated body" (*To Donatus* 8). As Peter Brown notes, Cyprian was also much exercised by the possibility of Christian "effeminacy" in the battle against the devil, who seeks to "soften Christian hardness [*ut molliat Christianam vigorem*]" out of envy and jealousy because of his fall. For Cyprian, according to Brown, the church itself was a hard, disciplined body that had trained itself through "daily martyrdom," and "ever-vigilant control" of its more unruly members.[25]

The deacon Pontius's laudatory account of Cyprian's own martyrdom (258) in his *Life of Cyprian* is apparently influenced by the *Martyrdom of Perpetua and Felicitas*, to which it disparagingly refers in the prologue as coming from "laity and catechumens," whereas this martyrdom is that of a bishop and consequently more important.[26] According to Amat, the *Martyrdom of Perpetua and Felicitas* had influenced two other martyr stories dating to the time of Cyprian, the *Passion of Marian and James* and the *Passion of Montanus and Lucius*.[27] This view is confirmed by Maureen Tilley, who asserts that "North African martyr stories owe a major debt to their shaping by the *Passion of Perpetua and Felicitas*."[28] The oft-repeated first vision of Perpetua, the ladder leading to heaven, which she mounts as she treads on the head of the serpent (*Martyrdom* 4.3–7), according to Johannes Quasten, is appropriated in a fresco depicting a male martyr in the Catacomb of Saints Marcus and Marcellianus.[29] So it is no surprise that Pontius was influenced by these narratives and shares some of their motifs. He depicts Cyprian as having a vision that predicts his martyrdom (12), and he probably refers to the scene in the *Martyrdom of Perpetua and Felicitas* in which Perpetua guides the shaking hand of the young tribune to her throat: Cyprian, too, tries to grasp the executioner's trembling hand to assist in his own beheading, but in the end God strengthens it and the martyrdom is accomplished (18). Pontius shares Cyprian's views of the thoroughly militant and masculine martyr: he depicts the bishop as the officer of Christ and of God, striding into the arena and followed by disciples as if by an army (16).

By the fourth century, when Catholic Christians in North Africa were in combat with Donatists as well as Montanists, the question was how martyrs should be appropriately honored, or more cynically, to be best employed in the service of the church. J. Patout Burns observes that the Donatists—who objected most strenuously to those who had, in their view, been traitors to the cause of Christ and avoided martyrdom—"had taken a particular interest in the cult and even imitation of the martyrs, making this heritage a characteristic of their communion."[30] There was the continuing presence of the Montanist influence, with its reverence for apocalyptic eschatological visions and women's ecstasy, coupled with a strong encratite strain. Perpetua, however, was a heroine not only to the Montanists but also to orthodox Christians.[31] How were the latter to deal with her example? If, as F. C. Klawiter and others note, the Christians who were merely imprisoned for the faith and thus became "confessors" were able to forgive the sins of Christians who sought their aid, restoring them to communion with the church—if these confessors included women, the Montanist emphasis on women's authority as martyrs and prophets, as well as the Donatist reverence for the martyrs, created a serious problem for the Catholic (orthodox) church, with its constitution of "ecclesiastical authority as male."[32] What better way to incorporate the authority of women martyrs into the service of the male-dominated Catholic church than to praise them as men? They would not be around to challenge the Christian male power structure as they had symbolically shattered that of the Roman pagan hierarchy.

The co-optation of Perpetua into the service of male-dominated Christian discourse, which uneasily saw itself, as we have seen with Cyprian and later with Augustine, as being too readily designated weak and effeminate, not only by its opponents but also by its own apologists, begins with the popularity of her first vision: the ladder extending into heaven, whose ascent is perilous and which symbolizes the martyr's attainment of her heavenly goal (*Martyrdom* 4.3–10). This image for communication between the human and divine realms is as old as the story of Jacob (Gen. 28:12–17) and as modern as Led Zeppelin's "Stairway to Heaven." Yet the image is appropriated in a fresco in the fourth-century catacombs of Saints Marcus and Marcellianus, which shows "a man climbing a ladder beneath which appears a threatening dragon or serpent," one of the "two eponymous martyrs."[33] We have seen how Perpetua is appropriated by Tertullian by attributing Saturus's vision of entry into the paradise of martyrs to her, even though he declares her the "bravest [*fortissima*]" woman martyr. But if the *Martyrdom of Perpetua and Felicitas* was in fact Montanist and accords authority and validity to female confessors as well as to visionaries, this authority had become a problem for the Catholic church in North Africa *post pacem* and remained a source of conflict for another two hundred years.

Augustine, who assuredly had no more elevated a concept of women than Tertullian or Cyprian, was engaged in combat with a number of challenges to the orthodox church in North Africa, including the unforgiving Donatism. Augustine nevertheless had to recognize the importance of the martyrdoms of Perpetua, Felicitas, and their companions, whose *passio* was being read aloud in his church (*Sermon 282.2*), probably as part of a celebration of the martyrs' feast day. At the same time he denied both the authority of women as leaders in the existing church and curtailed what he and other Catholic bishops, including his mentor Ambrose, abhorred as excessive reverence for the dead martyrs (*Confessions* 6). As Patricia Cox Miller observes, Augustine effectively translated the martyrdom of Perpetua and Felicitas into examples "of orthodox Christian courage and faith and . . . understood [their] fortitude as male."[34] Following the custom of commemorating the *dies natalis*, the "birthday" or day of martyrdom of the martyrs, Augustine preached three sermons on Perpetua and Felicitas between the years 400 and 420;[35] his successor Quodvultdeus (whose sermons were often attributed to Augustine) also preached at least one. According to Kenneth B. Steinhauser, Augustine was very well aware of the Montanist nature of the *Martyrdom* and the nature of the authority Montanists accorded to women, especially ecstatic women, on an equal basis with men.[36] I do not believe, with Steinhauser, that Perpetua's fourth and final vision, in which she becomes male, demonstrates "the insignificance of personal gender identity" that is a mark of Montanism (in fact, I believe that the vision demonstrates exactly the opposite, its very *significance*). Yet Augustine uses some very clever rhetoric in order to emphasize the martyrs as female and therefore having inherited the fallen nature of Eve, but as redeeming themselves through the manliness of their actions. Steinhauser also points out Augustine's use of this rhetoric of gender in citing Perpetua's visionary combat with the Egyptian in his "anti-Montanist" response to Vincentius Victor, in *The Nature and Origin of the Soul*. Augustine characterizes Perpetua's vision as a dream, in which she could be *in virum conversa* (changed into a man), but while her body, retaining its feminine sex, lay sleeping, her soul alone could be put into "the likeness of a man's body": her soul (*anima*) could change bodies, but her body could not be transformed.[37]

In his first sermon on their feast day, Augustine neatly puns on the names of the saints, who have "flourished in perpetual felicity [*perpetua felicitate*]" because they retained "the name of Christ" (confessed they were Christians) in battle (*in praelio*), obtaining his name as a reward (*in praemio*; *Sermon 280* 1.1). He expands on their example as one worthy of admiration but not capable of imitation: "What is more glorious than these women [*feminae*], whom men [*uiri*] may more easily admire than imitate?" Their service to Christ makes them, "according to the inner human [*interiorem hominem*] found to be neither male nor female [*nec masculus nec femina*]," and while they were "women in body [*feminae corpore*]," their strength (or manliness) of mind (*virtus mentis*) "took away the sex of their flesh [*sexum carnis abscondat*]." Augustine alludes to the ladder vision of Perpetua by saying that the same means (the "ancient serpent") that caused the first woman to fall was the step for her ascent, treading on the dragon's head with her "chaste foot," insinuating, as will be seen so many times in the future, that the power of chastity (and later virginity) is more than a match for the devil. Yet where is the woman who was oblivious of the attack of the mad heifer (4)? No longer on this earth. Again, Augustine plays down the importance of martyrdom in the current Christian world by means of a pun on Felicitas's name: "The happiness (felicity) of some martyrs is before, others after, the resurrection" (5). As throughout, his point is that current Christians are unlike these martyrs and cannot equal them (6), a difference from the stringency of the Donatists. There is no more martyrdom to imitate, only to celebrate. He outlines the "sober joy" for the celebration of their feast day (in contrast to the often carnival-like celebrations progressively restricted by the North African Catholic bishops),[38] but urges the martyrs to "have mercy on us" and "pray for us" as heavenly intercessors.

Augustine continues his rhetorically masterful emphasis on the ability of Christ to strengthen feminine weakness in his second sermon on the feast day of the martyrs Perpetua and Felicitas (*Sermon 281*). As in the first sermon, he calls them "*famulae*" (serving-girls) of God, not only equating Perpetua's noble status in the *Martyrdom* (which he does not mention) with the servile status of Felicitas, but also asserting their humble status, even as martyrs, before God, especially with regard to their gender: "For the crown (of victory) is more glorious, where the sex is weaker. For certainly a manly mind [*virilis animus*] accomplishes something greater in women, by as much as feminine fragility does not fail under so great a weight" (1). He goes on to praise them as "*univirae*," one-man women, the Roman and later the Christian ideal, but their spouse (*vir*) is Christ, like that of the chaste virgin, the church. It is from this husband that they draw their strength, their manliness [*virtus*], to defeat the devil, women defeating the enemy who first defeated "man [*virum*]"; the one who was weakened by them now appears "unconquered [*invictus*]." He (Christ) made women die "like men [*viriliter*]," faithfully (*fideliter*), and for their sake he consented to be born of a woman.

Augustine refers to Perpetua's own narrative (*de se ipsa revelatum esse narravit*), her vision of fighting the devil (2), so he must have known of the version of the *Martyrdom* that included it. He acknowledges that in that combat she was transformed into the image of "the perfect man [*virum perfectum*]," of the full age of Christ. The reference is to Ephesians 4:13; yet here, as in the *City of God* (22.18), Augustine implies that the women's resurrected and restored body will be one of Christ's age at death, but since it is only the *image*, the body will still be that of a woman. He also continues his image of female martyrs redeeming the weak Eve by proving stronger than men: the devil tries to deceive Perpetua through a man (her father), as he had deceived the man (Adam) through a woman. Augustine, unlike Cyprian or the later redactors of the *Acts of Perpetua and Felicitas*, believes that Perpetua's response to her father was "in moderation" and did not violate the commandment of honor owed to parents, yet "did not yield to his tricks, to which he was driven by an older enemy," responding perhaps to Perpetua's characterization of her father's arguments as "of the devil [*diaboli*]" (*Martyrdom* 3.3). Instead, although she pities him (as in the *Martyrdom*), according to Augustine Perpetua hates her father's obtuseness and faithlessness, not her father himself: she is driven by "a greater glory than a beloved father who persuades evil" when she bravely (*fortiter*) repels him. His grief does not draw her back from the "strength of her fortitude" and adds to the merit of her passion.

Furthermore, Augustine explains the lack of Perpetua's husband by saying that a husband had not been "added" to her lest she be distracted from heavenly matters by fleshly desire, perhaps alluding to 1 Corinthians 7:34. (He does not explain, however, how she got a nursing son.) As for Felicitas, her giving birth "gave testimony to the feminine condition with a feminine voice" (3). Augustine alludes to the painful childbirth: "The punishment of Eve was not absent," but refers to the redemption won by Mary: "The grace of Mary was present," perhaps echoing his teacher Ambrose's reverence for Mary as the one who redeems the sin of Eve (*Letter 22* 21). Felicitas endures what a woman must, but she receives the assistance won by the Virgin (another mother). Punning again on the names of Felicitas and Perpetua, Augustine asks, "Why do martyrs bear all things, unless to glory in perpetual felicity [*perpetua felicitate*]?" They have "been called" so that all may be called to this fate.

In his third sermon on the martyrs (*282*), Augustine continues to pun on their names but also cites the example that they have set for other Christians to imitate (1): perpetual felicity (*perpetua felicitas*) is

their reward if they engage "in the most glorious contest." In this sermon, Augustine makes it clear that the *passio* of these martyrs has just
been read (2), and he again thinks of the necessity for the congregation
to understand that these are women, and that their virtues are greater
because they are women. Saddled with the "infirmity of the sex," they
endure "hard and cruel works of persecution," because their "interior
human" (*interior homo*, which could also be translated, "interior man,"
but probably refers to the soul) gives them strength. Because of this, the
male martyrs who suffered with them are not given as great an honor,
even though they were the "bravest of men [*uiri fortissimo*]." He concludes, punning for the last time: "This is done not so much because
women [*feminae*] should surpass men in the dignity of their morals,
but because even a woman's weakness conquered the ancient enemy
[Satan] by a greater miracle and manly virtue [*virilis virtus*] fought for
perpetual felicity [*perpetuam felicitatem*]" (3). In this sense, the female
martyrs' deaths redeem their frailty as women.[39]

The presumed frailty of women also comes into play in a more
subdued fashion with Augustine's comments on the martyr Crispina.
According to Brent Shaw, Augustine did not feel compelled to offer a
special sermon to commemorate her *natalitia*, but he did use her example in sermons and writings that mention female weakness to point
out comparisons with males.[40] Crispina, whose martyrdom supposedly
occurred during the persecution of Diocletian in the early fourth century and whose *passio* may date from around that time, perhaps including elements of "oral report," was prominent enough to have a shrine
dedicated to her at the basilica in Thebessa, Algeria, the supposed site of
her martyrdom.[41] In his *Exposition on the Psalms* 137:7, a sermon coin-
cidentally preached on Crispina's feast day, Augustine asks rhetorically
whether there was anyone in Africa who did not know her (120.13). He
works in some typical tropes, including her noble birth, her delicacy,
her being unused to hardship because of her wealthy upbringing, and
of course being of the "weak sex [*sexu infirma*]," all to point out, rather
surprisingly, the support she receives from her *sponsus*, Christ, whose
left hand is under her head and whose right hand embraces her (neatly
conflating commentary on protection by God's right hand in Ps. 138:7
with the Song of Solomon 2:6). The "right hand" of God also saves
Crispina in *Exposition on the Psalms* 137.14. In both instances, it is the
mighty hand of God that saves the delicate woman.

Augustine also works the example of Crispina, together with that of
the virgin martyr Agnes, as a contrast to Peter, who initially appeared

weaker than either of these women (*Sermon 286* 2.2). Per contra, he
castigates the mother of the Maccabees for allowing her sons to die
before her, letting them teach her how to die (*Sermon 286.8*). Agnes and
Crispina are also paired as examples of servants of God: one a virgin, one
a married woman (*mulier*), who have not allowed pride, the ever-fertile
mother of envy, to triumph (*Sermon 354* 5.5). Augustine's picture of
Crispina is not the one we have from her martyrdom, in which Crispina
is arrested on the charge of "having contempt for [*contempsit*] the law of
our lords the princes" and defiantly refuses to sacrifice, causing the proconsul Annulinus to exclaim: "You are a hard [*dura*] and contemptuous
woman [*contemptrix*]," threatening the recalcitrant woman with "the
force of [our] laws" (1.5). Crispina ably refutes Roman idolatry; refusing
to sacrifice to "mute and deaf idols" (3.2) even after her hair is shaved in
order to shame her (3.1). The stubborn woman is finally beheaded.[42]

Why, one might ask, did Augustine appear to ignore Crispina's
"hardness," which he could have turned to good account, especially
since he appears to dwell on elements that may even be extraneous to
the account as we have it, such as Crispina's birth and "delicacy"? For
Shaw, Augustine did not employ the story of Crispina in the way he
did of Perpetua because she was not such a challenge: Crispina does
not speak in her own voice, nor does she relate visionary experiences
of empowerment.[43] Certainly Augustine's use of the story of Crispina
shows feminine frailty once more redeemed, not by becoming male
(only to die as a woman), but through the rescue of the weak female by
the powerful male Lord, who has become the martyr's spouse.

Quodvultdeus, fifth-century bishop of Carthage (sometimes called
Pseudo-Augustine because many of his writings have been attributed
to Augustine), refers in his sermon on the barbarian invasions (*The
Time of the Barbarians*) to the celebration of the "*natalitia*" of the martyrs Perpetua and Felicitas a "few days" previously. He, too, employs
the rhetoric of gender:[44] Why, he inquires, when there were so many
men among their comrades, are these two women mentioned above all
the others? Was it not simply that "their weaker sex not only equaled,
but surpassed, the fortitude of the men [*nisi quia infirmior sexus aut
aequauit, aut superauit virorum fortitudinem*]?" (5.6). He draws attention to the details of the *passio*: that Perpetua was nursing and Felicitas
was pregnant; but Perpetua herself in turn received "a morsel of milk"
from the shepherd/father in her vision, receiving the "sweetness" of
"*felicitatis perpetuae* [perpetual felicity]" (Quodvultdeus could not resist
punning on names, either) that enabled her to "despise her son, spurn

her father [*contemnere filium, spernere patrem*]," in order to lose her life for Christ.[45] Felicitas, who had pain when she gave birth (*parturiebat et dolebat*), while being thrown to the beasts "rejoiced rather than feared [*gaudiebat potius quam timebat*—quite a poetic line]."

Admiringly, Quodvultdeus remarks, "*Quam virtus in feminis* [what strength/virtue/manliness in women]!" Their actions showed that they received such grace that it prevents anyone from judging their sex unworthy: this grace, shown to women, has redeemed their sex. Quodvultdeus goes on to use traditional comparisons: Eve was conquered by the devil; Christ's birth from Mary "raised up many women." Perpetua (and Felicitas) trod on the head of the serpent that Eve had admitted "to her heart." While the devil rejoiced at ruining the delights of paradise, the martyrs made him fear because of the constancy of their courage (*fortitudinis constantiam*) in the midst of pain. For all of this, says Quodvultdeus, the women are justly the equals—nay, the superiors— of men, but he hastens to add, all really are one in Christ (Gal. 3:28) and all come together "in the perfect man, Christ" (Eph. 4:13). Once again, women achieve manliness only to have it taken from them. Shaw notes Perpetua's remarkable achievement, expressing her experience in her own words: "Even this exiguous voice could not be left alone. From the very start it was buried under an avalanche of male interpretations, rereading, and distortions. What chance, one must wonder, was there for any Perpetua to tell her story?"[46]

REJECTING FAMILIES FOR CHRIST

Quodvultdeus's sermon raises an important issue in the martyrs' stories that is emphasized in the brief *Acta* even more than in the longer *Martyrdom* and has interested many feminist commentators. He uses quite harsh words for Perpetua's rejection of her family: she not only "spurns" her father but also "despises" her own son. In the first version of the *Acta* (*Acta* I, J. Amat; *Acta* A, van Beek),[47] Perpetua is confronted by father, mother, brothers, and the husband (*maritus*), who is missing from the earlier, longer account, bringing Perpetua's infant son with them (6.1). Her father pulls out all the familial stops, pleading with her to have pity on him, her mother, her brothers, her "most unhappy husband," and her infant son; yet Perpetua stands looking up to heaven. When the proconsul urges her to consider the tears of her parents and the cries of her infant, she replies that it will be more of a matter of tears if she betrays her vision and is "found a stranger [*aliena inuenta*]" to the Lord and the community of the saints, to whom she will be united "as to good brothers" (6.4). As a last gesture, her father hangs her nursing infant from her neck, while he, her mother, and her husband stretch out their hands, weeping and kissing her, pleading once more that she have pity on them (6.5). With words that are as harsh as her gestures, Perpetua throws her son back at them (*proiciens infantum*), and thrusts them away (*repellens*) as she quotes the judgmental words of Jesus from Matthew 7:23 (//Luke 13:27): "Depart from me, workers of iniquity; because I do not know you" (6.6).

A similar scene prevails in the second version of the *Acta* (*Acta* II, J. Amat; *Acta* B, van Beek), with husband and son along with the rest of the family. Perpetua again stands adamant, unmoving, secure in her decision and completely caught up in "the desire for martyrdom [*inmobilis atque secura, et tota in martyrii desiderio*]" (6.3), ignoring their pleas, refusing to recognize "parents who are ignorant of the Creator of all, who if they were [my parents], would persuade me to persist in confessing Christ." Again she is pressed by proconsul and family; again she (here additionally called "*beata*," blessed, already a saint) violently rejects infant and parents with the same quote, adding that *they* are strangers (*alieni*) to *her*, having separated themselves from the redemption of Christ (6.6). Thus Perpetua, with her confessor status having given her the "power of the keys," uses it to condemn her pagan family rather than to forgive the penitent Christian or convert, perhaps a significant Catholic emendation in a story that might have Montanist resonances of the "ministerial status" of female as well as male confessors and martyrs.[48]

Felicitas is not to be outdone in contempt of family in the *Acta*: she is assigned a husband, only to reject him. In an exchange with the inquisitive proconsul, here called Minutius, in *Acta* I, Felicitas receives a bold speaking role that matches Perpetua's in the longer *Martyrdom*, and perhaps is in deliberate imitation of it. The proconsul has the male confessors deliberately taken away and addresses the women (5.1–8), Felicitas first. After he asks her for her name, he asks her, "Do you have a husband [*Virum habes*]?" She responds, "Yes, but I now despise him." The text uses the same harsh verb, *contemnere*, which Quodvultdeus used for Perpetua's rejection of her father. The rather plodding proconsul continues on the husband theme: "Where is he?" inviting Felicitas's sharp rejoinder, "He is not here." He continues, "What rank is he?" "Plebeian," she replies, thus establishing the fact that at least in the *Acta* I, Felicitas is probably not a slave. Further questioning reveals that she has no parents but is the sister of Revocatus: he is no help in persuading a recantation since he also is a Christian. Since the proconsul has run out of relatives, he asks Felicitas to have pity on herself, "especially since I see you have an infant in your womb." (Really, does this man miss anything?) Felicitas's reply is like that of Perpetua: "I am a Christian [*Christiana sum*]," and she adds, "I have been taught to despise [*contemno*, again] all of these things for the sake of God." Although Felicitas has less of a dialogue in *Acta* II, being threatened with torture, she replies, "I choose temporal torments for the sake of eternal life and everlasting light" (5.3–4).

The *Acta* of Perpetua and Felicitas are almost certainly later than the longer Latin version of the *Martyrdom*, may be extracts from a different version, and play down the role of Perpetua, especially her own account of her feelings and visions.[49] Conversely, they play up much more the rejection of family: both Perpetua and Felicitas are given husbands only to reject them,[50] while they demonstrate, even more than in the *Martyrdom*, "a surprising eagerness to abandon young infants," which Mary Lefkowitz has also observed in other martyr stories of women.[51] Is this another indication of the growing emphasis that we see in the sermons of Augustine and Quodvultdeus, on the "manliness" of these martyrs? At first glance it certainly seems odd that the stories and sermons about these martyrs, after the recognition of Christianity, would portray them as women so indifferent to a family life (and to having a family *and* a life) in a period when women were increasingly being instructed in proper Christian ways of attending to that life (e.g., 1 Tim. 2:8–15), and when, in North Africa especially, the Montanist disregard for family and reproduction was being attacked by Catholic Christianity. The contempt for worldly ties expressed by Perpetua and Felicitas could be understood, however, in characteristic Christian fashion, as following the stark commandment of Jesus: "Whoever comes to me and does not hate [the Greek verb is the strong *miseō*] father and mother, wife and children, brothers and sisters, yes, and even life itself, cannot be my disciple" (Luke 14:26 //Matt. 10:37). Other stern sayings about family in the Gospels, especially those in Luke, which in most cases preserve earlier versions, warn Christians that following Jesus will mean rejection and division among natal families (Luke 12:52–53 //Matt. 10:34–36; Luke 18:28–30) as Jesus' behavior toward his own implies (Mark 3:31–35 //Matt. 12:46–50 //Luke 8:19–27). Even respect for dead family members must be abandoned for the sake of discipleship: there is no looking back (Luke 9:59–62).

Yet while such Christian teaching can be used to provide a model and motivation for martyrdom as imitation of Christ, it does not explain why none of the familial relationships of the male martyrs are emphasized or even present, or why in the church's reflections on Perpetua and Felicitas, there is a growing emphasis on their harshness toward their families and their own children. Even in the *Martyrdom*, when Perpetua sees her father's arguments as "diabolical" and defies him by refusing to recant, in her own words she says that she feels as if stricken herself when Hilarianus has him beaten for being unable to persuade her, and she grieves "for his pitiful old age [*dolui pro senecta eius misera*]" (6.5). (Not, we hasten to add, enough to change her mind.) When she first is put into prison, she feels a similar torment for her nursing infant (3.6) and is relieved when she is allowed to have him with her in better quarters after "having suffered for several days" in this way (3.9). Later, when her baby is taken away from her by her father, she is also relieved because she is not "tortured" by worry for her baby and pain in her breasts: it is "as God willed" (6.8). Similarly, the pregnant Felicitas, who hopes to suffer with her fellow martyrs rather than with common criminals and thus to give birth early, has her daughter brought up by "a certain sister" (fellow Christian) who is attending her in prison (15.7), presumably as a Christian. Felicitas does not seem to have any other relatives unless one counts her fellow slave, Revocatus (2.1), who in the *Acta* is changed into her brother, together with an elevated status for both. (Their parents are presumably dead.) One of Perpetua's own brothers, a catechumen like herself, is also her brother in Christ. In the *Martyrdom*, what we have is a model for the new Christian *familia*, one in which slaves like Felicitas and Revocatus, matrons like Perpetua, and male leaders like Saturus are all "brothers and sisters."

In the Latin *Martyrdom of Saint Irenaeus, Bishop of Sirmium*, which supposedly occurred about one hundred years after that of Perpetua and Felicitas, during the Diocletian persecution (ca. 304),[52] Irenaeus is confronted by his relatives (*parentes*) and his children (*pueri*), and perhaps his wife (the reading is dubious), all of whom attempt to persuade him to have pity on them and himself (3.1–2), but he "despises" them for the sake of a "better passion [*melior cupiditas*]." Questioned by the prefect Probus about his wife and children, Irenaeus denies that he has them. When Probus asks, "Then who were the ones who were weeping at the last session?" Irenaeus quotes the saying of Jesus about hating the family (Matt. 10:37//Luke 14:26), adding that God will take care of his sons (4.5–8). An interesting inversion of this motif occurs in the

Martyrdom of Carpus, Papylus, and Agathonicē, in which Papylus replies under questioning that he has "many children through God" (27–32), presumably his converts. Agathonicē—portrayed in the Greek version as a bystander who is converted, and in the Latin version as a Christian who gives her testimony—rather more characteristically of these stories, refuses to yield out of pity for her son, replying that God will pity him.[53] In the Latin recension of the martyrdom, Agathonicē is also exposed naked (6.4–5) so that the crowd may gaze on her beauty.[54]

So far we have addressed actions rather than motives. The *Martyrdom of Perpetua and Felicitas* and the subsequent *Acta* give us little indication of why these women were motivated to undertake what after all was an avoidable death: Vibia Perpetua herself, being of free and even noble status, would not have been under the same compulsion as a slave girl like Felicitas. Moreover, other Christians seem to have been able to visit them freely in prison without themselves being arrested: the deacons Tertius and Pomponius, who procured better lodgings for the prisoners, may have been among them. All that Perpetua says by way of indicating why she resolutely faces martyrdom is in reply to her father's questioning: "I cannot be called other than what I am, a Christian" (3.2). In the defenses of Felicitas and Perpetua before the tribunal in the *Acta*, this motivation is also given. As Pliny's *Letter to Trajan* (*Letters* 10.96) shows us, the charge of being Christian was a capital matter, so to confess Christianity was to choose death. Perpetua does give us more of a motive in the *Acta* I: she wants to join the company of the saints in paradise, which she has seen in her vision of the heavenly ladder (the only vision referred to in the *Acta*). Martyrs win paradise.

But as Elizabeth Castelli has put it, "The discourse of martyrdom is also a discourse of power," the volatile and perilous means by which those who perceive themselves without power gain it.[55] One could certainly see how this might motivate the slave girl Felicitas, but what about Perpetua, who seems to have a considerable share of earthly status? W. H. C. Frend's statement that Perpetua's example (he ignores Felicitas) "shows just how Christianity appealed to the bored and frustrated intelligent women of the Greco-Roman world," suggests a reason, but the risk of bodily dismemberment seems a radical solution to an intellectual problem.[56] Frend might belong to Lefkowitz's catalog of male scholars who exhibit a "consistent failure . . . to acknowledge the positive significance of femininity in the performance of certain heroic acts," but given the manipulation of the stories of these acts by later church authorities, it is hardly surprising.[57] In Lefkowitz's "psychohistorical analysis," Perpetua's choice of "death as a means to life" is "a political act against her environment," reflected in rejection of family and in her dreams by a "concern with destroying threatening male figures." According to Lefkowitz, Christianity met a "social need" of Perpetua and women like her, not of relieving intellectual boredom but of "releasing women from the hierarchical structure imposed by patriarchal society, which the church in its own organization would increasingly incorporate and emulate."[58]

This desire, which we see reflected in the *Acts of Paul and Thecla* in the confrontation of Thecla with her family and male political authorities and thus in a work that may also have originated with women's stories, comes at a perilous price. The martyr saint becomes powerful, first as confessor and then as intercessor, but not on earth, and perhaps she *is* no longer on earth. Did women follow the example of Perpetua? Brent Shaw suggests that they did: "Later female martyrs who came to play such a dominant role at Carthage, could hardly have been unaware of her action. Others outside Carthage as, for example, the three females Maxima, Donatilla, and Secunda, whose martyrdom bore resemblances to hers, could hardly have been ignorant of her example."[59] Maxima and Donatilla were dedicated Christian virgins; according to their *passio*, they were on their way to be martyred when they are joined by the twelve-year-old Secunda, who leapt from the window of her parents' house to join them, having no regard for her parents' wealth and despising it, along with the rest of the world, in her desire to merit "finding the one whom she desired for eternity."[60] Maureen A. Tilley regards the *Passio of Maxima, Donatilla, and Secunda* as typically Donatist, especially in its valuing of female martyrs:

> The Donatists themselves valued martyrs by either sex over male hierarchical leadership. Donatist exegesis is different from contemporary [Catholic] practice in its use of feminine metaphors and models. In the ambient Christian literature, male figures in Scripture are models for the behavior of both men and women, and female figures model only institutions. Thus individuals, both men and women, find their models for Christian virtue only in masculine patterns. In Donatist literature, by contrast, female figures may be models for individual men's behavior.[61]

A faint, rather fantastic echo of the story of Perpetua may be found in the *Passio Salsae*, about a fourteen-year-old girl who was brought by her pagan parents to worship a dragon statue in Tipasa, Mauretania.

Salsa managed to take off and destroy the dragon's head, but on returning for the rest, she was caught and martyred.[62] The connections here
would be the pagan parents and dragon's head; everything else is fairly
standard fare in a martyrology.

One of the major factors in analyzing all these martyr stories cited
above and the related examples given by the Christian church authorities is that—with the exception of Perpetua's "own account"—in her
prison diary and record of her visions, except for the first vision, treading on the dragon's head as she climbs the stairway to heaven—they
tend to be slighted or omitted in most later versions; they are not written by the women themselves and probably not often by women at all.
And even Perpetua's own account is embedded in a larger *passio*, with
an obviously propagandistic bent, announced in the preface, which is
not by her hand. As Margaret R. Miles notes, "The *Martyrdom of Perpetua and Felicitas* is an unusually vivid example of the appropriation of
a woman's writing as support for theological and ecclesiastical concerns
that the text does not acknowledge as her own."[63] Where Perpetua's
own account leads toward her ultimate envisioned "virilization" and
conquest of a powerful man (the Egyptian) *as* a man (*Martyrdom* 10.7),
the description of her and Felicitas in the arena by a presumably male
hand continues to emphasize not only their female bodies, but also a
female sensibility on Perpetua's part that is appropriate to an upper-
class matron: in fact, she is described as a *matrona*, the *matrona Christi*,
the "wife of Christ" (as also the "darling of God [*Dei delicata*]"), as she
enters the arena (18.2). Perpetua has no earthly husband, but she has
two heavenly males to whom she is bound.

When Perpetua and Felicitas, at the former's request, are divested of
the clothing of priestesses of Ceres (18.4–6), in an action that is both
reminiscent and the reverse of Perpetua's unclothing to become a gladiator (10.7), they are brought out dressed only in nets (20.2), so that the
crowd is aghast to note that one is a "tender girl [*puellam delicatam*]"
(echoing the "*Dei delicata*" of 18.2): God's beloved is naked, as is Felicitas, whose dripping breasts are also mentioned. This exposure is even
too much for shameless pagans, and they are brought back reclothed.
This clothing enables another scene of feminine modesty to take place.
Tossed by the mad cow (or heifer), a beast pointedly "appropriate to
their sex" (20.1), Perpetua finds herself with a ripped tunic exposing
her thigh and hastily fixes her garment, "more mindful of shame [mod-
esty, *pudor*] than of pain [*dolor*]." This is from a woman who did not
jib at being divested of clothing to fight in the arena in her dream: she

had no modesty then because she saw herself as male. The reader (like the crowd) is now seeing her as a female behaving appropriately to her worldly and heavenly station, as a *matrona*. She also fastens up her inappropriately loosened tresses, which would not be appropriate for a female martyr (*martyra*; 20.5). All of this is despite the fact that in her exalted state she is supposedly unaware that she has been tossed by the cow and is only convinced of it because of some "marks" on her body and her clothing (20.8–9). The careful reader cannot help but respond here with Peter Dronke:

> The redactor indeed adds many edifying details that are quite alien to the Perpetua of the diary, and are almost certainly fictitious. His picture, for instance, of Perpetua in the arena, covering her legs and tidying her hair after being gored—consorts ill with the dream of the woman who strips naked and is anointed for combat: one who is unafraid to write like that will hardly have gone to her death in a fit of prudery.[64]

At the end, her being a woman is again emphasized, not only because of the classically feminine way she dies, guiding the sword to her throat, the woman's "weak spot,"[65] but also in the final comment: "Perhaps so great a woman, who was feared by the unclean spirit, could not have been felled in any other way than if she herself had willed it" (21.10).

What the conclusion does is to emphasize, not only the staged death of tragic heroines, as Nicole Loraux has shown, but to recall the noble deaths of Roman women like Arria celebrated by Pliny (*To Nepos*, in *Letters* 3.16), who were all the more noble because they overcame women's weakness. She is a woman who has escaped the destructive and threatening male authorities of the Roman Empire only to be rewritten by the male authorities of the Christian church. Perpetua is a great woman, but nonetheless a woman. She is all the greater *because* she is a woman and these actions are not expected of her, but as a woman she is doubly dead: her female flesh and her female gender are erased and only so can she be valued as male. It is perhaps irresistible for feminist scholars to applaud the depictions of Perpetua and Felicitas thrusting away social roles that define and confine them as women in a patriarchal society—wife, daughter, mother, slave girl—but we must also remember that these women are depicted as praiseworthy but "unnatural": their actions are "masculine," and in the world of late antiquity, the home of emerging Christianity, manly women are no better than effeminate men.

In the *Martyrdom of Perpetua and Felicitas*, as Judith Perkins notes, the text is unusual in that the "unruly woman" has not been put back in her hierarchical place: "society's power is not affirmed but radically reinterpreted."[66] Roman society, as intended by a Christian narrative that sees that world as fundamentally and always defeated, despite its gestures of dominance, by the Christian Kingdom of God, is indeed subverted; but as the story is told and retold, as Roman society becomes Christianized, the old values of male and female are reasserted, and there is no room for unruly women. As Augustine so pointedly said, they are (and perhaps for him should be) examples that are more to be admired or wondered at than imitated (*Sermon 280* 1.1). The prayers of the devout can certainly ask the saints who have entered paradise to be the means of canceling the sins of their female flesh, which they have sacrificed as flesh, and with it sacrificed their femaleness; but women on earth cannot, because of that same flesh, assume the roles of leadership in the church increasingly reserved to men.

Even Tertullian—who can praise the dead Perpetua for her example of opening paradise, as a martyr should, at the cost of her "heart's blood" (*The Soul* 55.4)—can condemn the "impudent" Quintilla for using the example of another female martyr, Thecla, as a license for authority in the church (*Baptism* 17.4–5). Like Perpetua, Thecla was an inspiration for women and men alike, but they saw her example differently. Preeminently, Thecla was a virgin martyr who not only continued to live but later also became the center of a thriving cult that was much greater than Perpetua's. The story of what Peter Brown calls the taming of the "wild virgin" into the saint who blesses an "orderly hierarchy" of women in John Chrysostom's *Panegyric of Thecla* is also the story of a woman's body.[67]

4

The Nakedness of Thecla

And when he heard [her say] these things, the governor ordered clothing to be brought and said, "Put on these clothes."
　But she said, "He who clothed me when I was naked among the
beasts will clothe me with salvation on the day of judgment." And taking the clothes she put them on.

　　　　　　　　　　　　　　　　　　　　—*Acts of Paul and Thecla* 38

VIRGINS TRIUMPHANT

In the previous chapter we examined examples of the manliness of
matrons: the mother of the Maccabean seven, Perpetua, and Felicitas. Their virile virtues were not simply ascribed to them by later male
authors, but at least in Perpetua's case her strength for the final combat
in the arena seems to have come from her own visualization of herself as
a man. In this guise she wrestles with and defeats the male Egyptian, the
powerful and frightening symbol of the devil, also portrayed as male.
But we have also seen that many of the Christian authors who praise
Perpetua and other women for their ability to overcome their female
nature must necessarily portray that nature as "infirm" (so Augustine
and Quodvultdeus), a nature weak and easily seduced, inscribed on
the female body. If that body is able to resist the assaults of masculine
power upon it, it becomes defeminized as a body. As Brent Shaw notes,
the Christian martyr's body became the site of a struggle to reject one
ideology and reinscribe another.[1] And as we have seen, a favored way to
represent this conflict was through the female body. Further, as Sarah
Barnett has observed, the portrayal of female martyrs was often "violently sexualized."[2]

　　Unlike Barnett, I see the examples of Perpetua and Felicitas as less
"sexualized" than as gender emphatic. They are unusual also in that
they both are mothers, and the maternal body is particularly important

for later interpretations of their story. Yet there are other examples, particularly of virgin martyrs, that emphasize them as sexual prey, only to show the inviolability of their intact bodies. Sabina in the late third-century *Acts of Pionius* is threatened with exposure in a brothel for refusing to sacrifice; she replies that the "holy [*hagios*]" God will take care of her.[3] The "famous [*periboēton*]" Potamiaena, whose story is mentioned in the account of her martyrdom in Eusebius's *Ecclesiastical History* 6.5 as one who is still being talked about among her own people,[4] endured a great struggle (*agōnisamenē*) seeing that so many men wanted to be her lovers because of the "holiness [*hagneia*] of her body and of her virginity [*partheneia*]." The judge Aquila, after tormenting her body with various tortures, threatens to have that same body (*sōma*, emphatically placed twice in the same sentence) handed over to be assaulted by his gladiators, a fate from which she is saved by the kind soldier Basilides, only to be martyred by having boiling pitch poured over her body: "Such was the contest [*athlos*] that the celebrated maiden [*korē*] won."[5] Another celebrated virgin martyr is Irenē, in a martyrdom that contains, unusually, only women, the *Martyrdom of Agapē, Irenē, and Chionē* of Thessalonica, with their four female companions, referring to the Diocletian persecution (304).[6] Most of the attention is focused on Irenē, whose interrogation and exposure naked in a public brothel by the prefect Dulcitius become the subject of the tenth-century nun Hrosvit of Gandersheim's melodramatic morality play, *Dulcitius*. Irenē's exposure, however, does not have the desired effect, at least from Dulcitius's standpoint, since instead of being sexually humiliated, she is kept pure (*katharos*) by God. No man dares speak to her or insult her (6.2). Sentenced to the flames like her older sisters, Irenē bravely climbs the pyre and throws herself into the fire (7.2).

This same holy shield or force field that protects the virgin saint is to reappear in other stories of virgin martyr saints exposed in brothels. Ambrose of Milan, in his work *On Virgins*, addressed to his consecrated sister Marcellina, gives her not only the examples of Mary and Thecla (under what circumstances we shall later see), but also a "recent" example of a virgin of Antioch whose modesty and chaste resolve was so great that she would not venture out in public. Naturally, pagan male lust being what it is in these tales, she is forced to appear in public to be tried for failure to sacrifice and is condemned to a brothel as punishment. Before she can be violated, however, she is rescued by a Christian soldier, who exchanges clothing with her to let her escape. A customer entering the brothel is astonished to see the chaste virgin changed into a man and is converted to chastity on the spot, while the virgin realizes that she has only escaped violation temporarily and would rather die. In the end, both virgin and soldier receive the "reward" of martyrdom, although she gallantly lets him be martyred first (*On Virgins* 2.4). Although Ambrose praises the fourth-century Agnes as another great example of a virgin martyr, he is apparently unaware of the legend that the fifth-century Prudentius attaches to her: that Agnes, too, is exposed in a brothel, but that her hair grows down to cover her modesty.[7] In the story of Thecla in particular, her decision to convert to celibate Christianity occasions her divine rescue on a number of occasions when she is about to be put to death in ways that in Barnett's terms are "violently sexualized."

In the longer fifth-century *Life and Miracles*, the elderly Thecla is even rescued from envious men who want to rape her and shame her when God encloses her in a rock, thereby literally enclosing her virginity in stone. Daniel Boyarin cites a rabbinic example of the daughter of R. Hanina ben Teradion's being sentenced to prostitution as a parallel tale to that of Ambrose's virgin of Antioch, suggesting that the former's virginity may have been miraculously preserved in order to marry (this daughter is either the famous Beruriah, wife of R. Meir, or her sister, whose virginity is marvelously preserved by God). Boyarin points out an essential difference between fairly contemporary Jewish and Christian virgin-martyr tales: for Christians, virginity is the value for which even life must be sacrificed, *the* essential virtue of Christian sanctity. In Jewish martyr stories, it provides a model for male behavior, but for women it is a necessary condition for marriage, the ultimate destiny for the Jewish virgin.[8]

Virginity thus symbolizes a virtue that can be distinctly feminine and also masculine. When it relates to the much-praised ancient virtue of chastity, virginity before and fidelity after marriage, it is characterized, advised, and admired as a virtue of women. For example, a Pythagorean moral treatise of the third to second centuries BCE, written in the name of a woman, Phintys, but almost certainly pseudonymous, advises women that "a woman's greatest virtue is chastity," particularly with respect to marriage.[9] "Life-long lay celibacy was rare" in the Greco-Roman pagan world, especially for women.[10] Thus, women's sexual restraint was seen as their gender's form of *sōphrosynē*, self-control, which was also one of the cardinal virtues for men, the highest task of the *psychē*, itself characterized as male. For men, the control of sexual satisfaction was also a means of preventing them from becoming, or being seen as, effeminate. Sanctioned marriage was functionally the only goal for women, as well as men who wished to participate in the respected public life of their cities. As both Peter Brown and Kate Cooper have observed, the Greco-Roman "romance" novels—which portray nobly born young men and women falling in love and, even though parted and tested by "dramatic trials," vowing (and keeping) fidelity to each other at the risk of death, but eventually being united happily in marriage—convey the ancient message that a solid marriage, fulfilled by children, is the cornerstone of society's continuity.[11] These literary romances—which are truly what even now we would find "romantic" in the classic sense of faithful lovers parted, threatened, and reunited in order to consummate their loving relationship—were written during the first to third centuries CE. As works of literature with known authors, we might suppose that only literate men and women were reading them, but Virginia Burrus and others have shown that the novels themselves have oral origins in legend and folklore, which would mean that many people knew them and their central theme of chastity.[12]

The framework that appears in these novels is adopted, albeit with an entirely different denouement—the active commitment to celibate Christianity and rejection of familial, civic, and social ties—by Christian apocryphal literature, which combines the themes of the romance novels with those of martyrologies. The most spectacular early Christian example of these is the *Acts of Paul and Thecla*, which Allison Elliott has called "the earliest full-fledged hagiographic romance," one that is opposed to the "hagiographic epic" in that it focuses on the life rather than the death of the central character, the saint.[13] And like the pagan romances, these romances of early Christians may have also originated in oral tales, perhaps told by women.[14] What was a script of commitment to the regulation of sexual desire, made difficult by the proneness of women to their passions and by men through their neglect of reason, became a call for freedom from sexual desire and its consequences, which in Christianity signaled the end of the present evil age.[15] As Peter Brown has observed, moreover, the bodies of women were once more used to "think with" in these apocryphal acts:

> The Christian authors of the Apocryphal Acts had only to replace a manifest destiny to the wedding bed, with which every pagan novel had ended, with the Apostle's call to continence. As in the Romances, danger followed from that first moment. For after the moment of conversion, the readers of the Acts were treated to a dramatic evocation of the towering force of the world, as it bore down on their heroes and heroines. The impression of its brutal power was

heightened by being seen from the viewpoint of the most vulnerable of all of its potential victims, the unprotected virgin woman.[16]

Yet these are not stories that have female characters merely for men to think with; we know that women, too, read or heard these acts and, as we shall see, found themselves in the roles of their celibate heroines. After persecutions by the Roman imperial government ceased, the female body remained a site of struggle between female and male authority within the church.

THE WAGES OF CELIBACY

In his first letter to the church at Corinth (at least as we have canonically recorded and received it), the urbane Hellenized Jew, Paul of Tarsus, writes, "It is well for a man not to touch a woman" (1 Cor. 7:1). Whether one believes that he is quoting a Corinthian slogan (as the NRSV use of quotation marks implies) or that he is giving the spiritually and sexually unruly Corinthian Christians a new maxim for their behavior, he could hardly have framed a more important—and more debated—discourse for Christians in the following ages. Earlier he had said, in his letter to the churches in Galatia, that in Christ (that is, in baptism, which signified entry into a new community of initiates) "there is no longer male and female" (Gal. 3:28), a clause that he significantly omits in a similar expression in 1 Corinthians 12:13: Jews and Greeks (Gentiles), slaves and free people may be equal in Christ, but apparently not males and females. What Paul meant by what we would call "gender equality" is not clear, especially since he seems to have taken pains to assert some kind of gendered spiritual hierarchy in his admonitions about married women's prayer and prophecy in 1 Corinthians 11:3–16.[17] What seems clear, however, is that Paul lived in an eschatological tension that anticipated an end of the present age, in which bodies would be transformed into spiritual ones and in anticipation of which those "in Christ" ought to behave as though they did not have social commitments or bodily desires. In Daniel Boyarin's terms, Paul was a "proto-encratite": he envisioned the coming spiritual life as anticipated by *enkrateia*, "self-control and withdrawal from sexuality."[18]

But Paul's injunctions, especially in 1 Corinthians 7, were mainly addressed to men. How did women understand them? According to Dennis R. MacDonald and others, the conflict in the second-century

Christian churches over Paul's legacy revolved around precisely what the apostle would advise about marriage and family life in the light of an end that had not arrived and in a period in which some Christians, particularly those of the literate upper classes, from which church leaders were increasingly drawn, were concerned with Christianizing Roman society rather than trying to destroy it with radical social alternatives.[19] The question was what to do about one of the most radical of these social alternatives, ascetic behavior, the hallmark of which was sexual abstinence. This stance presented a difficulty when it was combined with claims to authority over Christian communities. The New Prophecy (Montanism), which arose in Asia Minor in the second century and spread throughout the Eastern Christian world, was particularly problematic for Catholic Christians in that respect, since it granted ecclesiastical and spiritual authority to prophetic celibate women who had rejected marriage and household management in light of the return of Christ, as did two of the prophetic women leaders of the movement, Priscilla (Prisca) and Maximilla. The New Prophecy's emphasis on martyrdom, combined with visionary experience, and its popularity in North Africa, has often been associated with the *Martyrdom of Perpetua and Felicitas*, as we have seen. Yet, curiously, there are no women of whom we have record who deliberately chose Perpetua as an example to follow and wrote about it. But we do have women, perhaps Perpetua herself, who chose Thecla as an example.[20]

The choice, as well as the conflict it caused within Christianity, is first signaled by Tertullian in his *Baptism*, composed about 198 CE, in the period before his inclination toward the New Prophecy caused him to turn from defending Catholicism. In this work, Tertullian inveighs against a "female viper of the Cainite heresy" whose "most venomous doctrine" is to preach against the necessity of baptism for Christians (*Baptism* 17.4).[21] The Carthaginian presbyter and admirer of martyrs like Perpetua is exercised against two things that are really one: that this woman Quintilla, who shares a name with the Montanist prophet, presumes to teach *about* baptism, and that she uses for her authorization the example of Thecla (*exemplum Theclae*), contained in a scripture attributed to Paul (17.5). Tertullian quotes "the Apostle" from 1 Corinthians 14:33–35, a passage long assumed to have been interpolated, as forbidding women even to study, let alone giving them "the power to teach and baptize," the authority that women are claiming through Paul in their reading of what appears to be a version of the *Acts of Paul and Thecla*; Tertullian vehemently claims that an Asian presbyter who "made up [*construxit*]" this text, using "Paul in his title" and confessing that he did it "out of love of Paul," was dismissed from his position. This work therefore cannot be appealed to as authoritative Scripture. Tertullian is the only church father who insists that the *Acts of Paul and Thecla* is a fabrication; in this, he may be constructing his own fabrication in what he believes is a convincing and conclusive defense. If he had to prevaricate, perhaps he believed that the occasion demanded it. He may have believed that he had to defeat Quintilla by assaulting not merely her reference to authority but also the authority itself.

Nevertheless, what this reference to a pseudonymous work by Paul (or about Paul; I do not think we need to assume from Tertullian's phrasing that the Asian presbyter wrote it "as if" he were Paul)[22] shows is that there was not only a knowledge of some written version of the Thecla story current in North Africa at the close of the second century, but that its use for women's authority to teach church doctrine and to baptize also presented enough of a challenge that Tertullian had to launch a polemic against it that strains credibility. Regardless of the fact that we have one male church authority (the presbyter Tertullian) attacking another male church authority (the presbyter from Asia) over sanctioning female authority in the church, women, at least one of whom (Quintilla) is named, were indeed using Thecla's example as a model for their own behavior. What, specifically, was that example?

THE "EXAMPLE OF THECLA"

According to Ross S. Kraemer, the *Acts of Thecla* and the *Acts of Paul* (to which Tertullian refers) may have originally been separate works, the former serving as a "literary prototype" of other apocryphal acts like the *Acts of Xanthippe* and the *Acta* of other women converts.[23] MacDonald has posited that there were three separate stories contained in the early Christian versions of the *Acts of Paul* known to Tertullian, Origen, and Jerome: one was the Thecla narrative, one told the story of Paul and a lion in Ephesus, and the other reported Paul's martyrdom.[24] Catherine Burris and Lucas Van Rompay testify to the existence of several Syriac and Armenian manuscripts that indicate the popularity in Syrian Christianity of the *Acts of Paul and Thecla*.[25] There is also a complete Greek version of the *Acts of Paul*, containing what may originally have been a separate *Acts of Thecla* (or at least a "Thecla episode"), with fragments in Coptic, and a fifth-century expanded Greek version that also incorporates a cycle of miracle stories relating to Thecla, usually referred to as the *Life and Miracles of St. Thecla*, long attributed to Basil of Seleucia but now agreed to be a pseudonymous work.[26] The widespread manuscript evidence indicates the popularity of these *Acts* within the early Christian world, especially in those parts that valued a commitment to the faith along with demanding a commitment to virginity and abstinence, which we need not assume was solely female but included a goodly number of women, perhaps in some areas a greater number of women than of men.

These, like the Greek romances, are the *written* narratives; yet many scholars, as we have seen, do not presuppose an original written form but, as in the case of the romantic novels, an oral prehistory. Davies, MacDonald, and Burrus all assume that communities of celibate women were responsible for preserving and telling such Christian "anti-romance" narratives.[27] Esther Yue L. Ng, on the other hand, follows the example of Lynne Boughton in doubting the use of the *Acts of Thecla* as giving a mandate for female autonomy in Christian circles: instead, she believes that Thecla's example is used by the church as a "model confessor/martyr/and virgin."[28] I think that such conflicting interpretations of the evidence reveal not only the importance attached by feminist scholarship to finding ancient women's expressions of their own experiences or reactions to their portrayal, but also the fact that even early Christians, male and female, interpreted the literary experiences of women in different ways, as different models of authority and power. I also find Aymer's analysis of the conflicts that take place in the *Acts of Thecla* narrative to be compelling: she attributes the relative passivity and victimization of Thecla in the Iconian section of the narrative and the powerful voices of the women, together with Thecla's own newly found voice in the Antiochene section, to preexisting Christian oral stories that were redacted by an editor interested in reconciling conflicting narratives of identity in the early church.[29] At minimum, however, I think we can with a degree of confidence posit that women as well as men either were reading or knew of the *Acts of Paul and Thecla* in some version prior to Tertullian's polemic in 198.

But what, specifically, was the *exemplum Theclae* that he found so abhorrent? Tertullian is attacking one Quintilla, who appears to preach *against* the necessity of baptism (*Baptism* 17.2). Tertullian's argument therefore establishes a connection between women's teaching and baptizing; women do not have the right (*ius*) to do either (17.4): "It is the active connection of women with baptism, either denying it to others or administering it themselves, that he appears to condemn."[30] Moreover, this double authority is claimed by reference to some spurious "*Acta Pauli* [*Acts of Paul*]," which put forth "the example of Thecla for the license of women to teach and baptize" (17.5). Nonsense, claims Tertullian, quoting 1 Corinthians 14:34–35; the "authentic" apostle did not permit women even to *study* let alone speak in churches; the *Acta Pauli* containing this example of Thecla are fictions of the Asian presbyter, who confessed his deed. There are certainly many problems created by this passage, some of which have already been mentioned. In my view, one of the chief problems is that the *Acts of Paul and Thecla* that we now possess does not really show Paul giving Thecla the authority to baptize, only the authority to teach, which in Tertullian's view may have been bad enough.[31] Yet we need to pay attention to Tertullian's wording: the example of Thecla in the condemned *Acts of Paul* being claimed is one "of teaching and baptizing [*docendi et tinguendi*]," a phrase Tertullian repeats (17.4–5). The double right is claimed for women; it is denied by reference to the "real" Paul.

In the *Acts of Paul and Thecla*, as well as the longer version contained in the *Life and Miracles*, the apostle Paul comes to Iconium and starts preaching in the house next door to that of the "noble virgin" Thecla and her mother, Theocleia. What Paul preaches, here characterized as "the word of God concerning continence [*enkrateia*] and the resurrection" (5) seems initially fairly consistent with what he has to say about sexual restraint and the passing "form of this world" in 1 Corinthians 7:29–31, albeit intensified in the direction of virginity as well as abstinence even in marriage:[32]

> Blessed are those who have kept their flesh pure, for they will be God's temple.
> Blessed are the continent [*enkrateis*], for God will speak to them.
> Blessed are those who abandon this world, for they are well-pleasing to God. . . .
> Blessed are *the bodies of the virgins*, for they are well-pleasing to God and will not lose the reward of their purity [*hagneia*], for the word of the Father shall be for them a work of salvation for the day of his Son and they will have rest forever.[33]

Listening to Paul's preaching from the neighboring courtyard, Thecla modestly remains within her house yet daringly on the verge of it; she sits in the window "day and night," listening to "the word of purity [*hagneia*] spoken by Paul," and becomes "very joyful."[34] Thecla's joy is not mirrored in her mother's concern that her daughter has not eaten,

drunk, or moved for three days and three nights; she sends for Thecla's fiancé, Thamyris, sharing with him her "amazement" that such
maidenly modesty would be so seriously troubled. Jan Bremmer rightly
notes, "It is hardly surprising that Theocleia was getting anxious, since
Thecla displayed clear signs of lovesickness, as the pagan novels abun-
dantly show."[35] When Thamyris cannot get any response from Thecla
either, he and Theocleia (and the entire household) assume that she
is dead to them, lost through the bewitching erotic spells cast by the
apostolic invader of their homes. It is not simply one household (and a
future one, that of Thamyris and Thecla) that is destroyed by the word
of the celibate life; it is also the foundation of the city: the sorcerer
(*magos*) has "ruined all of our women [wives, *gynaikes*]" and therefore
must be properly punished (*APTh* 15). Interestingly, the traitorous
Christians Demas and Hermogenes vow to help Thamyris win Thecla
back by countering Paul's teaching with the teaching that the "resurrection" consists in having children and has already come (14).[36]

Curiously, Paul is allowed two occasions on which to defend himself
before the Roman governor of Iconium: at one his enemies suggest that
he be charged with Christianity, thus making quick work of him (16),
when the sympathetic governor would rather hear what he teaches; at
another Paul is accused of being a *magos* (20) by the crowd while the
governor hears him "with pleasure." Although this double trial scene
resembles others in the martyrologies, it seems to be modeled on the
trials of Paul in Acts 24–26 before sympathetic Roman authorities. At
his second trial in the *Acts of Paul and Thecla*, Paul is condemned to be
scourged and expelled from the city. Thecla, who is tried with him, is
not so lucky.

I do not find Bremmer's explanation of the difference between the
two sentences particularly compelling, that Paul is a Roman citizen,
whereas Thecla is not. After all, she and her family are among the "first
citizens of the Iconians."[37] Nor does the story, as Sheila McGinn contends, simply show that "Christianity is permissible for men but not
for women."[38] Thecla's crime is that she presents an even greater dis-
ruption to her family, city, and society than does Paul. Her story may
follow the erotic subtext of the Greek romance, but for a purpose that
is not clear to the other characters. She has abandoned her maidenly
modesty, not for the expected consummation of marriage, but in order
to boldly follow a "strange" new teaching out of love for a foreigner.
She does things that are simply not consistent with the public chastity
expected in a Greco-Roman city: she leaves her house, the upper-class

woman's sphere, at night, alone, in search of Paul, a man to whom she is not related.[39] Like the Christians who visited Perpetua and her companions in prison, Thecla bribes the jailors with symbols of her wealth, her bracelets (or anklets) and her silver mirror (18). Once she is in Paul's own presence, she is again mesmerized, sitting at his feet and kissing his chains. Once again, we appear to return to an erotic sub-text, but with a Christian "sexual logic": as Tertullian mentions in his letter *To His Wife* 2.4.2, pagan husbands (presumably even betrothed husbands) were hardly likely to allow their wives freedom to attend "nocturnal meetings," or to "crawl [*reptare*]" into prison to kiss a martyr's chains.[40] (This might have been an *exemplum Theclae* of which he might have approved, however.) He could also have added that the pagan husbands would not approve of such shameless behavior as rolling around in the place where Paul had sat.

It becomes clear that the reason Thecla, rather than Paul, is condemned to death is precisely because her behavior, much more than his, is a greater scandal to the Iconians. Her complete silence has already seemed to her family as signifying a kind of death: in an extreme move, her own mother calls for her to be burned as "lawless [*anomos*]," a lawlessness that is symbolized by her being a "nonbride" (*anymphos*, 20). Thecla is to be a public spectacle, burned in the theater, as an example for all women to fear, for not playing out the expected end of the romance: a marriage between two wellborn young people that will be a civic partnership.[41] Magda Misset-van de Weg even suggests that Thecla's removal of her bracelets, sale of her mirror, and kissing the fetters of Paul "symbolize that Thecla severs the ties that bind her to her family and everything that 'mirrors' the world (*kosmos*), including marriage," which includes jewelry as part of a dowry.[42] So far, Thecla is not playing by the rules of the marriage text: instead, she is headed for what would be a typical Christian female martyrdom. In fact, the governor has her brought in naked, a topos that appears in several other stories of Christian female martyrs. The body of the woman is exposed. But here we experience another reversal: the governor weeps and "is amazed," not because of her beauty, as a prominent English translation has it, and as we might expect (Agathonicē, Crispina, and Potamiaena in their respective *Acta* come to mind),[43] but "because of the power [*dynamin*] in her" (22). Still, Thecla appears not to realize her power because she keeps looking around for Paul (though absent, he appears in the likeness of Christ and then disappears; he does quite a bit of disappearing from Thecla).

Like Blandina at her martyrdom, Thecla "makes the figure of the cross";[44] then she mounts the pyre. But Thecla has not "spoken a martyrdom," as does Blandina. She does not even confess to being Christian: the question is whether that is, in fact, what she is. There is more to it than that: Thecla is an encratite Christian, at any rate the kind of Christian woman of whom the author of 1 Timothy would strongly have disapproved, one who "forbids marriage" (1 Tim. 4:3). Bremmer, however, considers the gesture of the cross made by Thecla not primarily a symbol that she has become Christ, as with Blandina, but a conqueror's gesture.[45] What has she conquered? Certainly in the paradoxical language and symbolism of martyrdom, her exposed, vulnerable female naked body has conquered the timidity of the flesh. If, as Maureen Tilley has asserted, the type of ascetic behavior elevated by Paul and adopted by Thecla was training that "allowed the martyrs to reconfigure their bodies as battleground," then Thecla and those she represents have conquered in the sign of the cross as forcefully as Constantine later was to do, remaking their world.[46] The "force" or power that the governor senses within Thecla is the power of her choice for fleshly integrity, on which spiritual authority is based. This is the power approved by God, who causes a hailstorm so violent that Thecla's persecutors are in danger of being killed, while she is saved (22). Thus ends the first part of her story, the destruction of a former identity and the emergence of a new one, as the unassailable and powerful virgin slave girl of God.

Once Thecla leaves Iconium, she has "abandoned the world" she once knew, along with its value. She is actually dead to it, as her mother, her betrothed husband, and the slave women of her *familia* have already assumed. The resurrection of the "blessed" body of the virgin preached by Paul in Iconium (*APTh* 5–6) has in a sense already happened and is underlined by the fact that when the newly rescued Thecla meets Paul, who is with the family of Onesiphorus, it is at an "opened tomb" (23), and she declares to him that she has been "saved" from the flames. The term she uses, *sōtheisa*, can mean "rescued" but also echoes the preaching of Paul that God will be "a work of salvation" (*sōtēria*) for the bodies of virgins. According to the narrative, it is now belatedly discovered that it was not Thecla's power but Paul's distant intercessory prayer that has saved her (24). Despite the great affection (*agapē*) that all in this impromptu family in Christ show for each other at an impromptu Eucharist (25), Paul refuses to let Thecla follow him. His reasons seem inexplicable for someone who preaches the strength of the celibate life to someone who has believed him and shown the strength of that choice in the face of death: "Times are ugly (shameful) and you are beautiful: may a trial (temptation) greater than the first one not seize you, so that you will not endure it, but act like a coward [*deilandrēsēs*]."[47]

What a curious rejection! The verb used here, *deilandreō*, has the same root as *andreia*, courage or manliness. As we have seen, women who show courage (*andreia*) are behaving like men. Has Thecla not already shown that courage? Is Paul afraid that she will also lack "manly" self-control, in other words, to act "like a woman"? As Misset-van de Weg points out, Paul's remark that *Thecla* might not be able to resist another temptation "debases this young woman who just bore the worst test," reducing her to "classical tropes" of women, virtually turning her triumphant virgin body back into "the body which is equated with her sexuality."[48] Why would he believe that she would be tempted, especially to become a *cowardly* male? Is it because she offers to cut her hair short (like a man's) and therefore would look like a man? Or is this cutting of the hair a mark of shame, like Crispina's shaved head? If so, it would not make her particularly beautiful, but it might make her seem more sexually available, in that it is not a mark of a respectable woman. The canonical Paul has a lot to say on the subject of female hair in 1 Corinthians 11:3–16: hair is a natural covering but ought to be covered in the case of a married woman, as a "sign of authority" over her. But here Paul clearly does not want Thecla to "belong" to him: he firmly disowns her when they are accosted in Antioch by the lustful Syriarch Alexander, subjecting her to a trial—a series of trials—that clearly are worse than the Iconian one (26). Or does it signal, as in the other apocryphal acts, that "the physical beauty of the heroine was not an unambiguous sign of spiritual beauty; it was also a temptation for celibate men?"[49] If this is the case, then Paul is the one in danger, yet when Thecla suggests that he give her the "seal" of baptism—the Christian force field that so effectively protects many a virgin martyr from losing her virginity (and is later to protect Thecla when she baptizes herself)—he refuses, saying she must be patient (25). In any event, Paul does take Thecla with him to Antioch, only to reject her once there. He has not allowed her to "follow" him as a disciple, yet she does.

There could be many reasons for Paul's distancing of himself from his latest disciple, and I have outlined some of them, but with respect to the narrative, and the narrative alone, Aymer's suggestion seems to be convincing, that Thecla's accompanying Paul to Antioch just after he has refused her is one of the seams betraying the hand of a redactor who was reconciling two compelling and competing Christian stories.[50] Nonetheless, Paul's inexplicable first rejection of Thecla, almost immediately followed by another, more serious one, emphasizes a recurrent theme in martyr stories: the paradoxical pointing to the woman's body as a source of strength, all the more remarkable because that same body should be a source of weakness and stumbling. Thecla's body is a temptation—one that she has overcome (and perhaps Paul needs to keep away from)—but one that needs to be tested over and over in circumstances that do not let the reader forget it is a *woman's* body. Neither among pagans nor among Christians are women supposed to act this way.

In Antioch, Thecla acts like no cowardly male, but instead "unmans" the chief of the Antiochenes, Alexander. As she and Paul enter the city, they are encountered by Alexander the Syriarch, an official who was probably responsible for entertainment, which as the fourth-century writer Libanius tells us, included wild-beast shows, several of which are going to star the unwitting Thecla.[51] The romance theme enters once again, as Alexander falls in love with Thecla at first sight (26), but since this is a Christian story and not a Greek romance, it is not love but lust. Alexander seems to assume that Thecla is Paul's property, perhaps his slave girl, and tries to get him on his side with the kind of money and gifts appropriate in such a situation. At this point Paul shamefully—there is no other word for it—betrays and abandons Thecla, saying, "I do not know the woman of whom you speak, nor is she mine." With complete license, especially since he is "very powerful [*poly dynamenos*]," Alexander lays hold of Thecla in the street (well, why not? Is she not a streetwalker?) and kisses her.

The language that describes this assault reminds us of the Iconian incident, in which Thecla, naked on the pyre, seeks the absent Paul: here, too, she "looks for Paul." This time, however, he is not even assisting her with prayer; she is on her own and finds a public voice. First, she screams, and then protests against this attack: "Do not force the stranger, do not force the slave girl of God. I am first of the Iconians, and because I would not marry Thamyris, I was cast out of the city." While this is not entirely true—she was rescued from death in Iconium by a spectacular miracle of God that left several fellow citizens dead—her protest nonetheless reflects the growing tendency in this part of the narrative for Thecla to act for herself as she speaks for herself, claiming her own new "male" identity. Because Alexander has tried to dishonor her publicly, she will also shame him publicly: she rips his cloak and removes the *stephanos*, the crown symbolic of his authority, from his head, thus triumphing over him.

This has now become a contest between "first citizens" over their public honor. To recover his lost honor (and, says the narrative, partly unwilling to abandon the romance theme, "because he loved her"), Alexander brings her to the governor, and upon her confession that she has in fact done what she has done, he condemns her to the beasts (27). While it is clear that, as in Iconium, Thecla's "crime" is one of refusal of marriage or sexual intercourse, the later inscription over her in the arena is "*hierosylos* [sacrilegious]" (28, 32), equating the decision for virginity with an affront to the social order. Here, as at Thecla's trial in Iconium, there are women present who comment on the judgment, but instead of crying out for her to burn, the women cry out, "An evil judgment, an unholy judgment!"[52] This cry is repeated five times in the course of the narrative, each one emphasizing another condemnation of Thecla by the authorities, and in response condemning them.

In the Antioch section of the *Acts of Paul and Thecla*, as Aymer has pointed out, the women characters are highlighted and all seem beneficial, as opposed to the male characters, which are at least menacing if not "evil."[53] Of particular interest is the wealthy "queen" Tryphaena, who is a foil for Thecla's punitive mother Theocleia, perhaps in the way that the Good Shepherd seen in Perpetua's first vision is a substitute for her earthly father.[54] Tryphaena takes Thecla into her house, in response to Thecla's request to be kept "pure [*hagnē*]" until her upcoming death (27), an echo of the threatened punishment of virgin martyrs like Potamiaena of being raped by gladiators or exposed, like Agnes, in brothels. Tryphaena's protection of Thecla is also the occasion for another reminiscence—or possibly anticipation—of martyrdom. Tryphaena's dead daughter, Falconilla, appears to her, begging her mother to let the imprisoned confessor pray for her, in order that she might be translated to "the place of the just" (28). Interestingly, we do not see the corresponding vision of the redeemed Falconilla, as we do in Perpetua's third vision of the redeemed Dinocrates. Instead, we see the rescued Thecla, who is "raised from the dead" after her final combat and taken into Tryphaena's house in Falconilla's place, as a substitute daughter (39).

In the upcoming combat, the once-more naked Thecla is matched first with female beasts, a she-lion and a she-bear, as Perpetua and Felicitas are matched with the mad heifer. Yet, as with all females (except the bear) in Antioch, the she-lion proves beneficial, first licking the feet of Thecla (28), and later fighting off all other animals, until she herself is killed, at which all the women "grieve the more" (33). Undaunted, the governor and Alexander bring forth "many beasts," the most remarkable of which are the seals, who appear in a pit filled with water that prompts Thecla to decide, "Now is the time to wash" (34), a phrase that reminds us of the "baptism of blood" received by the martyrs Felicitas and Saturus in the *Martyrdom of Perpetua and Felicitas.* Yet Thecla's is no baptism of blood, but a self-baptism that is probably the *exemplum Theclae* in the *Acts of Paul and Thecla* to which Tertullian so strenuously objected. Despite the pleas of the women, the crowd, and even the governor, another Roman official who weeps, this time at the destruction of such beauty, Thecla leaps into the water, first exclaiming, "I am baptized [or, 'I baptize myself'] in the name of Jesus Christ on the last day!" A second miracle, or perhaps two miracles, occur: Thecla's powerful action is such that God causes a lightning bolt to kill the seals and a cloud of fire to cover Thecla up, so her nakedness will not be seen. (God apparently approves of female modesty in the arena.) Finally Thecla has received the "seal," the mark of belonging to Christ through baptism that will defend her in the arena.

Impressive though this miracle is, it is nowhere near the denoue-ment: there are other wild beasts, whom the women overpower by a "feminine" tactic of pelting them with sweet-smelling (and apparently narcotic) flowers; in the finale Alexander as a last resort brings out two ferocious bulls that belong to him, and Thecla is tied between them while scorching irons are applied to their genitals in the hopes that in their rage they will destroy her. The symbolism of the beasts (and their owner) with their red-hot genitals is not difficult to read, but Thecla survives this last trial as well with another miracle: the rope that ties her is burned through, and she is "as one unbound." Once more the ties that bind have been overcome. Lust's last assault is finished; Try-phaena faints, causing Alexander to become quite concerned because of her prominence and relationship to Caesar, who might destroy the city because of her death (36). The governor now gives Thecla the opportunity to "speak her martyrdom," even though it is a martyrdom manqué: "Who are you, and what is it about you, that none of the beasts touched you?" Once more we have a Roman official marveling at the "power within her." As Thecla previously said to Alexander, she says again: "I am the slave girl of the living God." It is her confession of Christ that has saved her, as he will save all who believe in him. There is not a word about her celibacy; perhaps there is no need for any since in this narrative the decision for Christianity is a simultaneous decision for sexual continence. Thecla's baptism merely provides the formal "sealing" of a body that had already dedicated its integrity to Christ.

The happy ending is coming: Thecla has beaten off all suitors, she is reclothed and released, the city rejoices, and Thecla gets back a household, a mother, and even the maids that she lost in Iconium. Tryphaena takes her home and bequeaths her fortune to her, and Thecla manages to convert the maids. A Christian household has been substituted for the pagan household: "And there was great joy in the house" (39). The end? Unfortunately, not. Just as the reunion of the two chaste but sundered lovers must happen in the Greek romance, Thecla must be reunited with Paul, only to be turned away once more, but with his recognition of what she has done for herself through Christ (baptism) and his adding the apostolic functions of teaching and preaching (40–41). Thecla has transformed herself, not only spiritually but also physically: this time, taking her own initiative, she travels "like a man [*schēmati andrikō*]," a phrase that can mean either dressed like a man or looking like a man, with her own entourage of young men and maids, and finds Paul in Myra. Paul has not changed; he is "astounded" to see her (could he have hoped to have gotten rid of his pesky disciple once and for all?) and can only imagine "some other temptation (trial) was with her." Boldly Thecla now confronts her teacher: "I have taken the bath [baptism], Paul. For the one who worked for the gospel in you has worked with me to baptize" (40). Here may be Tertullian's problem: the baptism of Thecla is a charismatic baptism, given only by Christ and administered by a woman as a result of her confessor status. Paul has no more protests; he takes her with him to his host's house, where she astonishes him even more. Thecla, however, wishes to return to Iconium, whereupon Paul says, "Go and teach the word of God" (41), an apostolic commissioning if there ever was one. Thecla returns full circle to the house of Onesiphorus and preaches there in Paul's stead (42). Fortunately, Thamyris is dead (preventing an awkward encounter), but Theocleia is alive. We are not told her response in one version of the story; in another, longer version, she remains silent; in still another she will not listen. Undismayed, however, Thecla "having given her witness [*diamartyramenē*] in Iconium (at last!) goes to Seleucia, "and having enlightened many with the word of God fell asleep with a beautiful sleep."

WHO LOVES THECLA AND WHY?

So ends one version of the story.[55] And perhaps the most significant part of the interpretation of Thecla is the incorporation of the *Acts* in a lengthier, edited version from the fifth century, credited to Basil of Seleucia, *The Life and Miracles of Thecla*. Yet the story of Thecla, more than that of Perpetua, was important to a variety of people and used in a variety of ways long before that date and at one point possibly even considered scriptural.[56] The current debate over the circumstances of the composition of the *Acts*, whether all or part of the story arose in women's circles or proved a history of women's leadership in the early church, has tended to obscure the very different ways in which the early Christians themselves employed the story of Thecla. On the one hand, several scholars have seen in the *Acts of Thecla* the history of a counter-canonical tradition that valued women's leadership roles and validated them through the recitation of stories like that of Thecla.[57] On the other, this view has been questioned by scholars who see either no valid evidence for the existence of such women's communities and their composition of such oral narratives, or an advocacy for women's leadership in the *Acts of Paul and Thecla*.[58] Although the debate continues, scholarly opinion now tends to support the position articulated by A.-J. Levine in her summary introduction to the recent *A Feminist Companion to the New Testament Apocrypha*, that heroines like Thecla "are less representative of women's voices than they are reflections of male authors who expressed their concerns via the figures of women."[59]

But still the questions remain. Do stories like that of Thecla have to be by women and for women in order to be empowering stories for women in the past as in the present? And is it the same kind of power? For example, I find no instances of women in early Christianity who say they want to follow Perpetua's example: we do, however, have the powerful voice of Perpetua herself, who is determined to attain paradise. On the other hand, we have male voices, like those of Tertullian and Augustine, employing Perpetua as a model for male as well as female Christians. We do, however, have instances of women adopting the model of Thecla for themselves, and of men both praising Thecla's example for women (like Ambrose and Gregory of Nyssa) and attacking it (like Tertullian). We need to find out, however, what each gender found attractive and powerful and why.

The first and most obvious response of women to Thecla's story is the citation from Tertullian's *Baptism* 17.4–5 (ca. 198 CE). Whatever we may think of the existence of protofeminist communities and their use of this story, it seems that, minimally, at least one Christian woman (and probably others, as well as men) in Carthage's Christian community were using the example of Thecla to teach and to baptize; yet Tertullian finds both of these functions equally abhorrent for women. His solution is to declare falsely Pauline the text on which they base their mandate, and that's that for him. In a letter to Cyprian of Carthage, dated approximately 256, Firmilian of Caesarea in Cappadocia complains about Stephanus of Rome, the pope, for his stance on baptism, complaining that in Caesarea a woman prophet claimed to be filled with the Holy Spirit and not only performed miracles but also taught, celebrated the Eucharist, and baptized, using the proper ecclesiastical formulae. Firmilian attributes this woman's seductive power (she allegedly seduced even a presbyter and a deacon) to her possession by a demon, but he raises the question about baptism: "What, then, shall we say about the baptism of this woman, by which a most wicked demon baptized through means of a woman?" (Cyprian, *Letters*, 74; 75.10–11).[60] Needless to say, Firmilian thought that *this* baptism was invalid and those who received it needed to be rebaptized. Again, however, we have only the word of a man that a woman was performing ecclesiastical functions and that men also were listening to her and accepting her leadership.

The only other important literary record that we have of a woman using Thecla as an example for herself is also regrettably not by a woman. The remarkable Cappadocian family best known for Basil of Caesarea and Gregory of Nyssa also included their formidable sister Macrina, praised by her brother Gregory in his *Life of Macrina*, which he wrote in the form of a letter to the monk Olympius and in his treatise *The Soul and Resurrection*. Gregory tells the story of Macrina's "secret name," which was given to her in a vision or dream that her mother, Emmelia, had as she was about to deliver her first child. According to Gregory, Emmelia saw an angelic being who "addressed the child she was carrying by the name of Thecla, that Thecla, I mean, who is so famous among the virgins" (962B).[61] After confirming the name three times, the apparition vanished and gave Emmelia an easy delivery. One wonders why the name "Thecla" needed to be private and secret (surely not a nickname). Gregory relates the story as if Emmelia had her own reasons, apart from the vision, since she herself had wanted to follow the virgin life but might have suffered the fate that threatened virgin martyrs— rape—had she not sought a husband to protect her (962A). Similarly for Gregory, the name Thecla is significant not because it should be the child's actual name, but because it seals her fate. Did Emmelia want to name her child Thecla (as many in the Greek Christian East increasingly did), and had to name her something else (a family name)? As Francine Cardman notes, both Emmelia and Macrina are important and signifying names in this family: Macrina was the name of her father's grandmother, a Christian confessor; Emmelia herself bore the name of her own grandmother, who was a martyr.[62] Is this Emmelia's choice (or story) at all, or is it Gregory's? And might Emmelia have been marking her daughter for a destiny she herself wanted to fulfill?

This question of choice—and of voice—also arises in Gregory's laudatory biography of his sister, in which, like many other male writers who praise women, he cannot resist returning to her body, which is "marked" over and over again as female throughout a rather long section on preparing Macrina for her burial. This designation of Macrina's bodily femaleness happens despite or perhaps even because of Gregory's saying at the beginning of his letter to another male, the monk Olympius, that a woman is its subject, "If indeed she should be styled woman, for I do not know whether it is fitting to designate her by her sex, who so surpassed her sex" (960B). Throughout the funeral narrative, the reader looks with Gregory and others on Macrina's dead virgin body, which like Thecla's is continually exposed: as naked, as a bride, as maternal, as marked, as beautiful, as shining in the darkness. This constant visibility of Macrina's body contrasts strongly with Gregory's unwillingness to see the "common shame" of the disintegrated bodies of his parents when they open the family tomb (996A).

Distressed that he cannot find anything suitable with which to clothe her, Gregory consults the deaconess Lampadia. She tells him that Macrina had no "treasures" to be buried with her except her monastic's habit because she "resolved that a pure life should be her adornment" (990A). When Gregory tries to have Macrina's body dressed in linen, Lampadia protests that it is not fitting for her to appear as a bride before the other virgins, and she is rerobed in dark clothing that belonged to Emmelia, "that this holy beauty be not decked out with the unnecessary splendor of clothing." It turns out, however, that Macrina does have some "treasures"; like Thecla, she wears the "sign" of the cross, both in the form of an iron cross and an iron ring containing a fragment of the True Cross. Even more, as her noble friend Vestiana points out, she is "marked" or branded with a small scar, the sign of a healed cancer of the breast, for which Macrina had refused to see a doctor because like the virgins in so many martyrologies, she found death preferable to uncovering her body to a "stranger's eyes." Instead, she asks her mother Emmelia to make "the holy seal," the sign of the cross, on the tumor, which is effectual. Yet Macrina still carries that "seal" of her belonging to God, a choice that she has made, just as Emmelia, who had no choice but to marry, chose the emblematic name of Thecla for her daughter. Like Thecla also, Macrina chose the virgin life, seeing herself as a widow after her fiancé died before the marriage was consummated, and therefore as free to dedicate herself to become a monastic. As Virginia Burrus writes of "Macrina's tattoo," despite the insistence of Gregory's narrative that writes of her body, there are "traces" here of Macrina's inscription of her own life.[63] It may be that Gregory's description of the story of Macrina's secret name, like the secret she *almost* carries to her grave, reflects for her as well as for Emmelia a choice that, however prescribed and described by males, is a self-conscious one that reflects their own subjectivity.

Macrina is the "Teacher [*Didaskalos*]" in the dialogue *The Soul and Resurrection*, in which she, close to death herself, consoles Gregory for the death of their brother Basil, like Plato's charioteer skillfully "curbing" her brother's "disordered" soul with her reason.[64] Macrina, however, is not speaking in her own voice; Gregory is speaking "through" her, and he does not, even in the beginning of the dialogue when he notes her being weak and prostrate with illness, emphasize her female body. As Elizabeth Clark notes, for Gregory, Macrina is an ideal ascetic's image of "the primal rational human who is [for him] 'without sex,'" at the same time as she functions "as a shaming device for Christian men," if even a woman could reach "this summit of wisdom and rationality."[65] So while Macrina functions as Christian Diotima, or even as Christian Socrates in this dialogue (she is after all, near death, as Socrates is in Plato's *Phaedo*), she is not speaking in her own voice.

Another Christian writer, Methodius, uses virgin ascetic women, including Thecla, in a deliberate literary parallel to a Platonic dialogue. In his *Symposium*, drawing its name as well as its form from Plato's *Symposium*, the fourth-century bishop uses the knowledge of the pagan philosophical work—a discussion and praise of erotic attraction by Socrates and his male friends at a drinking party—to underline the contrast to his own work: a sober discourse on chastity (*hagneia*) by ten virgins, who symbolize the "wise and foolish virgins" of the parable about the unexpected arrival of the bridegroom-Messiah in Matthew 25:1–12 (*Symposium*, Discourse 6.2–4). Thecla, who is responsible for the eighth discourse, praises virginity (*partheneia*) as equality to God (*partheia*, 8.1) and speaks of the necessity for Christians to demonstrate the "drama of the truth" by coming into the *theatron* and combating the devil and the demons arrayed against them, perhaps a reference to the classic theme of the spectacle of the martyr, perhaps even to her own spectacle. Thecla also mentions giving up one's body to "beasts and flames" (8.2). In the epithalamium, the wedding song celebrating the marriage of the virgins and of the virginal church to their heavenly "celibate bridegroom" Christ (11),[66] Thecla is chosen to lead the other virgins as she sings of her own abandonment of home and marriage, mother and kin, passing through the beasts and fire, to come to the pure bridal chamber. She receives this honor and the largest "crown" from the leader of the virgins, Aretē, or personified Virtue, because her discourse has been the best. She is also praised by her sister virgins because she has been victorious in the contests of the martyrs with the strength of body that matches her strength of mind (8.17).

MacDonald regards Methodius's *Symposium* and the character of Thecla in it as one more example of the widespread knowledge of Thecla's story.[67] Clearly, Methodius presumes knowledge of some details of her martyrdom, both in Iconium (the fire) and in Antioch (the beasts), since he is familiar with and praises her choice of the virgin life. Nevertheless, Methodius's Thecla—even more than Gregory of Nyssa's Macrina, who at least we can be sure is a historical woman—is the representative of the bishop's own theological concerns. The discourse for which Thecla wins the largest prize from the hand of virtue is one that exegetes the figure of the Woman Clothed with the Sun in Revelation 12:1–6 as the church, who gives birth to the "male people [*laon ton arsena*]," the Christians who abandon the "passions of women" (8.7).[68] As for Gregory of Nyssa, who finds Thecla not only an appropriate name for his sister Macrina but also noteworthy as an example of destroying the "outward person,"[69] so Methodius finds in Thecla a symbol of the ideal Christian ascetic, one who is defined as either androgynous (rarely) or male. Palladius, in his *Lausiac History*, uses the phrase, "*hē anthrōpos tou theou*" to describe Melania (9). The feminine definite article used with the masculine noun could be translated as "this woman of God," but is usually translated as "this female man of God," in order to convey the "masculine and perfect mind" (Preface, 1) of the ascetic woman.[70]

Thus for most of the church fathers from the second to the fifth centuries, Thecla's main function was as a martyr who was willing to defend the virtue they valued—chastity—to the death. As such, she was a symbol of a woman who overcame, not merely the confines of her woman's body, but also woman's fallen nature, transforming that body into one that, like Macrina's, radiated sanctity. In his advice on virginity to his sister Marcellina, Ambrose recommends Thecla's virgin resolve to her, relating the story of a male lion (not a lioness) that would neither attack "the sacred body of the virgin" nor even look at her, keeping his eyes modestly lowered because of her nakedness. Therefore, he says, just as the Blessed Virgin Mary should teach Marcellina the "*disciplina vitae*," the necessary life-training of self-denial, so Thecla should teach her how to sacrifice herself in death (*Thecla doceat immolari*; *On Virgins* 2.3.19–21). Jerome, who doubted Luke's authorship of the *Acts of Paul and Thecla* (*On Famous Men* 3.7), was nevertheless not skeptical about the existence of Thecla, envisioning her enthusiastically greeting the virgin Eustochium in heaven (*Letters* 22.41) and even praising Melania the Elder as "the new Thecla" (*Chronicle*). Augustine calls Thecla "most blessed [*sanctissima*]," defends Paul's preaching to her on virginity against Manichean charges (*Against Faustus* 30.4), and in *Sacred Virginity* praises the martyrs Thecla and Crispina as examples of obedience, one as a virgin (*uirgo*), the other as a married woman (*mulier*; 1.44), as he had earlier praised the contrasting pair of Agnes and Crispina (*Sermon* 354 5.5).[71] The latter example provides a parallel to Augustine's use of Perpetua and to the employment of both Perpetua and Thecla as examples by the Fathers; these women are ideals because they see their lives aimed at the next world, not this one. The final transformations of Thecla will occur in the rewriting of her *Acta* by the fifth-century Pseudo-Basil of Seleucia, reflecting Thecla's transformation into an iconic martyr and intercessor. Pseudo-Chrysostom's panegyric to her as the model of asceticism and Severus of Antioch's praise of her "perfect body, . . . beautiful, powerful, and immense," in the sixth century are also elements of her ecclesiastical apotheosis.[72] But before we examine this ultimate metamorphosis of Thecla, there is one other woman's voice concerning her that we need to consider.

EGERIA'S ENCOUNTER

One of the remarkable writings from women in the first five centuries of Christianity is another diary, this time that of a pilgrim to the Holy Land, variously named Egeria, Aetheria, or even Silvia. The incomplete diary, known as the *Itinerarium Egeriae* (*Travels of Egeria*) or *Peregrinatio Aetheriae* (*Aetheria's Pilgrimage*), was by most accounts written by a Spanish woman of some means, perhaps a monastic herself, since she writes her account for her "sisters" (*sorores*), presumably sister Christians. It dates from near the end of the fourth century.[73] A good half of the work is taken up with Egeria's (as we will call her) visit to Jerusalem and her interest in the liturgy celebrated there. But for our purposes the most intriguing part of her voyage to numbers of holy places is a trip she took to Seleucia in Isauria in Asia Minor, where she chooses to visit "Saint Thecla," probably her *martyrium*, or tomb, which was probably more modest than the later basilica built in her honor by the Emperor Zeno about a century later. According to Egeria's account (23.3–5), she finds nothing at the "very beautiful" church there except a monastery "of men and women without number." There, she says, she encountered her "dearest friend," the renowned deaconess Marthana, whom she had known in Jerusalem, and who "was ruling [*regebat*]" over "the monastery of *apotactitae* or virgins." Marthana herself has left Jerusalem for Seleucia "for the sake of prayer." There a double monastery had been founded on a site of known holiness, sacred to Christian virginity of both men and women. Egeria also tells us that at Thecla's *martyrium* either a prayer or speech was made and that all of the *Acts of Saint Thecla* were read. She concludes by saying, "I gave infinite thanks to God for deeming me, unworthy and of no merit, worthy to fulfill all my desires." She stays there two days with the male and female virgins and then departs for Tarsus.

Her pilgrimage is imitated by two strenuously ascetic "desert mothers," Marana and Cyra, who only left their enclosure in Beroea, Syria, twice in forty-two years: once to visit Jerusalem, to which they walked, fasting; and once more to visit Thecla's *martyrium*, to which they also walked fasting, a distance of over two hundred miles. It is regrettable that, unlike Egeria, they left no account of what they did there; we only know the story from Theodoret of Cyrrhus's *Religious History* (29), but from this account it is clear that a visit to Thecla's shrine was as important as a pilgrimage to the Holy City.[74] We cannot automatically assume, although many have, that Egeria was a nun, but we do know that Marana and Cyra were. For each of these women, and one by her own writing, it was important to be in the presence of Thecla's enclosed body. For Egeria, to be with her friend the deaconess Marthana, reading or hearing the story of Thecla in the presence of other virgins, was the fulfillment of desire, perhaps a ratification of her own choice. For Marana and Cyra, Thecla's tomb was a significant site, again perhaps—even more than for Egeria—the ratification of their way of life, their own self-mortified yet soon-to-be-glorified virgin bodies. Is it significant that all three have become, like Thecla, independent itinerants? Stephen J. Davis thinks that such women were important in the development of the cult of Thecla not only in Asia Minor but also in its spread to Egypt: "Independent virgins [i.e., wandering itinerants] continued to play a surreptitious role in the development of the Thecla cult, . . . a role preserved in the witness of oral traditions about women, but subtly cloaked beneath the reticent rhetoric of male authors."[75]

REWRITING THECLA: PSEUDO-BASIL'S LIFE AND MIRACLES

One of the "rich paradoxes of Thecla's position in the imagination of the early church," as Kate Cooper has put it, is Thecla's powerful "afterlife" as the focus of pilgrimage at a variety of centers, most importantly Meriamlik, near Silifke (Seleucia), an already important site in the late fourth century, but also as the miracle-working patron saint of the church who supports the humble faithful and grants the prayers of the powerful as well.[76] In fact, Gregory of Nazianzus spent some time—three years—at the shrine in Seleucia, just before Egeria's pilgrimage, himself in need of physical if not spiritual healing, saying that he fled to Seleucia to "the Parthenon [*parthenōna*] of the famous maiden [*korē*] Thecla" (*Poems, On His Life* 547–549).[77]

But it is the *Vita ac Miraculis Sanctae Theclae*, the *Life and Miracles of Saint Thecla*, in two books, long attributed to Basil, bishop of Seleucia that transforms her from the independent virgin disowned even by Paul to the protector of virgins, healer of suppliants (especially but not exclusively women), and defender of her church, her territory, and of orthodoxy. In a lengthy preface, the writer declares that he is a historian who wants to write a *"parthenikē historia*," a "virgin's story," in which Thecla will be shown to be the "first of women" martyrs as Stephen was the first of men.[78] As Monika Pesthy comments, the first book is "a lengthy paraphrase of the Thecla story," which the author edits, in favor of long discourses and speeches (for example, Paul has a very long apologia before the proconsul about the iniquities of pagan worship compared with Christian), and either omitting or sanitizing objectionable material. Paul does not reject Thecla at Antioch; Thecla acknowledges him at length as her teacher (*didaskalos*) in the virtues of virginity and continence, but especially in the doctrines of the faith.[79] Paul thus judges that Christ has chosen her through himself as an apostle. Scott Johnson points out that the rewriting of the *Acta* by Pseudo-Basil thus gives Thecla "a character that she never had in the *ATh* [*Acts of Thecla*], that of one of Paul's disciples in Acts or in his letters," on a par with Timothy and Titus rather than with Stephen, connected to Paul only through Paul's assenting to his death.[80] This is undoubtedly the Thecla who supposedly guaranteed to the Byzantine emperor Zeno victory over his rival and for whom in turn Zeno built the votive church at the site of the *martyrium* in thanksgiving.

The first book of Pseudo-Basil's *Vita* ends, not with Thecla's "beautiful sleep" but with something more miraculous. After she has preached extensively, converted many, enrolling them in "Christ's army," and "sealing" them with baptism, she enters the earth "while still alive" (PG 85:558–60), apparently on the site where the church known to Egeria, Gregory, and Pseudo-Basil stood. A different version of the story expands her healing and teaching career in Seleucia and gives a reason for her disappearance.[81] Accompanied by a "bright cloud," Thecla travels to Seleucia, but appalled by the city's idolatry, she lives an ascetic life similar to that of the desert mothers in a nearby mountainous cave, resisting the devil's temptations by the help of God, but attracting the attention of some "wellborn" women who come to learn from her and subsequently live like her, perhaps forming the core of female monastics later associated with the shrine. The "virgin Thecla [*parthenos Thecla*]" appears here very much like a "divine woman" as she performs miracles of healing and casting out of unclean spirits "by the grace of God."

Her abilities make the physicians of Seleucia envious, since they are losing business, and they plot a way to steal her power. Thinking that she is a virgin priestess of Artemis, deriving her power from the virginity that makes her beloved of all of the gods, they hire some ruffians, getting them drunk, in order to rape her and thus steal her virgin power. These men are so wicked [*ponēroi*] that, like many men in the *Acts of Paul and Thecla*, they appear beastly; here they are like lions raging outside the cave. The "holy martyr," strengthened by the power of God, is not afraid; she asks them what they want, and when they tell her, she replies that even though she is a "lowly old woman [*tapeinē graus*], she is still the servant of Christ, and they will not be able to accomplish their design. Even when they insist, using force in order to "shame" her, she replies gently, "Wait, children, so that you may see the glory of God."

In her prayer to God, she enumerates the times that he has rescued her—from the fire, from marriage to Thamyris, from Alexander, from wild beasts, from the "deep waters" (the pit of seals?)—asking him to deliver her one more time, preserving the virginity that she has kept for him whom she loves and desires, "Father, Son and Holy Spirit for all eternity." Not only does this prayer return us in some sense to a reiteration of the Christian "chastity romance," with its theme of the heavenly bridegroom; it also takes us in the direction of the defense of orthodoxy found in the speech that Pseudo-Basil portrays Thecla speaking to Paul on their reunion in Myra. In response, a heavenly voice tells his "true slave girl [*doulē*]" not to fear, giving her a vision of her "eternal home." The wanderer, who left her earthly home, is enclosed in a rock, so that all they can grasp is a piece of her veil—apparently intended to become a relic, since it is given with the permission of God "for the belief of all who see this holy place, and for a blessing for future generations, to those who believe in their Lord Jesus Christ from a pure heart." Thecla's body is now protected: she has become a legacy and a sign. As Stephen Davis notes, moreover, this part of the story may be "apologetic," to explain the absence of her mortal remains at the *martyrium*: her body has been completely translated.[82]

In this collection of legendary material, edited though it may be to fit the concerns of fifth-century orthodoxy, Thecla stands as part of that church, but as a woman who is an apostle, a teacher, and who baptizes. The latter activity may be linked to the baptism of women, as it is with Mygdonia, one of the heroines in the apocryphal *Acts of Thomas*, and it is nobly born women who come out to join her in her desert isolation; yet there is no comment in the text about whether Thecla's baptisms are limited to women. Nor, in Egeria's account of her visit to Thecla's shrine, does it appear unusual that a woman is in charge of a double monastery of men and women. In the accounts of her miracles, many of which are performed for the sake of women and their concerns, the saint is sought by all sorts of people, as A.-J. Festugière asserts: "men and women, masters and servants, the aged and adolescent, rich and poor . . ."[83]

THECLA THE MIRACLE-WORKER

Although we do not have any record of miracles being performed at the site of the *martyrium* of Perpetua and Felicitas, the second book of Pseudo-Basil records many of the miracles Thecla's spiritual presence performed. In fact, the enclosure in the rock is the last of the "rescue" miracles Thecla will receive; for thirty-one others,[84] *she* (although disembodied, even her remains not present in her *martyrium*) is the powerful agent. Ironically, Thecla's disappearance from Seleucia meant that she could be present in a variety of venues: a Roman-based legend related that she was enclosed in the rock only to travel to Rome in time to see Paul's martyrdom, whereupon she also died. There, according to a seventh-century pilgrim itinerary, "her body rests in a cave" in a church near the basilica of St. Paul fuori le Mure (St. Paul outside the walls). Another contemporary account does not mention a body.[85] It does not seem to have been essential for her ability to work miracles, but it will reappear on a variety of pilgrim articles, often unclothed and definitely female.

Festugière sees an arrangement in the miracle stories of the shorter text. After the prologue, in which she defeats the local pagan deity Sarpedon, clearing the way for her own oracles and miracles, she works four miracles for women; "punishment" miracles (like the one performed against Ananias and Sapphira by Peter in Acts 5); miracles in which she defends her shrine and devotees, several healing miracles and favors for women, including the fascinating one in which the illiterate woman Xenarchis is able to read, thanks to Thecla's intercession.[86] Most of the miracles that she performs for women, however, have to do with assisting them with family difficulties: stopping the debauchery of an unfaithful husband, restoring the beauty of Callistē so she will get her husband back, for example. She also punishes two men who wanted to rape one of her consecrated virgins, thus anticipating her own divine "rescue." Even today, at the shrine to Thecla at Ma'alula in Syria, Christian women who believe Thecla brought Christianity to the area pray to the saint for children—an odd occupation for such a resolutely virgin saint.[87] In the final miracle of the longer text, Thecla actually does not perform a miracle at all, at least by action, but rather appears in a vision, "embracing" Dionysia, who has renounced in typical apocryphal fashion "husband, children, and household" to live at Thecla's shrine: in effect, to become another Thecla.[88] In addition, Thecla, the mute virgin of Iconium in the *Acts of Paul and Thecla*, also seems to have gained both a fondness and an ability to assist public speakers: she heals the rhetorician Alypius; she assists two pagan professors of rhetoric; and she helps Basil when he has to speak in public.

The legend of the miracle-working virgin saint and martyr spread throughout the Roman Christian world from the fourth to the seventh centuries, from Seleucia to Italy, Syria, Egypt, and northward even to as far as Wales, where she either became identified with or gave her name to the local saint Tegla, whose well is associated with healing miracles. Thecla, in short, did a good deal of traveling both before and after her death. As Davis observes, not only were women, particularly ascetic women who remained virgins or widows who would not remarry, attracted to Thecla as an example; but also the martyr and intercessory Thecla, whose power was exhibited through miracles, secured her "institutional power."[89] What is remarkable, however, is that in the material artifacts, including frescoes, bas-reliefs, and most importantly pilgrim articles from her various shrines, the body of St. Thecla, displayed and martyred, is most important. It seems as though there is a paradoxical relationship between the *absence* of a body in her chief *martyrium* and elsewhere and the presence of that *definitely* female body in art and objects relating to her. Claudia Nauerth and Rüdiger Warns have cataloged thirty-five images that they believe are genuine representations of Thecla, of which seven represent Thecla as nude or partially nude, while all, clothed or naked, make her breasts distinct, except for a relief from Etschmiadzin in Armenia, which represents Thecla with cropped hair and boy's attire, standing before a seated, teaching Paul (Tafel II.4), very much like pupil and teacher.[90] One remarkable example, also mentioned by Davis, is the grave stele of an Egyptian woman named Thecla. The representation of a woman on the stele is of a woman clothed only below the waist, with defined breasts and arms raised in prayer, a favored depiction of Thecla; but as Davis notes, "The artist seems to have actually conflated the image of Saint Thecla with that of the deceased."[91] So we have at least one woman, who imagined herself (or was imagined) as Thecla, complete with Thecla's exposed woman's body, like Dionysia, "becoming Thecla," a true identification with the saint.

Finally, there is an interesting fresco, probably dating from the sixth century, from the so-called "Grotto of St. Paul" at Ephesus. Once again, Thecla is associated with Paul: the figures in the fresco stand together, both with the right arms raised in a teaching attitude. Paul holds an open book, Thecla a scroll. John Dominic Crossan and Jonathan L. Reed, who put this fresco on the cover of their book *In Search of Paul*, use it as an indicator of the way in which Paul has been used by the church (and we might say, Thecla as well): although the figures of Paul and Thecla are of equal height, asserting their equality iconographically, and both are portrayed as teachers, some later hand has scratched out Thecla's eyes and raised, "authoritative hand." For Crossan and Reed, both the original fresco and its vandalized later version reflect graphically the conflict over Paul among Christians: Did he promote equality for women, or did the "real Paul" want them silenced and subordinate?[92] One might also point out, as Crossan and Reed do not, that the damage, depending on how one looks at it, may already have been done. Thecla is fully clothed in the apparel of a matron, with a head covering. Once more we ask, Where is Brown's "wild virgin girl"?[93] The later church was able to allow Thecla to be part of it because her body, resolutely brought back in the popular iconography, had vanished untouched. As Davis observes, from the frescoes of Thecla at El Bhagawat, Egypt, which depict Thecla in the flames, but curiously clothed, to the revisions of her story in the fifth-century *Life and Miracles*, Thecla symbolizes a move within the church to channel the ascetic impulse. Thus Thecla, as a model for female ascetic piety, embodies "a conflict between the ideals of female autonomy and forms of patriarchal constraint upon those ideals."[94]

5

Why Martyrs Matter

The blood of Christians is seed.

—Tertullian, *Apology* 50.13

God is using Rachel as a vehicle.

—Darrell Scott

I will die for my God, I will die for my faith.

—Cassie Bernall

Every Palestinian woman will give birth to an army of martyrs.

—Dareen Abu Aysheh[1]

PERPETUA AND THECLA IN MODERN DRESS

In the first year of Rhodes College's core humanities course, "The Search for Values in the Light of Western History and Religion," both the *Acts of Paul and Thecla* and the *Martyrdom of Perpetua and Felicitas* are read. [2] The former has had a shorter existence in the course; the latter has been an integral part of it for twelve years and has reached the status of a classic, defined as a text that still has the emotional power to move its readers and to provide enduring models by which they continue to interpret their own experiences. One of the hopes for including a text that for some time had been recovered and reclaimed by feminist scholars as a classic was that it would help to resonate with the experiences of young women students, who now are the majority in college classrooms, to provide a "different voice" in a curriculum that traditionally features women as characters in texts scripted by men, reflecting male concerns and motifs like that of the Quest.[3] Discussions of the text raise questions of individualism, obligation, and religious belief, familiarity and unfamiliarity with the contexts of history and culture. Student reactions to and discussions of the *Martyrdom*, both in the Search class and in upper-level classes that also read it as part of an entire spectrum of early Christian literature, remain surprisingly uniform, despite (or because of) attempts to find contemporary analogues. First-year students, especially the women, who before reading about

103

Perpetua and Felicitas have read, discussed, and reacted fairly positively to the stories of the Maccabean martyrs, are seldom sympathetic to Perpetua's cause.

The *Martyrdom of Perpetua and Felicitas* might seem a remote and alien tale, a sad, gruesome, and rather grotesque story of a newly married woman with a baby, a slave woman, and their friends who are imprisoned, tried, and executed in a Roman arena in 203 CE because they practice a religion that has been outlawed. In a nation that prides itself on separation between church and state, if it does not always practice it, the concept of an illegal religion is hard to understand. The celebrated visions contained in Perpetua's diary, even if understood as dreams, are also quite alien and questionable in a modern context. Some regard this story, albeit in the remote past, as one that is familiar in the context of their own Christian history: yes, the early Christians were persecuted; they died bravely for their faith; their faith eventually was victorious. Many students in 2004 attended packed showings of Mel Gibson's graphically blood-soaked *The Passion of the Christ* and found themselves identifying with what to them was a viscerally familiar story, although their own death for the faith in imitation of Christ was not a sacrifice any longer required of them. The question became how one defamiliarizes the Christian story as "past" history or even unique history and brings that story forward into familiar space and time, and whether any resonances with the present seem shallow and contrived.

One of the ways in which I as an instructor attempted to do this was through reference to the story of the "martyrs" of Columbine High School, including the legendary death of Cassie Bernall, the born-again Christian teenager celebrated for the confession of her faith in the best-selling book *She Said Yes*. Although I did not realize it at first, Rachel Scott, the other celebrated martyr, had like Perpetua written a diary before her death, which became published by her parents, along with their reminiscences of her, called *Rachel's Tears*.[4] Though this analogy might have made some sense in 1999, when the tragedy occurred, for most of my students, who would have been nine or ten years old at the time, it has been obscured to a great degree by the far greater calamity of September 11, 2001. The "Columbine martyrdom" is part of the past for most students, who have not seen much connection between it and Perpetua's story, and perhaps rightly so. Cassie and Rachel were not being tried by the government for their faith; sadly, they probably would have been shot anyway; yet once again several students said "of course" they would have acted as these two young women did.

With another, more contemporary, and ongoing analogy, I had greater success in provoking discussions about the understanding of martyrdom, its motivations and forms, and the limits of religious fidelity: that of female suicide attackers. Bruce Springsteen's powerful song "Paradise"[5] begins by evoking the image of a young female suicide attacker of high school or college age, an image that occurred to him after reading newspaper accounts of such women's actions.[6] These stories and others like them, as we will see, raise questions similar to those in the story of Perpetua's martyrdom: religious motivation, reaction to perceived political oppression, defiance of gender, family, religious, and political norms. Some of the questions students often ponder involve the limits of religious conviction exhibited in martyr tales: Can one who is a "faithful witness (martyr)" to God also fight against an evil power and kill its representatives? The Maccabean warriors in 1 Maccabees 2:44, 50 do just that. Is martyrdom a form of suicide? What about Perpetua guiding that gladiator's sword to her throat, "willing" her death? Is there a limit to religious dedication and fidelity? If so, where does it lie? Who defines it? What are the most appropriate forms of its expression? Who, ultimately, defines who is a martyr?

Responses to these questions that focus on male martyrs and even on one female martyr (the mother of the seven in 2 and 4 Maccabees) overwhelmingly praise the decision for martyrdom while remaining cautious about armed resistance. In one response, "Is Martyrdom the Answer?" the author speculated whether, in the case of the Maccabean martyrs, there was any response that could be faithfully made. While noting that other alternatives were possible, all but martyrdom, the voluntary suffering of death rather than denying one's religion "by words or deeds," had to be rejected because of the belief in the sacredness and inviolability of the Law. In the case of Jesus' martyrdom in the Gospel of John 18–20, the same author noted that no other alternative presented itself: Jesus sacrificed his own life as a religious obligation.[7] Many others found that, even though the mother in 4 Maccabees encourages her sons to be tortured and to die rather than submit to an unjust "tyrant" who demands they renounce their faith, conduct that the author of 4 Maccabees sees is most unmaternal of her and therefore "manly," her actions were the only ones possible.

Something usually interferes with a similar approach to the story of Perpetua, however: that "family thing," as some describe it. Perpetua, they have noted, has a family, most of whom, including her infant son, will not be sharing her fate but are eminently affected by it. Most of the women in my classes, unexpectedly (to my mind, at least), translated what they saw as a decision in favor of the same religious obligation chosen by the Maccabean martyrs and Jesus as a form of selfishness in Perpetua's case, conflicting as it did with familial obligations and responsibilities; even the few who approved of it did not see Perpetua's decision as a particularly liberating one. They did, however, see it as a "power trip." More than one said, "She's made that decision to be imprisoned, to suffer and die for her faith—that's because she knows she'll get to heaven." In their opinion, it was better to forfeit a sure chance in heaven than fail to sacrifice yourself for your family on earth.

Thecla, on the other hand, fares quite a bit better. Despite the fact that many of the students in classes that studied asceticism and martyrdom and its relationship to gender had some difficulty in understanding a decision for lifelong celibacy, most of them, particularly the women, had experienced enough of the power of sexuality, positive and negative, and had struggled enough with their own bodily integrity that they could understand why one might see total abstinence as a kind of freedom, depending only on God. One student wrote, "Thecla is the best example of [stripping away the false gods of our world in order to achieve higher spirituality] for she knew what it was like to escape death by fire or beasts, or [to] escape rape, purely by God's grace. I was truly amazed by her example."[8] This statement reinforces my impression that students could relate better to Thecla despite her asceticism because she is a character in fiction and they were freer to engage imaginatively with her story. Perpetua's personality is a more daunting one.

Besides actively engaging modern representations of Perpetua and Thecla in class, it seems that there are few ways in which either figure has a direct impact on popular culture. Daniel Boyarin introduces his chapter "Thinking with Virgins," in *Dying for God*, with the opening scene in the 1990 Richard Benjamin film *Mermaids*, in which Rachel Flax, the lead character played by Cher, passes her daughter, Charlotte (Winona Ryder) "genuflecting ecstatically at her private shrine to St. Perpetua." Charlotte's admiration for Catholicism and her desire for the celibate life, despite the fact that her family is Jewish, is a reaction to the open, promiscuous sexuality of her mother. As Boyarin notes, Perpetua is an odd choice as a "model and ego ideal" for a modern American Jewish teenager; Charlotte later abandons her worship of Perpetua, "with a rather dramatic effect on her nascent sex life."[9] Apart from this interesting comic nod to Perpetua, the story has inspired at least two novels. One is a work of Christian fiction, *In Perpetua: A Bride, a*

Martyr, a Passion (2004), by Amy Rachel Peterson. The novel is published by The Relevant Media Group, a publishing house that aims at
"God-hungry twentysomethings" and especially women, according to
its publicity. "Based on a true story," the novel takes place three years
before the martyrdom of Perpetua and follows the *Martyrdom* in that
it is narrated in the first person, except for the "Postscript" narrated
by Tertius, who records the martyrdom for the son of Perpetua and
Saturus (Peterson follows Osiek's suggestion that Saturus is Perpetua's
absent husband).[10]

Another retelling of the story is the graphic novel *Climbing the Dragon's Ladder: The Martyrdom of Perpetua and Felicitas* (2006), by Andrea
Lorenzo Molinari, with illustrations by Tyler J. Walpole. In an article
in the Society of Biblical Literature's online *Forum*, Molinari, a profes-
sor of theology whose previous books were academic monographs on
the apocryphal acts, describes his desire to create the kind of "theological art" that early Christian writers had created in the apocrypha and
martyrologies for modern audiences. His "meeting" with Perpetua in
the course of his academic studies inspired him to write his version of
her story, which also includes Saturus as a husband, and is illustrated,
because of the "essential component" of Perpetua's visions. Molinari
connected with her "in a powerful way" because of two "devastating
losses" in his own experience: "I learned that anachronism might not
only be inevitable, but perhaps is also absolutely necessary for us to
connect with the past and absorb its lessons as our own."[11] Although it
is not the first time that male writers have been inspired by the example
of Perpetua, it is intriguing that this modern theologian would connect with her story in a way that does not try to write Perpetua as a
man. Peterson's retelling of Perpetua's story from the perspective of
a confessing Christian woman seems somehow more consistent with
modern sensibilities.

PERPETUA AND THE CONSTRUCTION
OF THE COLUMBINE MARTYROLOGIES

Both of these novels appeared after the 1999 Columbine High School
shootings in Columbine, Colorado. On April 20, two teenaged gunmen, Eric Harris and Dylan Klebold, shot thirteen people, twelve of
their fellow students and a teacher, before killing themselves. They
had planned the event for over a year. Materials in their diaries and

Day-Planners, as well as home videos, one made approximately one-half hour before what they called "judgment day," reveal their motives: general hatred for humanity (Eric), revenge for slights and bullying, hatred for living "in this world" (Dylan). Although they had planned to blow up Columbine High School and shoot the staff and students as they fled the building, their plans went awry, and they ended up entering the school, shooting as they went. One of the students they shot, Rachel Joy Scott, was having lunch on the grass with a friend. They closed in on two particular places, the cafeteria, which was practically empty, and the library, which was full of students, most of whom sought shelter under tables. Two of these students were Cassie Bernall and Valeen Schnurr, hiding under different tables.

According to all surviving witnesses, including Valeen, there was a conversation between a young woman and one of the gunmen about whether she believed in God. The reported text of the conversation has varied ever since the day following the shootings, but there are two main variants. In one, the gunman asks, "Do you believe in God?" and the female victim replies, "Yes." The gunman then asks, "Why?" and shoots her, or says, "Then go be with him now," and shoots her.[12] In the second variant, reported by virtually all of the survivors, the gunman asks the same question. A female voice (later, by all survivor accounts, that of Valeen Schnurr) first says "No," but immediately changes to "Yes." The gunman asks, "Why?" and she replies, "Because I believe and my parents brought me up that way."[13] One survivor, Joshua Lapp, who was responsible for the earlier story of Cassie Bernall's "confession," later reported that "several" students were asked whether they believed in God and "the answer did not seem to dictate whether they got shot or not."[14]

Within days, the voice who said yes was identified by most as that of Cassie Bernall, a born-again Christian teen who was killed for confessing her faith. Others identified the dead confessor—now called a martyr—as Rachel Scott, another evangelical Christian teen, who was not in the library at the time of the shooting. Some said—and still maintain—that both girls had died for their faith. The pastor at Cassie Bernall's memorial service, Franklin Graham, and Bruce Porter, the pastor at Rachel Scott's funeral service, both claimed the status of martyr for the students, with Porter enrolling Rachel with "the martyrs from the very first day of the Church's existence."[15] Yet within a few months after the first martyrology, *She Said Yes: The Unlikely Martyrdom of Cassie Bernall*, was published, it became clear that Cassie was not the one who said yes, that the one who said yes was survivor Valeen Schnurr, who had been shot several times and was praying not to die. Most investigators have believed that Valeen's unvarying testimony is the true story of the one who said yes. And yet, as several studies have noted, the actual fact of Valeen's confession, the inaccuracy and tenuous nature of the testimonies of Cassie and of Rachel, seem to be unimportant in the construction of what quickly became the narrative of "the Columbine martyrs."[16]

The rhetoric of martyrdom was part of a reading of the event that portrayed evangelical Christianity as "an embattled subculture," with the bodies of Cassie and Rachel on its front line.[17] As Elizabeth Castelli notes, one of the intriguing factors in the recasting of these two deaths as martyrdoms is the fact that Protestant evangelicalism is "markedly devoid of anything approximating the Catholic cult of saints."[18] Justin Watson agrees that "the martyr stories of Cassie and Rachel differ sharply from the elaborate patterns of classic martyrologies."[19] Neither Cassie nor Rachel had specific models of martyrdom—other than Jesus—which they followed, although one of Cassie's favorite movies was Mel Gibson's *Braveheart*, the story of the Scottish William Wallace, whose torture and death at the hands of the English has "implicitly Christian" overtones.[20] Rachel had no such explicit media or literary models but kept journals that have entries in which one cannot tell whether she is speaking to a human beloved or to God. In one entry, specifically addressed to God, she asks, "Why can't I be completely consumed by you? Why can't I be used by you?" Yet there are other entries in which she insists, "I will create my own dream, my own image, my own future," and a disturbing poem in which she envisions the ways in which she may be killed, ending with, "Please hand me a gun. Finish what you have started."[21] More dramatic is a journal drawing that later was interpreted as a prophetic vision, in which a pair of eyes wept over or watered a rose, the teardrops changing from clear to opaque as they fell. This drawing, recovered from a journal in Rachel's backpack the day she died, was later interpreted as symbolic of the deaths at Columbine.[22] Another journal drawing, of a hand with long, red-painted nails that apparently pierces or embraces a bloody heart with a rose, has not received any attention or interpretation, as far as I am aware.

All of these dreams, poems, and admirations would be completely understandable in the case of any teenaged girl, but in the rhetoric of martyrdom, clergy and academics alike compared the death of Cassie Bernall directly to that of Perpetua: for example, the conservative writers William Kristol and J. Bottum in *The Weekly Standard*; Jean Bethke Elshtain in her review of *She Said Yes* for the *New Republic*. Cassie's youth pastor, Dave McPherson, had a "vision" of Cassie in which he saw her becoming the bride of Jesus, although he did not compare it to Perpetua's *Martyrdom,* of which he may well have been unaware.[23] The most recent and explicit comparison of Cassie with Perpetua is a sermon from January 13, 2008, in which the Reverend Thomas C. Pumphrey, pastor of St. Mark's (Episcopal) Church in Honeybrook, Pennsylvania, compared Cassie's profession of faith to Perpetua's "*Christiana sum*" in the *Martyrdom*, and in Augustinian fashion advocated it as an example for all Christians. Rachel Scott has only been associated with Perpetua in one instance: a woman named Bethany who wrote to the Christian women's online magazine *Radiant*, also published by the evangelical Relevant Media Group, wanting to see more about both of her heroines.[24]

Neither Columbine martyr has been compared to Thecla, perhaps because Thecla's story required a radical rejection of home and family, and the story of Cassie, a rebellious teen who thought of killing her parents, is one of a radical reintegration into Christian home and family, with a rejection of the satanic values of the outside world. Neither Columbine martyr has had miracles associated with her burial site, another interesting but probably unintentional parallel with Perpetua, who has no recorded miracle stories associated with her or with her *martyrium.* One of the surviving students, Mark Taylor, another born-again Christian, has described his experiences in a book entitled *I Asked, God Answered: A Columbine Miracle* (Tate, 2006), the title taken from his cry when shot, "Oh my God! Help me!"[25] Taylor, who appeared in Michael Moore's 2002 antigun documentary, *Bowling for Columbine*, later repudiated Moore and his own appearance in the film and left Columbine for a Christian high school. But none of the male students, even those who were killed, have been specifically and directly designated as martyrs; the Catholic priest at the funeral of Daniel Mauser and (female) Kelly Fleming, who were killed at Columbine, simply referred to their being greeted by the "martyrs" in heaven.[26]

The unexpected preaching of "martyrdom" to young Protestant evangelical Christians also has had its commercial side, not unlike the earlier relic trade of pilgrim flasks and other memorials, in the form of T-shirts, videos, bracelets, and other jewelry.[27] Although this aspect of the Columbine martyrdoms has considerably diminished, due in part to the overwhelming number of deaths and the negative association of the name of "martyrdom" with the bombing of the World Trade Center and the Pentagon on September 11, 2001, there are still quite active Web sites commemorating Cassie Bernall and Rachel Scott, and very active ministries by their parents and siblings, including "Rachel's Challenge," a program for reducing violence and bullying in high schools by promoting the Christian-influenced kindness embodied by Rachel in her own life. It is also particularly illuminating to note that after the worst school shooting in American history—the massacre of thirty-two at Virginia Tech by lone gunman Cho Seung-Hui on April 16, 2007, a date chillingly close to the eighth anniversary of the Columbine shootings—there are few references to the dead as "martyrs," and no one person particularly stands out.[28] The discourses that have emerged from this disaster concern psychological profiling, gun control, and campus safety, rather than religious issues.

Despite many of the obvious differences between the deaths of Cassie and Rachel and those of Perpetua and Felicitas, and the "martyrdom" of Thecla, there are similarities that are seriously claimed. One of the most striking is the fact that young women are the focus of these stories, another instance of using the bodies of women "to think with." The death of these young Christian women, portrayed as the polar opposites of the gun-toting, anti-Christian, disturbed, and spiritually unanchored young men, creates inevitable and poignant fodder for propaganda. For evangelical Christians, the deaths of Cassie and Rachel gain meaning because they were killed, not senselessly but purposefully: the blood of the martyrs is once again "seed." Unlike the emphasis in the martyrdoms of Perpetua, Felicitas, and Thecla, among other women martyrs, the bodiliness of these young women seems curiously absent, until one realizes that in descriptions of Cassie and Rachel, their bodies are delicately tangential to the spiritual narrative, representing the kind of sexual intactness and embodied spirituality that is assaulted and penetrated by the bullets of their executioners, in much the same way as Ambrose conceived of the virgin martyr's body as representative of the intact and embattled church.[29] Moreover, as Castelli has it, "the archetype of martyrdom" of early Christianity serves, inaccurately as it is often applied to these cases, as "a narrative resource, and an object of ambivalent nostalgia," a nostalgia that may trivialize the truth of the event in favor of "making truth."[30] This truth is often historically and dangerously inaccurate, made by portraying dualistic and apocalyptic forms of absolute opposition and accomplished over the dead bodies of women, most of them young; such a tradition is disturbing—and ongoing.

AN ARMY OF MARTYRS

Judaism and Christianity, particularly the latter, are not alone in acknowledging the martyrs and their power. Although, as we have seen, American evangelical Protestant Christianity is relatively new to the discourse of martyrdom, that language is nevertheless deeply embedded in its history and can be recovered and reinterpreted to fit new circumstances. American Christians also found, to their shock and dismay, that the discourse of martyrdom, part of Islam almost from its inception, could also be applied in ways that characterize Americans as "other" and as the forces of darkness and domination. While Americans characterize attackers like the September 11 hijackers as "suicide terrorists," they also respond to the claims of organizations like al-Qaeda and Hamas and their leaders that these people were "martyrs," by assuming that the rhetoric comes solely from Islam and what is characterized as "Muslim fundamentalism." Robert A. Pape, a political scientist who has studied worldwide suicide bombings and attacks from 1980 through 2003, finds that "there is little connection between suicide terrorism and Islamic fundamentalism, or any of the world's religions," although religion is "used as a tool by terrorist organizations in recruiting and in other efforts in service of the broader [political] strategic objective."[31] And in many cases, this tool, caught fast in its cultural web, has been used to employ the bodies of women in its service by using the rhetoric of martyrdom.

On January 27, 2002, Yasser Arafat spoke to more than a thousand Palestinian women in the West Bank city of Ramallah. Calling the women to sacrifice themselves as "an army of roses," he also coined a new term in Arabic, *shahida*, a female martyr, in contrast to the male *shahid*, and that very day the first *shahida* in the Palestinian conflict, a twenty-eight-year-old volunteer with the Red Crescent from the Amari Refugee Camp near Ramallah, Wafa Idris, detonated herself in a shopping district on Jerusalem's Jaffa Road, killing one elderly Israeli and injuring several others.[32] This was not the first female suicide attacker nor the first to be termed a "martyr," but Wafa Idris's suicide martyrdom was a subject of widespread interest because of the religious complications in Islam of a woman performing this kind of action. The ideologies as well as the motivations of female suicide attackers are different, but as we shall see, there seem to be some common threads, as there are in the martyrologies, ancient and present, of Jewish and Christian female martyrs.

Arafat's "army of roses" speech occurred seventeen years after the first female suicide attacker, sixteen-year-old Sana Youssef Mhaydali, a member of the Syrian Socialist Nationalist Party, blew herself up in Lebanon on April 9, 1985, stating as her intention the desire to "liberate the south from the occupation of the Zionist [sic] terrorists . . . who are not like us."[33] This rhetoric, while not overtly religious, expresses both a militancy of the sort that comes from a dualistic stance between "us" and "them (the occupiers)," with an apocalyptic program of "liberation" through death. In some cases, the liberation that takes place is described as the liberation of the woman from an impossible social situation; or at least that is the speculation of many Western journalists who have studied the phenomenon of female suicide attackers. I choose the term "attacker," as reflecting neither the pejorative term "terrorist" nor the honorific "martyr," in order to be able to examine the rhetoric of female suicide attack from those inside as well as outside, although many would argue that the term "suicide" is itself pejorative. As is the case with ancient noble deaths and martyrdoms, and as with the Columbine martyrs, so also James Bennet observes of the suicide attack by Palestinian Hiba Daraghmeh: "After a suicide bombing, the mythmaking begins almost as soon as the ambulances start their wailing rush to the scene. The how and the why blur as wondering friends and relatives of the bomber retrieve and burnish memories, at times conflicting, that might explain how their loved one became a willing 'martyr.'"[34]

In the welter of rhetoric on both sides of the issue, what seems relatively clear in most cases is the use of terminology that equates women attackers with men, but at the same time points to the extraordinary nature of the women's actions. In some cases it is something so contrary to cultural norms for women (perceived as "natural" or "God-given") that it is not praised but condemned. For example, the first suicide attack by an Iraqi woman, Iman Salih Mutlak, against U.S. forces in Zaqaniyah, Iraq, in May of 2003, was disowned by her own family, particularly her father, because the unmarried young woman, like Thecla, left the house unaccompanied and thus brought shame to her family and her tribe: "When she left the house, she lost her innocence," declared her father, saying that if she had returned, he himself would have killed her and "[drunk] her blood."[35] With this story for comparison, Theocleia's call for her daughter to be burned seems less remote and more understandable if not acceptable. Most recently, however, the 44th Iraqi female suicide attacker, thirty-year-old Wenza Ali Mutlaq, reveals a trend toward the recruitment of women by al-Qaeda, long known for virtually no use of women as attackers.[36] Initially also the religious leader of the Palestinian Hamas, Sheikh Ahmad Yassin, objected to the participation of women in suicide attacks, despite the glorification of the first, Wafa Idris, in the streets and by some of the Arab media. In 2004, however, he approved of the suicide attack by Reem Salih al-Rayasha, a twenty-two-year-old mother of two.[37]

Although it is becoming increasingly clear that there is no one pro-file—religious, educational, political, psychological, ideological, or even gender—that fits all suicide attackers, there has been much more of an interest in women because of their relative rarity and, again, the expec-tation that women do not readily take lives or give up their own. These women become objects of sometimes horrified speculation and interest in the motives that would allow them to do so, along with justification by their respective cultures for the taking of such extraordinary steps, as Barbara Victor puts it, "from bearer of life to killing machine."[38] Even these words suggest an expectation of what a woman's body—a woman herself—*should* be. Once again, writing about women who become des-ignated as "martyrs" focuses on societal roles and familial relationships, especially on gender, and sometimes on body. Usually the Palestin-ian, Lebanese (Hezbollah), and increasingly Iraqi women have received most of the publicity for their attacks and most of the speculation by Western journalists; yet the Tamil Tigresses of Sri Lanka, the Chechen so-called "Black Widows," and the PKK (Kurdistan Workers' Party) all have included large numbers of women. Pape's 2005 study showed that the latter in particular had a 71 percent participation of women in its suicide attacks, followed by the Chechens, the Tamil Tigers (or Tigresses), Hezbollah, and the Palestinians. Most of these women were in their midtwenties or older, usually older than men who became sui-cide attackers.[39] The oldest female suicide attacker to date has been Fatima Omar Mahmud al-Nazar, a fifty-seven-year-old mother of nine and grandmother of forty-one children.[40]

Regardless of how repugnant the rhetoric of "martyrdom" when applied to such suicide attacks may be, we need to examine how these women speak of themselves and their motivations (when we know them) and how their deaths are woven into the general fabric of what constitutes the ideal martyr in the public discourse of their societies. For purposes of comparison with the stories of Perpetua and Thecla, for whom religion is a major factor, I will use sparingly accounts of women who have undertaken what they and others call "martyrdom" for nonreligious (or apparently nonreligious) purposes. My aim here is to look at these women *as* women, to see how the rhetoric of gender and body functions in the martyr discourse, both in terms of women's comparison with men and in their exceeding what is expected of other women or of men. As with the discourse regarding ancient martyrs and modern as well, we must always remember that such language is embedded in a context but that it also attempts to offer radical alternatives to what is perceived as unsatisfactory within that context. Pape notes that modern attackers often fit Durkheim's model of "altruistic suicide" because they are bound to their own communities by "goals viewed as legitimate" and have reason to believe that "the willing acceptance of a voluntary death" will be supported and honored by that community with "elaborate ceremonies and other rituals" identifying that death "with the good of the community."[41] Very few of the potential (failed) suicide attackers among the many studied by Rosemarie Skaine have demonstrated a psychopathological bent to hurt or kill others.[42]

One question is whether female suicide attackers have choice, more than the young women who were executed at Columbine High School did, or less than the Maccabean mother, Miriam bat Tanhum, Perpetua, Thecla, and others like them did. We Westerners may, for example, wish to explain if not justify many of the suicide attacks by women because of our perception of Middle Eastern societies as "patriarchal," and thus the women acted out of atonement, revenge, or despair, but that does not much differ from our attempts to delve into the psychology of a Perpetua or a Thecla; this is the framework within which we interpret. For Marie-Louise von Franz, Perpetua's visions symbolize the internal struggle for individuation, one that reflects "the transformation which was then being fulfilled deep down in the collective stratum of the human soul: the transformation of the image of God."[43] For Mary Lefkowitz, Perpetua's story reflects "how Christianity in its earlier stages also met a social need of releasing women from the hierarchical structure imposed by patriarchal society."[44] For many feminist scholars, the widespread versions of the Thecla story and its condemnation by Tertullian symbolize more of a "transmission of a censored historical tradition" than a mere reflection of "second-century cultural values."[45] When Debra Zedalis notes of modern attackers, "Suicide bombers . . . see their own actions as being driven by a higher order; they believe their sacrifice will provide rewards for them in the afterlife," we need to determine whether, and how, the language for this motivation is any different from the language in the third-century Christian vision of Saturus in which Perpetua, labeled by some as "suicidal" in her determination to die as a Christian, says she is "much happier" in paradise than in "this life."[46]

MARTYRS AS WIDOWS, MOTHERS, AND BRIDES

In the case of the Chechen suicide attackers studied by Anne Speckhard and Khapta Akhmedova, the name "Black Widow" was applied by the press to these women not only because in their most widely publicized action, the takeover of the Dubrovka Theater in Moscow in October 2002, they wore the black dress of mourning, but also because in the case of the twenty-six women (and eight men) studied, nearly all had lost family members in the Chechen conflict with the Russians.[47] Although clearly this traumatic loss provides both political and personal motives, especially those of revenge, for these women as with other female suicide attackers, Speckhard and Akhmedova's study is illuminating because they observed that for a high percentage (73 percent) of these women, already Muslim, the "shattering of world assumptions" by their trauma led them to seek a sectarian form of Islam, Wahhabism, that promotes a return to an idealized original pure Islam and has been used to promote a "jihadist ideology." The women became "more religious," and psychologically they seemed to have adopted "a comforting view of an afterlife expressed in glorified terms for those who die on behalf of God (i.e., martyrs)."[48] As Zedalis has noted, this "invok[ing] religion to invest personal trauma with social meaning" is also a source of recruitment for the Palestinian suicide attackers.[49] This has occurred despite initial opposition from Palestinian male religious leadership to women's active participation in the attacks and despite the fact that the Qur'an forbids suicide. But it does not forbid martyrdom for either men or women, especially if they die in the cause of God, thus enabling an interpretation of what is forbidden as what is praised.[50]

For some Muslim Palestinian women, there also needed to be a translation of the language of martyrdom into a feminist stance. According to Mira Tzoreff, earlier rhetoric from the Palestinian male leadership "nationalize[d] the body of every Palestinian woman" by insisting that women had their honor (modesty), like that of the Roman *matrona*, in supporting the honor of the male *shahid* or martyr, and that their place in the struggle was in the home, bearing male children to become *shahids*, ready to embrace "the exalted status of 'Mother of a *Shahid*.'"[51] In fact, one of the more celebrated Palestinian women and reputedly the inspiration for female suicide attackers, known as Um Nidal ("Mother of the Struggle") Farhat, appeared with her son, Mahmoud, in the customary preattack video, and when interviewed by Barbara Victor, as well as by Lisa Ling of *National Geographic*, said that she encouraged her son to become a *shahid*, telling him, "Act with your mind, not your emotions. Be a man."[52] Victor observed that Um Nidal appeared typical in absorbing the maternal rhetoric, since in all of her visits to and interviews with the families of successful or would-be martyrs, the male relatives were always silent: the mothers and daughters were becoming "the voice of the [Palestinian] nation."[53]

In Tzoreff's view, the rhetoric changed between the first (1987) and the second (2000) *intifada* (uprising), so that women began demanding more rights as contributors to the struggle, but also increasingly rejected the idea of being "mother of a martyr"; a related factor was the appearance of the women martyrs, the *shahidat*.[54] Nearly all Westerners who have written about the first Palestinian *shahida*, Wafa Idris, have noted that her suicide attack may have been (and for some, was) undertaken not for religious reasons because of her lack of status in a static, patriarchal society as a divorced woman whose only child, a girl, had died, and who could never have other children, living again in her parents' home. Tzoreff's view is typical: "Wafa Idris's only way of redeeming herself from the inferior status ordained by her surroundings was by choosing to become a *shahida* for the sake of her nation."[55] The inability to marry, dishonor to the family by rape or adultery, failure to produce children—this logic of despair is also applied, not only to several Palestinian women *shahidat*, but also to Hindu Tamil Tigresses and Chechen Black Widows as well. Mia Bloom of the University of Cincinnati asserts that her research, conducted before 2006, shows that female attackers "have chosen to do so in order to atone for sins [like adultery] or wrongdoings by one of their family members" and that the attacks enable them to "reinvent themselves," cutting them off from an undesirable past, so that "the women become saints."[56]

The rhetoric on the other side is not unexpectedly different, although there is a similar sense of "honor" that is bestowed: honor to women as well as to the communities for whom they undertake their action. Once more women's bodies, by their death and dismemberment, are still, pointedly, women's bodies, claimed by women as their own, claimed by men as certifying the honor that women usually ensure for their husbands and families. Egyptian feminist and physician Nawal al-Sa'adawi, no apologist for Islamist extremism, nevertheless identifies fully with female suicide attackers "who fought with their own bare hands."[57] Saba Mahmood, another Muslim feminist from Egypt, criticizes Western notions of feminism and human agency as "the drive to rise up against authority and . . . male control," leading Rivka Yadlin to the conclusion that "female martyrs" are "not marginal but central" in their societies, and that their actions are "consensual," constituting "the ultimate embodiment" according to Islamic piety, "the sacrifice of their body."[58] Thus, as much as outside observers may ascribe to them other motives, these women had choice, not to openly defy their social goals and norms, but to integrate themselves fully into them. This perspective of the liberation of the *shahida*'s body is fulsomely sounded by an article in the Egyptian newspaper *al-Akhbar*, which at the same time depicts that body as partitioned and expendable: "The body parts of the *shahida* outlined the change on the earth of the fatherland, and in the ideology of the struggle. . . . Palestinian women will write the history of the liberation with their blood."[59] A failed *shahida* explained, "The [suicide] belt with which I had practiced had become part of my body."[60] The first "suicide belt," fitted with explosives, was in fact designed for the female body.[61]

Despite many journalists' initial view of such women as social failures because of their inability to fulfill their patriarchal "destiny" to marry and bear children, some of the *shahidat* were portrayed by their own communities as eminently able to fulfill that role. In fact, in some cases, the near-militant decision of a woman to protect her chastity, defined as public modesty, is also a factor, as in the stories of the virgin martyrs. The death of the woman is praised as validation of her decision for sexual integrity. Dareen Abu Aysheh, for example, described as "nihilistic" and depressed by Victor after her family tried to talk her out of her university studies to marry a cousin she was forced to kiss in public at an Israeli checkpoint near Nablus,[62] was characterized by a Fatah operative who tried to talk her out of her suicide operation as "a pretty and successful girl studying at the university, a future mother, who should marry and bear children, and help her people in other ways."[63] In an essay she wrote, Dareen had characterized herself as a "liberated Muslim woman" who wore modest dress because she felt that her physical appearance should not be an issue, who believed "her body belongs to her alone."[64] Nineteen-year-old Hiba Daraghmeh, asserting a "rare religious devotion," even in the West Bank, veiled herself since the age of ten, was never seen unveiled, and associated with women only, turning down proposals of marriage in order to pursue her studies in English. Stories of her suicide attack vary, but her death was claimed to be the result of a violation of her modesty when Israeli soldiers forced her to raise her veil. A woman student praised Hiba's action for its courage: "She made us feel proud."[65]

On the other hand, the criticism from both sides that followed the suicide attack of Reem Salih al-Rayasha (Rim Riashi), a Hamas operative, was unusual, but so was her action. She was in her early twenties, a university student and a mother of two, including a still-nursing infant. According to journalist Avi Issacharoff, members of the Palestinian organization Fatah criticized her actions in terms reminiscent of my own students' criticism of Perpetua: "A twenty-two-year-old girl, mother of two children, one of them a baby and the other a little girl, carried out an act of self-sacrifice. Who issued a Muslim religious ruling depriving the baby of its mother?" The writer returned to the rhetoric of the earlier attitude toward women's involvement in such missions: "On the basis of which passages in the Qur'an and the Hadith does a young mother abandon her true jihad role, which is raising two children, one of whom needs her milk?" Even by members of Hamas, Reem was assumed to have been having an affair with a Hamas official, making her suicide attack an act of what Bloom would identify as "atonement," an assertion angrily denied in the Arab journal *al-Quds*.[66] But if one looks at a still portrait of Reem from her suicide videotape, she has conceived of herself, if only for this purpose, as a male martyr: except for her hair covering, she is posed in an attitude typified by the popular "suicide tapes" made by the male *shahid*: wearing a green headband, the Prophet's color, with verses from the Qur'an, dressed in combat gear, prominently displaying a rifle, grenade, and grenade-launcher. Her face is entirely visible. In her videotape she says that as a martyr she envisioned parts of her body "flying all over"; that her love for her children was strong, but her "love to meet God is stronger still."[67] In her videotape a similar pose is adopted by the oldest Palestinian woman suicide attacker so far, fifty-seven-year-old Fatima Omar Mahmud al-Najar, disparagingly called "the suicide granny," but although she is holding an M-16 rifle, she is appropriately "feminized" by her distinctly feminine dress, which has in many cases become a convenient package for weaponry. Carolyn Wheeler, a reporter for the Canadian newspaper *The Globe and Mail*, was roundly criticized for her "sympathetic" reporting of the attack on November 29, 2006, including the words of her eighteen-year-old granddaughter, who praised Fatima as "not an ordinary woman," but nevertheless as a "good mother and a good grandmother."[68]

Yet in very few or none of the descriptions of these attackers by writers, male or female, from their own societies is the image of "becoming male" promoted, although, as with the preaching of the church fathers, and the "marketing of martyrdom" in modern evangelical teen circles, they "are also used to motivate men to follow their example."[69] Especially for Palestinian women suicide attackers, the language of martyrdom has been expanded to include a special place for women. Even in the case of Reem al-Rayasha, her "masculine" bomber stance includes the *hijab* under her martyr's headband, and her toddler son is outfitted in a coordinated costume.[70] As more than one commentator has noted, bridal imagery is used in descriptions of the martyrs. One of the first female suicide attackers, sixteen-year-old Lebanese Communist Sana Youssef Mhaydali, was designated "Bride of the South" and even starred in a movie called *The Bride*; she and Sumayah Sa'ad, who may actually have been the first female suicide attacker by two weeks, have also been called by the honorific title "Brides of Blood [*Arous ad-Damm*]."[71] Twenty-seven-year-old Hanadi Jaradat, a lawyer from Jenin, who attacked a restaurant in Haifa in October 2003, was given the title "Bride of Haifa," as compensation in Tzoreff's view for her unmarried and thus assumed "nonnormative" status in her community.[72] What seems to have happened here is that in the context of these women's societies, the rhetoric that includes them and honors them as martyrs is the same that defines them in female roles—not necessarily putting the same value on those roles as outsiders, primarily from the West, might assign to them. These terms, along with the "spectacle" provoked, not only by the public nature of the attacks but also by the videos and statements by the "martyrs" themselves, have tended to glamorize female suicide martyrdom for propaganda purposes.

The terminology "Black Widow" for the Chechen suicide attackers has already been discussed; it does not fulfill a similar propaganda function, but it also has served to glamorize somewhat or at least to highlight the phenomenon of these women as attackers. It is not a term that is assigned by the women's own communities but is a term in the Russian and the Western press that attempts to evoke a certain fascination with these women and their motives in the truest sense of the word "fascination," intriguing and terrifying simultaneously. This fascination, or perhaps "bewilderment" is a better word, seems often to be the attitude adopted when reading the stories of women who become martyrs through choice. Anne Marie Oliver tries to explain that when Western analysts try to offer the motive of empowerment for the choice

to become a martyr, they are acting upon the same type of Enlighten-
ment individualism criticized by Mahmood as foreign to the way in
which such women regard themselves; a woman's martyrdom instead
"strip[s] her of her identity—including, to some degree, her gender—
and turn[s] her into a rallying symbol for the living."[73] The martyr
herself, now dead, has been absorbed by a cause that does not advance
gender empowerment, however that is envisioned, for the living. As
Yoram Schweitzer observes, martyrs become tools of propaganda:
"Despite the rhetoric and the temporary honor these women enjoy in
implementing their tasks, they have not succeeded in promoting any of
the egalitarian agendas that hovered around them."[74] Even assuming
that the purpose of women martyrs, wherever they occur, is to achieve
equality or leadership for women, this motive is seldom given in statements by the women themselves but is often assumed by others who try
to examine their motives. The dead woman is once more at the mercy
of those who reinscribe her story, even if like Perpetua she has already
written her own.

Martyrdom, moreover, can only function as a valid discourse in
a society that sees itself in apocalyptic terms, living on the borders
between life and death, engaged in a struggle between good and evil,
in which perceived enemies that currently have the upper hand are
even now defeated by the cumulative actions of the martyrs, as they
will be in some hoped-for and eternally soon-to-be-achieved future. As
Castelli observes, the "glamorization of suffering" allows the martyr to
be elevated "beyond the human" while those in the same community
who survive continue to demonize the ones they deem responsible for
that suffering, fixing their sights on an idealized world beyond instead
of the undesirable present world that is already in the process of passing
away.[75] The very process of making martyrs does not allow them to live
among us, because a martyr by definition crosses boundaries not normally crossed, including those of acceptable gender and sexual behavior. Women martyrs in all cases must renounce their social identity
as women only to have that identity emphasized as they are ironically
exalted for becoming more than women in death. In fact, as the case
of Thecla shows, the martyr must ultimately be "domesticated" to support social norms once the value system desired by the opponents of the
previous system, now dominant in turn, is in place. Only extraordinary
situations would allow women to leave behind their children, as the
reactions to the story of Perpetua and Reem al-Rayasha show. Further,
although narratives of martyrdom, as in the Columbine case, function

to give the "monstrous meaning,"[76] we tend to lose sight of their own monstrosity, sometimes even their grotesqueness, especially when the rhetoric of "dying for God" becomes the rhetoric of "killing for God." The "stairway to heaven" that is bought at the cost of one's own "heart's blood," as Tertullian would have it, ultimately proves that women as well as men can be encouraged to die, but the martyr lives on, "at the mythologizing disposal of others."[77]

Notes

Chapter 1: The Power of Bodies

1. Since published as *The Divine Man: His Origin and Function in Hellenistic Popular Religion* (Berlin: Peter Lang, 1986).

2. This archetype for understanding the relationship of Jesus and the disciples, particularly in the book of Acts in the New Testament, to Greco-Roman charismatic miracle-workers, originated with Ludwig Bieler (*ΘΕΙΟΣ ΑΝΗΡ* [Vienna: Oskar Hofels, 1935–36]) and continued to provide a useful if criticized means of comparison throughout the 1970s and 1980s (e.g., David Tiede, *The Charismatic Figure as Miracle-Worker*, SBLDS 1 [Missoula, MT: Scholars Press, 1972); Carl R. Holladay, *Theios Anēr: A Criticism of This Concept in Hellenistic Judaism*, SBLDS 60 [Missoula, MT: Scholars Press, 1977]; and Eugene V. Gallagher, *Divine Man or Magician?* SBLDS 64 [Chico, CA: Scholars Press, 1982]).

3. Scott Fitzgerald Johnson, *The Life and Miracles of Thekla: A Literary Study*, Hellenic Studies 13 (Cambridge: Center for Hellenic Studies, 2006), 10.

4. As far as I have been able to discover, the phrase "a usable past"—first used by Van Wyck Brooks in an article in *The Dial* (April 1918), "On Creating a Usable Past"—was first used in connection with Christian feminist historical research by Eleanor McLaughlin in an article, "The Christian Past: Does It Hold a Future for Women?" in the *AThR* 57 (January 1975). See Angela Pears, *Feminist Christian Encounters: The Methodological Strategies of Feminist Informed Theologies* (Aldershot: Ashgate, 2004), 23.

5. Jan N. Bremmer, "Drusiana, Cleopatra, and Some Other Women in the *Acts of John*," in *A Feminist Companion to the New Testament Apocrypha*, ed. Amy-Jill Levine with Maria Mayo Robbins (London: T&T Clark, 2006), 77. Also on this subject, see in particular Lynne C. Boughton, "From Pious Legend to Feminist Fantasy," *JR* 71, no. 3 (1991): 362–83. Shelly Matthews has an excellent summary of the controversy that includes Boughton's critique, in "Thinking of Thecla: Issues in Feminist Historiography," *JFSR* 17, no. 2 (Fall 2001): 39–55.

6. Elizabeth A. Clark, "Holy Women, Holy Words: Early Christian Women, Social History, and the 'Linguistic Turn,'" *JECS* 6, no. 3 (1998): 430.

7. Several authors posited the development and transmission of these stories within communities of celibate women, most influentially Stevan L. Davies, *The Revolt of the Widows: The Social World of the Apocryphal Acts* (Carbondale: Southern Illinois University Press, 1980); Dennis R. MacDonald, *The Legend and the*

Apostle: The Battle for Paul in Story and Canon (Philadelphia: Westminster Press, 1983); and Virginia Burrus, *Chastity as Autonomy: Women in the Stories of the Apocryphal Acts* (Lewiston, NY: Edwin Mellen Press, 1987).

8. Peter Brown, *Society and the Holy in Late Antiquity* (Berkeley: University of California Press, 1981), 131–32. See also my discussion of this archetype in "Women as Sources of Redemption and Knowledge in Early Christian Traditions," in *Women and Christian Origins*, ed. Ross Shepard Kraemer and Mary Rose D'Angelo (New York: Oxford University Press, 1999), 345–46.

9. Gail Paterson Corrington (Gail Streete),"The 'Divine Woman'? Propaganda and the Power of Chastity in the New Testament Apocrypha," in *Rescuing Creusa: New Methodological Approaches to Women in Antiquity*, ed. Marilyn B. Skinner, *Helios* 13, no. 2 (1986): 151–62.

10. Burrus, *Chastity as Autonomy*, 60.

11. Gail P. Corrington (Gail Streete), "The 'Divine Woman'? Propaganda and the Power of Celibacy in the New Testament Apocrypha: A Reconsideration," *AThR* 80, no. 3 (July 1988): 218.

12. The *Acts of Paul and Thecla* (or at least a version of them) was contested as early as 198 CE, by Tertullian in his *On Baptism* 17.4–5, where he charges a "certain presbyter of Asia" as having "constructed" them *sub titulo Pauli*, representing them as Pauline.

13. The historical circumstances of the martyrdom and the Greek and Latin manuscript traditions are discussed extensively by Jacqueline Amat in her *Passion de Perpétue et de Félicité suivi les Actes*, SC 417 (Paris: Les Éditions du Cerf, 1996), 19–27; and by Åke Fridh in *Le problème de la passion des Saintes Perpétue et Félicité*, Studia Graeca et Latina Gothoburgensis 26 (Stockholm: Almqvist & Wiksell, 1968), 5, 8, 83; both conclude that there is no reason to suppose the work, including the prison diary, is entirely fictitious.

14. Jan Willem Van Henten and Friedrich Avemarie, *Martyrdom and Noble Death: Selected Texts from Graeco-Roman, Jewish and Christian Antiquity* (London: Routledge, 2002), 1.

15. Jan Bremmer, "The Motivation of Martyrs: Perpetua and the Palestinians," in *Religion im kulturellen Diskurs*, ed. B. Luchesi and K. Von Stuckrad (Berlin: Walter de Gruyter, 2004), 535–54.

16. John K. Elliott, review of *A Feminist Companion to the New Testament Apocrypha*, ed. Levine with Robbins, *RBL* 2 (2008), http://www.bookreviews.org/pdf/5408_5702.pdf.

17. Elizabeth A. Castelli, *Martyrdom and Memory: Early Christian Culture Making* (New York: Columbia University Press, 2005), 8.

18. E.g., the best-selling *She Said Yes: The Unlikely Martyrdom of Cassie Bernall*, by Misty Bernall, with an intro. by Madeleine L'Engle (Farmington, PA: Plough Publishing House, 1999); and Beth Nimmo and Darrell Scott, with Scott Rabey, *Rachel's Tears: The Spiritual Journey of Columbine Martyr Rachel Scott* (New York: Thomas Nelson, 2000). According to Jody Veenker, "Marketing Martyrdom

to Teens," *Christianity Today* 43, no.14 (December 6, 1999): 22, http://www
.christianitytoday.com/ct/9te/9te22a.html; the theme of martyrdom provided "a
business opportunity for retailers." Both Columbine martyrs continue to have
well-maintained and visited Web sites in their name: www.racheljoyscott.net and
www.cassierenebernall.org.

19. Castelli, *Martyrdom and Memory*, 200–201.

20. To name a very few lengthy studies within the last fifteen years, Jan N.
Bremmer, ed., *The Apocryphal Acts of Paul and Thecla* (Louvain: Peeters, 1996);
Joyce Salisbury, *Perpetua's Passion: The Death and Memory of a Young Roman
Woman* (New York: Routledge, 1997); Stephen J. Davis's monumental *The Cult
of Saint Thecla: A Tradition of Women's Piety in Late Antiquity* (Oxford: Oxford
University Press, 2001); P. Habermehl, *Perpetua und der Ägypter oder Bilder des
Bösen im frühen afrikanischen Christentum*, 2nd ed. (Berlin: Walter de Gruyter,
2004); Castelli, *Martyrdom and Memory*; Scott Johnson, *Life and Miracles of
Thekla*. Most fascinating perhaps is a recently published graphic novel by Andrea
Lorenzo Molinari, *Climbing the Dragon's Ladder: The Martyrdom of Perpetua and
Felicitas*, illustrations by Tyler J. Walpole (Eugene, OR: Wipf & Stock, 2006).

21. Francine Cardman, "Women, Ministry and Church Order in Early Christianity," in *Women and Christian Origins*, ed. Kraemer and D'Angelo, 302.

22. Linda Honey, review of Johnson, *Life and Miracles,* in *BMCR*, August 19,
2006, quoting Johnson, 221, http://ccat.sas.upenn.edu/bmcr/2006-D8-19.html.

23. Carol Meyers, "Where the Girls Are: Archaeology and Women's Lives in
Ancient Israel," in *Between Text and Artifact: Integrating Archaeology in Biblical
Studies Teaching*, ed. Milton Moreland (Atlanta: SBL, 2003), 33.

24. Greek text in M. Bonnet and R. A. Lipsius, *Acta Apostolorum Apocrypha*, vol. 1 (reprint ed., Darmstadt: Wissenschaftliche Buchgesellschaft, 1959),
235–72; ET in Edgar Hennecke and Wilhelm Schneemelcher, *New Testament
Apocrypha*, vol. 2 (Philadelphia: Westminster Press, 1966), 353–64.

25. Daniel Boyarin, *Dying for God: Martyrdom and the Making of Christianity
and Judaism* (Stanford, CA: Stanford University Press, 1999), 50.

26. Jan N. Bremmer, "Magic, Martyrdom and Women's Liberation in the
Acts of Paul and Thecla," in *The Apocryphal Acts of Paul and Thecla*, ed. Jan N.
Bremmer (Kampen, Netherlands: Kok Pharos, 1996), 44.

27. In Thecla's case, she is depicted "more often naked than usual," according
to Gilbert Dagron, *Vie et miracles de sainte Thècle* (Brussels: Société des Bollandistes, 1978), 26; quoted by Allison Goddard Elliott, *Roads to Paradise: Reading
the Lives of the Early Saints* (Hanover, NH: New England Press for Brown University, 1987), 50. Many of the "souvenirs" from pilgrimages to Thecla's shrines
favor representations of her partially nude, with her breasts clearly showing. The
breasts of both Perpetua and Felicitas are emphasized, particularly as nursing
(*Martyrdom* 6.8 and 20.2).

28. Elaine Scarry, *The Body in Pain: The Making and Unmaking of the World*
(New York: Oxford University Press, 1985), 14.

29. Maureen A. Tilley, "The Passion of Perpetua and Felicity," in *Searching the Scriptures*, vol. 2, *A Feminist Commentary*, ed. Elisabeth Schüssler Fiorenza (New York: Crossroad, 1994), 829.

30. "Martyrs" need not actually die, as the case of Thecla, "the first female martyr," shows. G. W. Bowersock, in *Martyrdom and Rome*, Wiles Lectures, Queen's University, Belfast (Cambridge: Cambridge University Press, 1995; reprint, 1998), makes the highly contestable claim that "martyrdom" in its present understanding did not really arise until the Christianity of the 2nd century, most likely among the churches of Asia Minor, and reflected the teachings of Montanus (17). He also claims (9) that the idea of martyrdom in Judaism that he identifies by the phrase *qiddush ha-shem* (lit., "sanctification of the Name [of God]") "does not occur until after the Tannaitic period" (i.e., end of the 2nd century). That his rather narrow definition excludes on principle both the martyrs of 2 Maccabees (probably 2nd–1st century BCE) and 4 Maccabees (probably 1st century CE) and the martyrs of the NT book of Revelation (end of 1st century CE) is, to say the least, problematic. But he does raise the question of the fluidity of definition of the Greek term *martys*.

31. Boyarin, *Dying for God*, 75.

32. Ibid., 67.

33. Castelli, *Martyrdom and Memory*, 121.

34. Carlin A. Barton, "Savage Miracles: The Redemption of Lost Honor in Roman Society and the Sacrament of the Gladiator and the Martyr," *Representations* 45 (Winter 1994): 57; cf. Erin Ronsse, "Rhetoric of Martyrs: Listening to Saints Perpetua and Felicitas," *JECS* 14, no.3 (2006): 305.

35. Teresa M. Shaw, *The Burden of the Flesh: Fasting and Sexuality in Early Christianity* (Minneapolis: Fortress Press, 1998), 6.

36. Elliott, *Roads to Paradise*, 24.

37. Scarry, *The Body in Pain*, 14.

38. Margaret R. Miles, "Patriarchy as Political Theology: The Establishment of North African Christianity," in *Civil Religion and Political Theology*, ed. Leroy S. Rouner (Notre Dame, IN: Notre Dame University Press, 1986), 175.

39. Averil Cameron, *Christianity and the Rhetoric of Empire*, Sather Classical Lectures 55 (Berkeley: University of California Press, 1991), 78–79.

40. Eusebius, *History of the Church* (*Historia Ecclesiastica* 5.1.41, NPNF[2], 1:215. Greek text of the *History* in PG 20:45–906, online from *Documenta Catholica Omnia*, http://www.documentacatholicaomnia.eu/03d/0265=0339,_ Eusebius_Caesariensis,_Historia_Ecclesia,_GR.pdf. There are many resonances between this 4th-century retelling of events occurring in the 2nd century and the stories of Perpetua and Felicitas, including the emphasis on persuasion and gender, some of which are noted by Elizabeth A. Goodine and Matthew W. Mitchell, "The Persuasiveness of a Woman: The Mistranslation and Misinterpretation of Eusebius' *HE* 5.1.41," *JECS* 13, no.1 (2005): 3.

41. The descriptive term, "athlete" (*athlētēs*) is also used for ascetics, whose practices are often spoken of in terms of athletic training or discipline (*askēsis*).

42. As Brent D. Shaw notes in "Body/Power/Identity: Passions of the Martyrs," *JECS* 4, no. 3 (1996): 309, Blandina is thus portrayed as the successful athlete, "no less than a male martyr like Maturus who is labeled a noble contestant (*gennaios agōnistēs*)."

43. Goodine and Mitchell, "Persuasiveness," 19. For a comparison of the stories of Blandina and Perpetua, see W. H. C. Frend, "Blandina and Perpetua: Two Early Christian Heroines," in *Les Martyres de Lyon (177)*, Colloques Internationaux du Centre National de la Recherche Scientifique, no. 575 (Paris: Éditions de Centre National de la Recherche Scientifique, 1978), 167–77.

44. Sarah Barnett, "Death and the Maidens: Women Martyrs and Their Sexual Identity in the Early Christian Period," *culture@home,* http://www.sydney anglicans.net/culture/thinking/369a.

45. The Latin text and ET of this letter may be found in K. C. Hanson, *Collection of Latin Documents,* http://www.kchanson.com/ANCDOCS/latin/pliny.html.

46. E.g., the conflict over the introduction of Bacchic rites during the Republic, in Livy, *From the Founding of the City* 39.8–18; and the scandals accompanying the introduction of Isis worship in Flavius Josephus's apologetic *Jewish Antiquities* 18.65–80.

47. Ignatius of Antioch, *To the Romans* 1; ET of the shorter version, *ANF* 1:73–79, in *Early Christian Writings* http://www.ccel.org/ccel/schaff/anf01.v.v.html. The longer version merely has "unless you spare me." Greek text from PG 685–96, in *Roads of Faith: Digital Patrology,* http://patrologia.ct.aegean.gr/PG_Migne/Ignatius%20of%20Antioch_PG%2006/Epistulae%20vii%20genuinae.pdf.

48. The translation in *Early Christian Fathers,* ed. Cyril D. Richardson, in the Library of Christian Classics (Philadelphia: Westminster Press, 1953), reprinted in Bart D. Ehrman, *The New Testament and Other Early Christian Writings: A Reader* (New York: Oxford University Press, 1998), 329, has "manhood will be mine" as the translation for "*anthrōpos esomai*," which may be translated by the less masculine "I will be truly human."

49. R. Ferwerda, "The Meaning of the Word σῶμα (Body) in the Axial Age: An Interpretation of Plato's *Cratylus* 400C," in *The Origins and Diversity of Axial Age Civilizations,* ed. Shmuel Noah Eisenstadt (Albany, NY: SUNY Press, 1986), 112.

50. Aristotle, *De anima, Books II and III (With Passages from Book I),* trans. with an intro. and notes by D. W. Hamlyn (Oxford: Oxford University Press, 1993),14.

51. Quoted in Page du Bois, *Sowing the Body: Psychoanalysis and Ancient Representations of Women* (Chicago: University of Chicago Press, 1987), 184. Other relevant passages in Aristotle's *On the Generation of Animals* 716a.5–23, 727a.2–30, 727b.31–33, 728b.l8–31, 765b.8–20, 766a.l7–30, 783b.26–784a.l2, trans. A. L. Peck, LCL, are enumerated in *WLGR,* #339, adapted for *Diotima: Materials for the Study of Women and Gender in the Ancient World,* http://www.stoa .org/diotima/, by Suzanne Bonefas and Ross Scaife.

52. J. J. Crump, "Syllabus on Medieval Women," University of Washington History Department, HSTAM 340 (Winter Quarter 2003), http://home.myuw .net/jjcrump/courses/medWomen/aonwomen.html.

53. The literature on this subject, and its relationship to Christian designations of what appear to be "effeminate" men, is vast. Particularly instructive is Bernadette Brooten, *Love between Women: Early Christian Responses to Female Homoeroticism* (Chicago: University of Chicago Press, 1996), 6.

54. References to the ET of Epictetus's *Enchiridion* are from the *Classics Archive*, by Elizabeth Carter, http://classics.mit.edu/Epictetus/epicench.html.

55. Seneca, *Ad Lucilium Epistulae Morales*, trans. Richard Gummere (London: William Heinemann, 1918), from the *Sophia Project*, http://www.molloy.edu/ sophia/seneca/epistles/ep24.htm.

56. Tacitus, *Annales* 15A, trans. Alfred John Church and William Jackson Broadribb, http://classics.mit.edu/Tacitus/annals.html, *Internet Ancient History Sourcebook*, http://www.fordham.edu/halsall/ancient/tacitus-ann15a.html.

57. Pliny the Younger, *Letters* 3.16, *To Nepos*, ET, http://ancienthistoryabout .com/library/bl/bl_text_plinyltrs3.htm#XVI.

58. Kari Vogt, "Becoming Male: One Aspect of an Early Christian Anthropology," in *Women—Invisible in Church and Society*, ed. Elisabeth Schüssler Fiorenza and Mary Collins, *Concilium* 182 , no. 6 (Edinburgh: T&T Clark, 1985), 72.

59. Translation by Stephen Patterson and Marvin Meyer, from *The Complete Gospels: Annotated Scholars Version* (Santa Rosa, CA: Polebridge Press, 1992; rev., expanded ed., 1994), online version, http://users.misericordia.edu//davies/ thomas/Trans.htm.

60. A more extensive discussion of the "head/body" metaphor can be found in Gail Paterson Corrington (Gail Streete), "The 'Headless Woman': Paul and the Language of the Body in 1 Cor. 11:2–16," *PRSt* 18 (1991): 223–31; and in Gail Streete, *The Strange Woman: Power and Sex in the Bible* (Louisville, KY: Westminster John Knox Press, 1997),132–33.

61. Patricia Cox Miller, *Women in Early Christianity: Translations from Greek Texts* (Washington, DC: Catholic University of America Press, 2005), 8.

62. Brooten, *Love between Women*, 8.

63. See "A Benefactor of Many and of Me Also," my unpublished paper delivered at the International SBL Annual Meeting, Vienna, Austria, July 22–26, 2007.

64. Sebastian P. Brock and Susan Ashbrook Harvey, intro and trans., *Holy Women of the Syrian Orient*, 2nd ed. (Berkeley: University of California Press, 1998), 25.

65. Boyarin, *Dying for God*, 67.

66. Kate Cooper, "A Saint in Exile: The Early Medieval Thecla at Rome and Meriamlik," *Hagiographica* 2 (1995): 2.

67. Ibid., 13, quoting variant endings in manuscripts of the *APTh*, A, B, and C (Parisinus graecus 520; 1454, and 1468, respectively) from the 10th and 11th

centuries. The existence of a church in Rome dedicated to Thecla also is attested in writings from the 7th century.

Chapter 2: Body Talk: The Martyr's "Voice"

1. Much of the material in this section comes from a paper, "Speaking and Silencing: The Female Martyr's 'Voice,'" delivered to the "Women in the Biblical World" Section, AAR/SBL Annual Meeting, Toronto, Ontario, November 23–26, 2002.

2. Jan Willem van Henten and Friedrich Avemarie, *Martyrdom and Noble Death: Selected Texts from Graeco-Roman, Jewish and Christian Antiquity* (London: Routledge, 2002), 2.

3. Ibid., 4–5. The authors also cite here a similar argument made by Arthur Droge and James Tabor, *A Noble Death: Suicide and Martyrdom among Christians and Jews in Antiquity* (San Francisco: HarperCollins, 1992).

4. Daniel Boyarin, *Dying for God: Martyrdom and the Making of Christianity and Judaism* (Stanford, CA: Stanford University Press, 1999) 94–95.

5. Allison Goddard Elliott, *Roads to Paradise: Reading the Lives of the Early Saints* (Hanover, NH: New England Press for Brown University, 1987), 24–25.

6. Boyarin, *Dying for God*, 95; Elliott, *Roads to Paradise*, 24.

7. Richard Valantasis, "A Theory of the Social Function of Asceticism," in *Asceticism*, ed. Vincent L. Wimbush and Richard R. Valantasis, with the assistance of Gay Byron and William S. Love (Oxford: Oxford University Press, 1995), 548.

8. Van Henten and Avemarie, *Martyrdom*, 4.

9. Amy-Jill Levine, *The Misunderstood Jew: The Church and the Scandal of the Jewish Jesus* (New York: HarperOne, 2007), 3.

10. Page du Bois, *Sappho Is Burning* (Chicago: University of Chicago Press, 1995), 157.

11. *WLGR* #43, p. 23.

12. Gail P. Corrington (Gail Streete), "The 'Divine Woman'? Propaganda and the Power of Chastity in the New Testament Apocrypha," in *Rescuing Creusa: New Methodological Approaches to Women in Antiquity*, ed. Marilyn B. Skinner, *Helios* 13, no. 2 (1986): 153.

13. Elaine Scarry, *The Body in Pain: The Making and Unmaking of the World* (New York: Oxford University Press, 1985), 215–19.

14. Van Henten and Avemarie, *Martyrdom*, 4.

15. Sebastian P. Brock and Susan Ashbrook Harvey, intro. and trans., *Holy Women of the Syrian Orient*, 2nd ed. (Berkeley: University of California Press, 1998), 22–23.

16. Karen Jo Torjesen, *When Women Were Priests: Women's Leadership in the Early Church and the Scandal of Their Subordination in the Rise of Christianity* (San Francisco: HarperSan Francisco, 1993), chaps. 4, 6–7.

17. Boyarin, *Dying for God*, 71, asserts per contra that in the case of rabbinic tales of martyrdom, the martyred rabbi's behavior is "feminized," in the sense that Jews under Roman rule, for their survival, are to act like women, hidden, silent, and "veiled" against the bloody gaze of the dominant, masculine Rome. Thus, the rabbi martyr, like a female martyr, has abandoned the appropriate gendered behavior.

18. Shelley Matthews, "Thinking of Thecla: Issues in Feminist Historiography," *JFSR* 17, no. 2 (Fall 2001): 48.

19. Nicole Loraux, *Tragic Ways of Killing a Woman*, trans. Anthony Forster (Cambridge, MA: Harvard University Press, 1987), vii, 23.

20. Robin Darling Young, "The Woman with the Soul of Abraham: Traditions about the Mother of the Maccabean Martyrs," in *"Women Like This": New Perspectives on Jewish Women in the Greco-Roman World*, edited by Amy-Jill Levine, SBLEJL 01 (Atlanta: Scholars Press, 1991), 66–81.

21. In rabbinic accounts—*Lamentations Rabbah* 1.16; *b. Gittin* 57b; *Pesiqta Rabbati* 43—the mother is called Miriam bat Tanhum and the persecutors are Romans; driven mad by the death of her sons, she commits suicide by jumping off a roof. See van Henten and Avemarie, *Martyrdom*, 145–51; Robert Doran, "The Martyr: A Synoptic View of the Mother and Her Seven Sons," in *Ideal Figures in Ancient Judaism: Peoples and Paradigms*, ed. John J. Collins and George Nickelsburg, SBLSCS 12 (Chico, CA: Scholars Press, 1980), 189–221.

22. Young, "Woman with the Soul of Abraham," 69.

23. Ibid., 70.

24. The term *aretē*, "excellence," often translated by the Latin *virtus*, "virtue," also can mean manliness, particularly in battle (LSJ).

25. Van Henten and Avemarie, *Martyrdom*, 70–72.

26. Jan Willem van Henten, *The Maccabean Martyrs as Saviours of the Jewish People: A Study of 2 and 4 Maccabees*, Supplements to the Journal for the Study of Judaism 57 (Leiden: E. J. Brill, 1997), 176.

27. Elliott, *Roads to Paradise*, 24.

28. Young, "Woman with the Soul of Abraham," 73.

29. Ibid., 76.

30. Ibid., 78.

31. Ibid., 79.

32. For the textual history and translation of this story, see van Henten and Avemarie, *Martyrdom*, 145–51; and Doran, "The Martyr," 189–221.

33. Van Henten and Avemarie, *Martyrdom*, 137.

34. Ibid., 151.

35. Doran, "The Martyr," 200.

36. Boyarin, *Dying for God*, 181, n. 59. More instructive here in terms of public/private, male/female representation is the fate of R. Hanina's (also unnamed) daughter, who is condemned to a brothel. Since one of the reasons R. Hanina was arrested was for publicly pronouncing the ineffable name of God in his teaching, Boyarin observes that the reasons given for punishment of the

rabbi and his daughter are "highly gendered in their implications. Rabbi Hanina himself was condemned for doing in public that he should have done in private." His daughter drew attention to herself by her immodest manner of walking, and her punishment by exposure supposedly fits the crime (*Dying for God*, 70).

37. Corinna Hasofferett, "The Woman and Her Seven Sons," "Time in Tel-Aviv," December 15, 2004, par. 1, http://timeintelaviv.blogspot.com/2004_12_01_timeintelaviv_archives.html.

38. Galit Hasan-Rokem, *Web of Life: Folklore and Midrash in Rabbinic Literature*, trans. Batya Stein (Stanford, CA: Stanford University Press, 2000), 121–23; cf. Boyarin, *Dying for God*, 117.

39. Maureen A. Tilley, "The Passion of Perpetua and Felicity," in *Searching the Scriptures*, vol. 2, *A Feminist Commentary*, ed. Elisabeth Schüssler Fiorenza (New York: Crossroad, 1994), 846.

40. Ibid., 829.

41. Elliott, *Roads to Paradise*, 24.

42. Mary Rose D'Angelo, "*Eusebeia*: Roman Imperial Family Values and the Sexual Politics of 4 Maccabees and the Pastorals," *BibInt* 11, no. 2 (2003): 139–65.

43. Brock and Harvey, *Holy Women*, 24–25.

44. The Greek text of the *passio* has only "bride of Christ." See Jacqueline Amat, *Passion de Perpétue et de Félicité, suivi les Actes* (Paris: Les Éditions du Cerf, 1996), 164, and commentary, 250.

45. Loraux, *Tragic Ways*, 3.

46. Lisa M. Sullivan, "I Responded, 'I Will Not': Christianity as Catalyst for Resistance in the *Passio Perpetuae et Felicitatis*," in *Rhetorics of Resistance: A Colloquy on Early Christianity as Rhetorical Formation*, guest ed., Vincent Wimbush, *Semeia* 79 (Atlanta: Scholars Press, 1997), 73.

47. Jan N. Bremmer, "Magic, Martyrdom and Women's Liberation in the *Acts of Paul and Thecla*," in *The Apocryphal Acts of Paul and Thecla*, ed. Jan N. Bremmer (Kampen, Netherlands: Kok Pharos, 1996), 44.

48. Margaret P. Aymer, "Hailstorms and Fireballs: Redaction, World Creation and Resistance in the *Acts of Paul and Thecla*," *Femeia* 79 (1997): 45–48.

49. Elliott, *Roads to Paradise*, 48–51. The "happy ending" in Thecla's case is not a marriage (from which she is fleeing) but a brief reunion with Paul, which confirms her celibate independence, quite a different ending, but positive for Thecla.

50. Thus ends the *Acts of Paul and Thecla* in the Tischendorf edition, preserved in R. A. Lipsius and M. Bonnet, eds., *Acta Apostolorum Apocrypha*, vol. 1 (Leipzig: Hermann Mendelssohn, 1891), 234–72. The 5th-century *Life and Miracles* by Pseudo-Basil has Thecla return to her home (10.10), but she continues on to Seleucia, working many miracles before her eventual "death" (11.16).

51. Gilbert Dagron, *Vie et miracles de sainte Thècle* (Brussels: Société des Bollandistes, 1978), 26; cited by Elliott, *Roads to Paradise*, 50.

52. Brock and Harvey, *Holy Women*, 24–25.

53. Stephen J. Davis, "Crossed Texts, Crossed Sex: Intertextuality and Gender in Early Christian Legends of Holy Women Disguised as Men," *JECS* 10, no.1 (2002): 19.

54. The Greek "*baptizomai*" is here clearly reflexive, "I baptize myself," but some translators take it as a passive, "I am baptized," as does Stephen J. Davis, "A Pauline Defense of Women's Right to Baptize? Intertextuality and Apostolic Authority in the *Acts of Paul*," *JECS* 8, no. 3 (2000): 453–59.

55. Boyarin, *Dying for God*, 74–77.

56. Brock and Harvey, *Holy Women*, 24–25.

57. Ibid., 25.

Chapter 3: Tough Mothers and Female Contenders: Perpetua and Felicitas

1. Author's translation from Latin text as found in Jacqueline Amat, *Passion de Perpétue et de Félicité, suivi des Actes* (Paris: Les Éditions du Cerf, 1996).

2. There are various terms for these stories of martyrs: the descriptive English terms "martyrology," "martyrdom"; and the commonly used literary terms in Latin, *Acta* (acts) and *passio* (passion, suffering). Although these are used interchangeably in the literature, *passio* is the narrowest, usually referring only to the suffering and death itself.

3. Gillian Clark, "Bodies and Blood: Late Antique Debate on Martyrdom, Virginity and Resurrection," in *Changing Bodies, Changing Meanings: Studies on the Human Body in Antiquity*, ed. Dominic Montserrat (London: Routledge, 1998), 99.

4. Elizabeth Castelli, *Martyrdom and Memory: Early Christian Culture Making* (New York: Columbia University Press, 2005), esp. 68–69.

5. Herbert R. Musurillo, intro., text, and trans., *Acts of the Christian Martyrs* (Oxford: Oxford University Press, 1972), xxv.

6. In the Latin text from a ninth-century manuscript—discovered and translated by J. A. Robinson, who supposed it to be the earliest account of the *passio*—the three women who have speaking parts are named in the indictment before the proconsul, but the sentence of execution includes the other two women. "Introduction to the Passion of the Scillitan Martyrs," *Early Christian Writings*, http://www.earlychristianwritings.com/scillitan.html.

7. Eusebius, *HE* 5.16; Epiphanius, *Panarion* 49, 79.

8. Timothy Barnes, *Tertullian: A Historical and Literary Study* (Oxford: Clarendon Press, 1971), 131.

9. Ibid., 80. Åke Fridh, *Le problème de la passion des Saintes Perpétue et Félicité*, Studia Graeca et Latina Gothoburgensis 26 (Stockholm: Almqvist & Wiksell, 1968), 11, posits the editor as a contemporary of Tertullian, but not the presbyter himself.

10. Amat, e.g., believes that the Montanist character of the *Martyrdom* is "barely perceptible [*peu sensible*]"; *Passion*, 269.

11. Ibid., 89–91; Fridh, *Le problème*, 5, 45.

12. Texts of the Latin *Acta* in both versions may be found in Amat, *Passion*, 277–303.

13. Ibid., 25. Curiously, the inscription puts Felicitas before Perpetua, so one might wonder whether the names were given in order from the least to the most important, at least in terms of their commemoration in the later church that built the basilica. But that is mere speculation.

14. Jacopo da Voragine, *Golden Legend* (1273, published 1470), trans. William Caxton, 1483, Temple Classics, ed. F. S. Ellis (1900; repr., 1922, 1931), in *Internet Medieval Sourcebook*, http://www.fordham.edu/halsall/basis/goldenlegend/GoldenLegend=Volume7.htm#Saturnine.

15. Francine Cardman, "Acts of the Women Martyrs," *AThR* 70, no. 2 (1988): 144.

16. Joyce E. Salisbury, *Perpetua's Passion: The Death and Memory of a Young Roman Woman* (New York: Routledge, 1997), 175–76.

17. Marie Turcan, "Être femme selon Tertullien," *Vita Latina* 119 (September 1990): 15–21, repr. in French with ET, in Roger Pearce, *Tertullian Project*, http://www.tertullian.org/sources.htm.

18. Ibid.

19. The examples of Cleopatra, the wife of Hasdrubal, and the "Attic prostitute" appear also in Tertullian's *To the Nations* 1.18; the prostitute appears also in the list of the pagan martyrs in the *Apologetic* 1.5–9; and Lucretia and Dido in the "Montanist" *Exhortation to Chastity* 13. See Herbert Musurillo, ed. and comm., *Acts of the Pagan Martyrs (Acta Alexandrinorum)* (Oxford: Clarendon Press, 1954), 243–44.

20. Here Tertullian uses the adjective *mollis* (soft, weak) and the diminutive *lectulus* (lit., "little bed"). *Mollis* was sometimes used to mean "effeminate," whereas diminutives that were not used as endearments were used pejoratively as put-downs.

21. Dom G. D. Schlegel, "The *Ad Martyras* of Tertullian and the Circumstances of Its Composition," *DRev* 61 (1943): 127–28. Several others who endorse the connection between the martyrs of *Ad Martyras* and those of the *Martyrdom of Perpetua and Felicitas* are mentioned by Amat, *Passion*, 39 n. 3.

22. Euripides, *Medea* 248–51. See Helen King, *Hippocrates' "Woman": Reading the Female Body in Ancient Greece* (New York: Routledge, 1998), 124.

23. Amat, *Passion*, 79, 82–83.

24. Cyprian, *ANF* 5.579–87.

25. Cyprian, *On Jealousy and Envy* 2, quoted by Peter Brown, *The Body and Society: Men, Women, and Sexual Renunciation in Early Christianity* (New York: Columbia University Press, 1988), 194–95.

26. Emanuela Prinzivalli, "Perpetua the Martyr," in *Roman Women*, ed. and with a new intro. Augusto Fraschetti, trans. Linda Lappin (Chicago: University of Chicago Press, 2001), 138.

27. Amat, *Passion*, 82.

28. Maureen A. Tilley, *Donatist Martyr Stories: The Church in Conflict in North Africa* (Liverpool: Liverpool University Press, 1996), 16 n. 5.

29. Johannes Quasten, *Byzantion* 15 (1940–41), 4–5; quoted in Stephen B. Luce, "Archaeological News and Discussions: Early Christian and Byzantine," *AJA* 47, no. 1 (January–March 1943): 120.

30. J. Patout Burns, "Authority and Power: The Role of the Martyrs in the African Church in the Fifth Century," Version: June 12, 1998, from "Devotion and Dissent: The Practice of Christianity in Roman North Africa," Interdisciplinary Working Group for the Study of Christianity in North Africa during the Second through the Seventh Centuries, Vanderbilt University, http://people.vanderbilt.edu/~james.p.burns/chroma/saints/martburn.html.

31. Frederick C. Klawiter, "The Role of Martyrdom and Persecution in Developing the Priestly Authority of Women in Early Christianity: A Case Study in Montanism," *CH* 49, no. 3 (September 1980): 257.

32. Ibid., 131; see also Patricia Cox Miller, *Dreams in Late Antiquity* (Princeton, NJ: Princeton University Press, 1994), 173.

33. Quasten in Luce, "Archaeological News," 120.

34. Miller, *Dreams in Late Antiquity*, 174.

35. Kenneth B. Steinhauser, "Augustine's Reading of the *Passio sanctarum Perpetuae et Felicitatis*," in *Proceedings of the 12th Annual Conference on Patristic Studies, Held in Oxford, 1995: Augustine and His Opponents: Jerome, Other Latin Fathers after Nicea, Orientalia*, ed. Elizabeth A. Livingstone, St Patr 33 (Louvain: Peeters, 1997), 245.

36. Ibid., 244.

37. Ibid., 248; Augustine, *On the Nature and Origin of the Soul* 4.18.26; cf. Brent D. Shaw, "The Passion of Perpetua—Christian Woman Martyred in Carthage in A.D. 203," *Past and Present* 56 (May 1993): 21.

38. Maureen A. Tilley, "Harnessing the Martyrs: Social Control of Hagiography in Roman North Africa," North American Patristics Society, Chicago, May 30, 1998, http://www.people.vanderbilt.edu/~james.p.burns/chroma/saints/martilley.html.

39. A fourth, very short sermon (394), contains similar puns on the martyrs' names; despite Shaw's claim that it "enunciates similar themes," it emphasizes the concord of the two martyrs, now joined in one feast day as they were joined in martyrdom; and the reception of milk by Perpetua from the Good Shepherd, which is pure teaching and power to endure martyrdom (see Shaw, "Passion of Perpetua," 28 n. 85 and below, n. 42).

40. Shaw, "Passion of Perpetua," 28 n. 79.

41. Musurillo, *Acts of the Christian Martyrs*, xliv.

42. Although there is dispute over the part of the martyrdom in which Crispina's head is shaved, the first part of the account, in which Crispina is called a "hard woman," is not disputed (ibid.). See also Shaw, "Passion of Perpetua," 1.

43. Shaw, "Passion of Perpetua," 18.

44. Ibid., 43.

45. Ibid., 22, points out that this action on the part of the "Good Shepherd" counters Perpetua's own maternal nursing and "trumps the 'weakness' of motherhood." The heavenly Father thus takes over the parental role.

46. Ibid., 23.

47. C. J. M. J. [Cornelius Johannes Marra Joseph] van Beek, ed., *Passio Sanctarum Perpetua et Felicitatis*, vol. 1 (Nijmegen: Dekker & Van de Vegt, 1936); vol. 2 (Bonn: [Peter Hanstein], 1938). Van Beek was the classic edition of the versions of the *passio* and *acta*.

48. Klawiter, "The Role of Martyrdom," 254.

49. Amat, *Passion*, 268.

50. In my view the addition of and emphasis on husbands for both Perpetua and Felicitas argues strongly against Carolyn Osiek's suggestion that Saturus is Perpetua's husband in the original *Martyrdom*, a connection that she herself admits is never made explicit. See Carolyn Osiek, "Perpetua's Husband," *JECS* 10, no. 2 (2002): 287–90.

51. Mary R. Lefkowitz, "The Motivations for St. Perpetua's Martyrdom," *JAAR* 44, no. 3 (1976): 419.

52. Dating and text from Musurillo, 295–301.

53. Ibid., Greek recension, 22–28; Latin recension, 28–37.

54. The theme of the beauty of the exposed or naked female martyr is important, particularly in the stories of the virgin martyrs (Thecla, Potamiaena, Irene, and others), as we shall see in the next chapter.

55. Castelli, *Martyrdom and Memory*, 197.

56. W. H. C. Frend, *Martyrdom and Persecution in the Early Church: Study of a Conflict from the Maccabees to Donatus* (Garden City, NY: Doubleday/Anchor, 1967), 211.

57. Lefkowitz, "Motivations," 421 n. 13.

58. Ibid., 417–21.

59. Shaw, "Passion of Perpetua," 5.

60. Author's translation of the Latin *passio*, edited by C. Smedt, *Analecta Bollandiana* 9 (1890): 110–16, cited by Alan Dearn, "Voluntary Martyrdom and the Donatist Schism," in *Papers Presented at the 14th International Conference on Patristic Studies Held in Oxford 2003: History, Biblical et Hagiographica*, ed. F. Young, M. Edwards, and P. Parvis, St Patr 39 (Louvain: Peeters, 2003): 29 n. 10.

61. Maureen A. Tilley, trans. with notes and intro., *Donatist Martyr Stories: The Church in Conflict in Roman North Africa* (Liverpool: Liverpool University Press, 1996), x.

62. James Everett Seaver, *The Persecution of Jews in the Roman Empire (300–428)*, University of Kansas Publications, Humanistic Series 30 (Lawrence: University of Kansas Press, 1952), 45–46. Seaver believes that the tale results from the misunderstanding of an inscription on the Christian church, a former Jewish synagogue, at Tipasa.

63. Margaret R. Miles, *Carnal Knowing: Female Nakedness and Religious Meaning in the Christian West* (Boston: Beacon Press, 1989), 62.

64. Peter Dronke, *Women Writers of the Middle Ages: A Critical Study of Texts from Perpetua (†203) to Marguerite Porete (†1310)* (Cambridge: Cambridge University Press, 1984), ACLS (American Council of Learned Societies) Humanities E-Book, 15.

65. Nicole Loraux, *Tragic Ways of Killing a Woman*, trans. Anthony Forster (Cambridge, MA: Harvard University Press, 1987), 52.

66. Judith Perkins, *The Suffering Self: Pain and Narrative Representation in the Early Christian Era* (London: Routledge, 1995), 105.

67. Brown, *The Body and Society*, 329.

Chapter 4: The Nakedness of Thecla

1. Brent D. Shaw, "Body/Power/Identity: Passions of the Martyrs," *JECS* 4, no. 3 (1996): 311.

2. Sarah Barnett, "Death and the Maidens: Women Martyrs and Their Sexual Identity in the Early Christian Period," *culture@home* 9/23/2002, http://www.sydneyanglicans.net/culture/thinking/369a.

3. *Martyrdom of Pionius the Presbyter and His Companions* 7, in Musurillo, 136–67.

4. Musurillo, xxviii; *Martyrdom of Potamiaena and Basilides*, in Musurillo, 132–35.

5. The Greek adjective translated as "celebrated" (*aoidimos*) can also mean "sung about." Potamiaena is famous in the way an athlete or epic hero is famous: she is the subject of "much report" (*polys ho logos*) and song. She even appears to her rescuer Basilides after her death, wearing the crown (wreath) of her victory/martyrdom and promising that he will join her. This time the woman precedes the man. Palladius, in his *Lausiac History* 3, also tells her story (Musurillo, 133 n. 2).

6. The supposed Greek original is contained in Musurillo, 280–93.

7. Useful information on the Agnes legend, with references, is found in the online Catholic Encyclopedia under "St. Agnes of Rome," http://www.newadvent.org/cathen/01214a.htm.

8. The stories are told in *Sifre Deuteronomy* 307 and *b. Avodah Zarah* 17b–18a. See Daniel Boyarin, *Dying for God: Martyrdom and the Making of Christianity and Judaism* (Stanford, CA: Stanford University Press, 1999), 87. See also Jan Willem van Henten and Friedrich Avemarie, *Martyrdom and Noble Death: Selected*

Texts from Graeco-Roman, Jewish and Christian Antiquity (London: Routledge, 2002), 157–66.

9. Pythagorean Treatise in H. Thesleff, ed., *The Pythagorean Texts of the Hellenistic Period* (Abo, 1965), 15–24; quoted in *WLGR* #107, pp. 104–5.

10. Walter Burkert, *Greek Religion*, trans. John Raffan (Cambridge, MA: Harvard University Press, 1985), 78, quoted in Gail Corrington (Gail Streete), "The 'Divine Woman'? Propaganda and the Power of Chastity in the New Testament Apocrypha," in *Rescuing Creusa: New Methodological Approaches to Women in Antiquity*, ed. Marilyn Skinner, *Helios*, 13, no. 2 (1987): 160 n. 24.

11. Peter Brown, *The Body and Society: Men, Women, and Sexual Renunciation in Early Christianity* (New York: Columbia University Press, 1988), 14–15; Kate Cooper, *The Virgin and the Bride: Idealized Womanhood in Late Antiquity* (Cambridge, MA: Harvard University Press, 1996), 28.

12. Virginia Burrus, *Chastity as Autonomy: Women in the Stories of the Apocryphal Acts* (Lewiston, NY: Edwin Mellen Press, 1987), 25.

13. Allison Goddard Elliott, *Roads to Paradise: Reading the Lives of the Early Saints* (Hanover, NH: New England Press for Brown University, 1987), 45–48.

14. See esp. Stevan L. Davies, *The Revolt of the Widows: The Social World of the Apocryphal Acts* (Carbondale: Southern Illinois University Press, 1980); Dennis R. MacDonald, *The Legend and the Apostle: The Battle for Paul in Story and Canon* (Philadelphia: Westminster Press, 1983); and Burrus, *Chastity as Autonomy*.

15. *The Conversion and Marriage of Aseneth* (*Joseph and Aseneth*), variously ascribed to the 1st and 4th centuries CE and as either of Jewish or Christian composition, is one work influenced by the Greek romances that does preserve marriage as an ending to the trials of the heroine. See Ross S. Kraemer, *When Joseph Met Aseneth: A Late Antique Tale of the Biblical Patriarch and His Egyptian Wife* (New York: Oxford University Press, 1998), 5–6.

16. Brown, *Body and Society*, 156.

17. Gail Corrington Streete (Gail Streete), "Sex, Spirit and Control: The Corinthian Women and Paul," in *Ritual, Power, and the Body: Historical Perspectives on the Representation of Greek Women*, ed. C. Nadia Seremetakis (New York: Pella Press, 1993), 95–117.

18. Daniel Boyarin, "Body Politic among the Brides of Christ: Paul and the Origins of Christian Sexual Renunciation," in *Asceticism*, ed. Vincent L. Wimbush and Richard R. Valantasis, with the assistance of Gay Byron and William S. Love (Oxford: Oxford University Press, 1995), 472.

19. Dennis R. MacDonald, *Legend and the Apostle*, 97–103.

20. Jan N. Bremmer, "Magic, Martyrdom and Women's Liberation in the *Acts of Paul and Thecla*," in *The Apocryphal Acts of Paul and Thecla*, ed. Jan N. Bremmer (Kampen, Netherlands: Kok Pharos, 1996), 44.

21. Much of the discussion here is anticipated in Gail P. C. Streete, "Authority and Authorship: *The Acts of Paul and Thecla* as a Disputed Pauline Text," *LTQ* 40, no. 4 (Winter 2005): 265–76.

22. Stevan L. Davies, "Women, Tertullian, and the *Acts of Paul*," in *The Apocryphal Acts of the Apostles*, ed. Dennis R. MacDonald, *Semeia* 38 (1986): 141; Streete, "Authority and Authorship," 267.

23. Ross S. Kraemer, ed., *Maenads, Martyrs, Matrons, Monastics: A Sourcebook on Women's Religions in the Greco-Roman World* (Philadelphia: Fortress Press, 1988), 407.

24. MacDonald, *Legend and the Apostle*, 18.

25. Catherine Burris and Lucas Van Rompay, "Thecla in Syriac Christianity: Preliminary Observations," *Hugoye: Journal of Syriac Studies* 5, no. 2 (July 2002) http://syrcom.cua.edu/syrcom/Hugoye/Vol5No2/HV5NBurrisVanRompay.html; and "Some Further Notes on Thecla in Syriac Christianity," *Hugoye* 6, no. 2 (July 2003), http://syrcom.cua.edu/syrcom/Hugoye/Vol6No2/HV6N2BurrisVan Rompay.html.

26. Gilbert Dagron, *Vie et miracles de sainte Thècle: Texte grec, traduction et commentaire*, Subsidia Hagiographica 62 (Brussels: Société des Bollandistes, 1978), 140–47.

27. Davies, *Revolt of the Widows*; MacDonald, *Legend and the Apostle*; Burrus, *Chastity as Autonomy*, 67–77.

28. Esther Yue L. Ng, "*Acts of Paul and Thecla*: Women's Stories and Precedent?" *JTS*, NS, 55, no. 1 (April 2004): 27; Lynne S. Boughton, "From Pious Legend to Feminist Fantasy," *JR* 71, no. 3 (1991): 365. I see no reason, however, with Ng to regard Tertullian's allusion in *Baptism* to women's use of the Thecla narrative as "dubious."

29. Margaret P. Aymer, "Hailstorms and Fireballs: Redaction, World Creation and Resistance in the *Acts of Paul and Thecla*," in *Rhetorics of Resistance: A Colloquy on Early Christianity as Rhetorical Formation*, ed. Vincent L. Wimbush, *Semeia* 79 (1997): 45–61.

30. Streete, "Authority and Authorship," 267.

31. Ibid., 274.

32. See MacDonald, *Legend and the Apostle*, 45.

33. *Acts of Paul and Thecla*, 5–6. Translation from the Greek text of the *Acta Pauli et Theclae*, in *Acta Apostolorum Apocrypha*, ed. R. A. Lipsius and M. Bonnet, vol. 1 (Leipzig: Hermann Mendelssohn, 1891), 235–72. Unless otherwise noted, translations are mine; italics added.

34. Burrus, *Chastity as Autonomy*, 89–91.

35. Bremmer, "Magic, Martyrdom," 41.

36. Lipsius and Bonnet, *Acta Pauli et Thecla*, 245 n. 4, point to 14 as a reference to the "heresy" of the realized resurrection mentioned in 2 Tim. 2:18, but it seems also likely that in context this may be in opposition to 1 Tim. 2:15, where woman is "saved" by childbearing.

37. Bremmer, "Magic, Martyrdom," 48.

38. Sheila E. McGinn, "The Acts of Thecla," in *Searching the Scriptures*, vol. 2, *A Feminist Commentary*, ed. Elisabeth Schüssler Fiorenza (New York: Crossroad, 1994), 814.

39. See Burrus, *Chastity as Autonomy*, 91, on Thecla's violation of the rules of chastity.

40. This is from the ET cited by Patricia Cox Miller, *Dreams in Late Antiquity* (Princeton, NJ: Princeton University Press, 1994), 172.

41. Andrew S. Jacobs, "'Her Own Proper Kinship': Marriage, Class and Women in the Apocryphal Acts of the Apostles," in *A Feminist Companion to the New Testament Apocrypha*, ed. Amy-Jill Levine, with Maria Mayo Robbins (London: T&T Clark, 2006), 18–23.

42. Magda Misset-van de Weg, "Answers to the Plights of Thecla," in Levine, *A Feminist Companion*, 150.

43. The Jeremiah Jones translation (1693–1724) of the *Acts of Paul and Thecla*, preserved in the Saint Pachomius Orthodox Library, has the governor "with surprise beholding the greatness of her beauty" (*APTh* 5.13). St. Pachomius Library, September/October 1995, available through http://www.fordham.edu/halsall/basis/thecla.html. Bremmer, "Magic, Martyrdom," 51, suggests other comparisons between the martyrdom of Agathonicē and that of Thecla.

44. Bremmer, "Magic, Martyrdom," 49 n. 48, prefers the translation, "She assumed the shape of the cross," following the strong suggestion of the Latin text, rather than the possible translation from the Greek, "making the sign of the cross."

45. Ibid.

46. Maureen A. Tilley, "The Ascetic Body and the (Un)Making of the World of the Martyr," *JAAR* 59, no. 3 (1991): 467.

47. For the translation and comments, see Streete, "Authority and Authorship," 270; and Gail P. C. Streete, "Of Martyrs and Men: Perpetua, Thecla, and the Ambiguity of Female Heroism in Early Christianity," in *The Subjective Eye: Essays in Culture, Religion, and Gender in Honor of Margaret R. Miles*, ed. Richard Valantasis, in collaboration with Deborah J. Haynes, James D. Smith III, and Janet F. Carlson, Princeton Theological Monograph Series 59 (Eugene, OR: Pickwick Publications, 2006), 260.

48. Misset-van de Weg, "Answers to the Plights," 153.

49. Margaret R. Miles, *Carnal Knowing: Female Nakedness and Religious Meaning in the Christian West* (Boston: Beacon, 1989), 70; quoted in Streete, "Of Martyrs and Men," 260.

50. Aymer, "Hailstorms and Fireballs," 51.

51. Scott Bradbury, trans. with intro., *Selected Letters of Libanius from the Age of Constantius and Julian* (Liverpool: Liverpool University Press, 2004), 27.

52. Bremmer notes that this same phrase recurs in virtually identical form in *The Martyrdom of Carpus, Papylus, and Agathonicē*, when Agathonicē is condemned ("Magic, Martyrdom," 51), but the difference in the latter is that the entire crowd, not just the women, cry out, and only after Agathonicē has thrown herself on the fire.

53. Aymer, "Hailstorms and Fireballs," 48.

54. Miller, *Dreams in Late Antiquity*, 176.

55. Subtitle adapted from a paper by Marianne B. Kartzow and A. Rebecca Solevag, "Who Loves the Pastorals and Why?" Disputed Paulines second session, SBL Annual Meeting, San Diego, CA, November 19, 2007.

56. The 4th-century pilgrim Egeria's travel diary mentions a reading from the *Acts of Thecla* at the saint's shrine in Seleucia (Siflike). Whether this is considered scriptural or simply a reading from the *passio* of a martyr saint is unclear.

57. These include Burrus, *Chastity as Autonomy*; Davies, *Revolt of the Widows*; MacDonald, *Legend and the Apostle*; and Elisabeth Schüssler Fiorenza, *In Memory of Her: A Feminist Reconstruction of Christian Origins* (New York: Crossroad, 1983). Sheila McGinn, "The Acts of Thecla," in Schüssler Fiorenza, *Searching the Scriptures*, 800–28, provides a good discussion and summary of the manuscript tradition and criticism of the *Acts of Thecla* and supports the view, adopted in large part by Aymer, "Hailstorms and Fireballs," that a male redactor "took a woman's folktale about Thecla and 'domesticated' it, giving Paul more prominence in the story" (805).

58. This is the view advocated by Boughton, "Pious Legend," *JR* 71, no. 3 (July 1991): 363–83. Boughton's view and others critical of the women's leadership/women's communities hypothesis are summarized by Shelley Matthews, "Thinking of Thecla: Issues in Feminist Historiography," *JFSR* 17, no. 2 (Fall 2001): 39–55.

59. Amy-Jill Levine, "Introduction," *Feminist Companion to the New Testament Apocrypha*, 2.

60. Quoted in Léonie Hayne, "Thecla and the Church Fathers," *VC* 48 (1994): 210; Gail P. C. Streete, "Buying the Stairway to Heaven: Perpetua and Thecla as Early Christian Heroines," in Levine, *Feminist Companion to the New Testament Apocrypha*, 202 n. 58. ET, *ANF* 5:390–97, Christian Classics Ethereal Library, http://www.ccel.org/schaff/anf05.iv.iv.lxxiv.html.

61. Section numbers are from PG 46:462–998; ET by W. K. Lowther Clarke is found in Paul Halsall, *Medieval Sourcebook*, http://www.fordham.edu/halsall/basis/macrina.html.

62. Francine Cardman, "Whose Life Is It? The *Vita Macrinae* of Gregory of Nyssa," in *Papers Presented at the 13th International Conference on Patristic Studies, Held in Oxford, 1999: Cappadocian Writers; Other Greek Writers*, ed. M. L. Wiles and E. J. Yarnold, with the assistance of P. M. Parvis, St Patr 37 (Louvain: Peeters, 2001), 36.

63. Virginia Burrus, "Macrina's Tattoo," *Journal of Medieval and Early Modern Studies* 33, no. 3 (2003): 412–13.

64. ET from *New Advent*, "Church Fathers," http://www.newadvent.org/fathers/2915.htm.

65. Elizabeth A. Clark, "Holy Women, Holy Words: Early Christian Women, Social History, and the 'Linguistic Turn,'" *JECS* 6, no. 3 (1998): 429.

66. Elizabeth A. Clark, "The Celibate Bridegroom and His Virginal Brides: Metaphor and the Marriage of Jesus in Early Christian Ascetic Exegesis," *CH* 77, no. 19 (March 2008): 1.

67. MacDonald, *Legend and the Apostle*, 91.

68. See Streete, "Buying the Stairway to Heaven," 190.

69. Gregory of Nyssa, *Homilies on the Song of Songs* 14, in PG 44:1068, cited by Monika Pesthy, "Thecla among the Fathers," in Bremmer, *The Apocryphal Acts of Paul and Thecla*, 167.

70. See Patricia Cox Miller, "Is There a Harlot in This Text? Hagiography and the Grotesque," *Journal of Medieval and Early Modern Studies* 33, no.3 (Fall 2003): 430 n. 7; quoting Gillian Cloke, *This Female Man of God: Women and Spiritual Power in the Patristic Age AD 350–450* (London: Routledge, 1995), 214. The alternate translation is by W. K. L. Clarke, *Palladius' Lausiac History* (London: SPCK, 1918), as contained in the *Internet Medieval Sourcebook*, Paul Halsall, ed., http://www.fordham.edu/halsall/basis/palladius-lausiac.html.

71. See Hayne, "Thecla and the Church Fathers," 211; Cloke, *This Female*, 10, 214; Pesthy, "Thecla among the Fathers," 167–68.

72. Pesthy, "Thecla among the Fathers," 173.

73. Patricia Wilson-Kastner, ed., *A Lost Tradition: Women Writers of the Early Church* (Lanham, MD: University Press of America, 1981), 74–83. Latin text, *Siluiae aut potius Aetheriae peregrinatio*, ed. W. Heraeus (Heidelberg, 1908), in *Bibliotheca Augustana, Itinerarium Egeriae*, ca. 380, http://www.hs-augsburg.de/ ~harsch/Chronological/Lspost04/Egeria/ege_it23.html.

74. See MacDonald, *Legend and the Apostle*, 93; Laura Swan, *The Forgotten Desert Mothers* (New York: Paulist Press, 2001), 88.

75. Stephen J. Davis, *The Cult of Saint Thecla: A Tradition of Women's Piety in Late Antiquity*, Oxford Early Christian Studies (Oxford: Oxford University Press, 2001), 72–73.

76. Kate Cooper, "A Saint in Exile: The Early Medieval Thecla at Rome and Meriamlik," *Hagiographica* 2 (1995): 2.

77. PG 37:1067, quoted in John A. McGuckin, *St. Gregory of Nazianzus: An Intellectual Biography* (Crestwood, NY: St. Vladimir's Seminary Press, 2001), 229–31.

78. PG 85:481A–C; a newer edition is Gilbert Dagron, *Vie et miracles de sainte Thècle* (Brussels: Société des Bollandistes, 1978).

79. Pesthy, "Thecla among the Fathers," 168–71.

80. Scott Fitzgerald Johnson, *The Life and Miracles of Thekla: A Literary Study*, Hellenic Studies 13 (Washington, DC: Center for Hellenic Studies, 2006), 63.

81. This version, from Codex G, edited by Grabe, is found in Lipsius and Bonnet, *Acta*, 271–72.

82. Davis, *Cult of St. Thecla*, 46.

83. A.-J. Festugière, trans. and commentary, *Sainte Thècle, saints Côme et Damien, saints Cyr et Jean (Extraits), saint George*, Collections grecques de miracles (Paris: Éditions A. et J. Picard, 1971), 37.

84. How many miracles does Thecla perform? In the text preserved in the Patrologia Graeca under the name of Basil of Seleucia (PG 85:473–618) and

mentioned by Festugière, 31; according to Gilbert Dagron, *Vie et miracles*, quoted by Johnson, *Life and Miracles*, 46. Monika Pesthy ("Thecla among the Fathers," 168–69) refers to the earlier text as a "bad and incomplete edition."

85. *Notitia ecclesiarum urbis Romae*, in Roberto Valentini and Giuseppe Zucchetti, *Codice topografico della città di Roma*, 2:20 (Rome, 1942), 69; quoted in Cooper, "A Saint in Exile," 15.

86. *Codice topografico*, 25. The number and arrangement of the miracles by Festugière follows the ordering in Pseudo-Basil's book 2 in PG 85; Dagron, *Vie et miracles*, who is followed by Stephen Davis, *Cult of St. Thecla*, and Scott Johnson, *The Life and Miracles of Thekla*, has a different ordering and number than does Festugière.

87. "As Christians Vanish from Their Cradle," *Zenda* 4, no. 19 (July 27, 1998), reprinted with permission from *The Economist*, July 18, 1998, http://www.zendamagazine.com/html/archives/1998/july27_1998.htm. Catherine Burris and Lucas van Rompay, "Thecla in Syriac Christianity: Preliminary Observations," *Hugoye* 5, no. 2 (July 2002), attest to Thecla's popularity in this area from a probable early date.

88. Johnson, *Life and Miracles*, 145.

89. Davis, *Cult of St. Thecla*, 80.

90. Claudia Nauerth and Rüdiger Warns, *Thekla: Ihre Bilder in der frühchristlichen Kunst*, Göttinger Orientforschungen II. Reihe: Studien zur spätantiken und frühchristlichen Kunst, Bd. 3 (Wiesbaden: Otto Harrassowitz, 1981), 93–99.

91. Davis, *Cult of St. Thecla*, 193; Nauerth and Warns, *Thekla*, Tafel IX.18.

92. John Dominic Crossan and Jonathan L. Reed, *In Search of Paul: How Jesus's Apostle Opposed Rome's Empire with God's Kingdom: A New Vision of Paul's Words and World* (San Francisco: HarperCollins, 2004), xii–xiii.

93. Brown, *Body and Society*, 329.

94. Davis, *Cult of St. Thecla*, 53.

Chapter 5: Why Martyrs Matter

1. Quote from Darrell Scott, father of Rachel Joy Scott, killed at Columbine High School, in S. C. Gwynne, "An Act of God?" *Time Magazine*, Monday, December 20, 1999, 12–20, retrieved from "Rachel Scott," http://en.wikipedia.org/wiki/Rachel_Scott; quote from Cassie Bernall, in Misty Bernall, *She Said Yes: The Unlikely Martyrdom of Cassie Bernall* (Farmington, PA: Plough Publishing House, 1999), 140; quote from Dareen Abu Aysheh, "Palestinian Women Martyrs against the Israeli Occupation," http://www.aztlan.net/women_martyrs.htm.

2. This section and its heading are taken from my unpublished paper, "Perpetua's Passion: The Ethics of Martyrdom," delivered at ACTC (Association for Core Texts and Courses) Annual Conference, Dallas, TX, April 15–18, 2004.

3. Daniel Levinson et al.'s study of moral development (*Seasons of a Man's Life*, 1978), as Carol Gilligan notes, *In a Different Voice: Psychological Theory and Women's Development* (Cambridge, MA: Harvard University Press, 1982; reprint, 1994), 152, uses the Quest or "Dream" model and applies it to males.

4. Beth Nimmo and Darrell Scott, *Rachel's Tears: The Spiritual Journey of Columbine Martyr Rachel Scott* (Nashville: Thomas Nelson, 2000). The relevance of this literature and these events to understanding modern Christian martyr-making has been brilliantly expressed by Elizabeth Castelli, *Martyrdom and Memory: Early Christian Culture Making* (New York: Columbia University Press, 2005), esp. 172–96, and will also be discussed later in this chapter.

5. Bruce Springsteen, "Paradise," from *The Rising*, Bruce Springsteen, Columbia Audio compact disc CK 86600.

6. Mark Godfrey, review of Bruce Springsteen, *The Rising*, http://cluas.com/music/albums/bruce-springsteen.htm.

7. Mark Erskine, "Is Martyrdom the Answer?" unpublished paper, Humanities 102, Rhodes College (Spring 1999), 1 and 5.

8. Katharene Papathopoulos, "Christian Asceticism," unpublished paper, Religious Studies 301, Rhodes College (Spring 2007), 3.

9. Daniel Boyarin, *Dying for God: Martyrdom and the Making of Christianity and Judaism* (Stanford, CA: Stanford University Press, 1999), 67.

10. Carolyn Osiek, "Perpetua's Husband," *JECS* 10 (2002): 287–91.

11. Andrea Lorenzo Molinari, "Climbing the Dragon's Ladder: Perpetua, Felicitas, Graphic Novels, and the Possibility of Writing Modern Hagiography," *SBL Forum* 1/30/2007–3/8/2007, http://www.sbl-site.org/publications/article.aspx?articleId=624.

12. Events are pieced together from a variety of sources, including Justin Watson's excellent analysis, *The Martyrs of Columbine: Faith and the Politics of Tragedy* (New York: Palgrave Macmillan, 2002), and the informative Web site maintained by Cyn Shepard, *A Columbine Site*, http://www.acolumbinesite.com.

13. Dave Cullen, "Who Said 'Yes'?" *Salon.com News*, September 30, 1999, http://www.salon.com/news/feature/1999/09/30/bernall.

14. "Injured and Survivors: Valeen Schnurr," from Shepard, *A Columbine Site*.

15. Watson, *Martyrs of Columbine*, 53 n. 7.

16. Ibid.; Castelli, *Martyrdom and Memory*, 172–96; Gail P. C. Streete, "Buying the Stairway to Heaven: Perpetua and Thecla as Early Christian Heroines," in *A Feminist Companion to the New Testament Apocrypha*, ed. Amy-Jill Levine, with Maria Mayo Robbins (London: T&T Clark, 2006): 186–205.

17. The term "embattled subculture" comes from Frances Fitzgerald, "The New Evangelicals," *The New Yorker*, June 30, 2008, 29.

18. Castelli, *Martyrdom and Memory*, 173.

19. Watson, *Martyrs of Columbine*, 20.

20. Ibid., 18.

21. Beth Nimmo, "Rachel's Legacy," *Rachel Joy Scott.com*. http://www.rachel joyscott.com/rachelslegacy.htm.

22. Watson, *Martyrs of Columbine*, 76–77.

23. Castelli, *Martyrdom and Memory*, 182–83.

24. *Radiant Magazine*, http://www.radiantmag.com/article.php?id=254.

25. "Injured and Survivors: Mark Taylor," Shepard, *A Columbine Site*.

26. James B. Meadow, "Teens 'Radiant,' Forever Young," *Rocky Mountain News.com*, April 26, 1999, http://denver.rockymountainnews.com/shooting/0426doub5.shtml.

27. Jody Veenker, "Retailers: Marketing Martyrdom to Teens," *Christianity Today*, 43, no. 14 (December 6, 1999): 22; Castelli, *Martyrdom and Memory*, 189.

28. Cho, on the other hand, referred to Harris and Klebold as "martyrs" in a video made before the massacre: "Columbine Families Mourn for Virginia Tech," *CBS News.com*, April 20, 2007, http://www.cbsnews.com/stories/2007/04/20/columbine/main2709495.shtml. One Web blog, "Shine for Peace," went so far as to characterize Cho as a martyr, in that he was a divinely sent agent to make us all think about peace, http://isshine.blogspot.com/2007/04/why-i-l-o-v-e-virginia-tech-martyr.html.

29. Peter Brown, *The Body and Society: Men, Women, and Sexual Renunciation in Early Christianity* (New York: Columbia University Press, 1988), 363–64.

30. Castelli, *Martyrdom and Memory*, 193–95.

31. Robert A. Pape, *Dying to Win: The Strategic Logic of Suicide Terrorism* (New York: Random House, 2005), 4.

32. Barbara Victor, *Army of Roses: Inside the World of Palestinian Women Suicide Bombers* (Emmaus, PA: Rodale Press, 2003), 19–20; "Palestinian Women Martyrs against the Israeli Occupation," http://www.aztlan.net/women_martyrs.htm.

33. Pape, *Dying to Win*, 138.

34. James Bennet, "A Scholar of English Who Clung to the Veil," *New York Times*, May 30, 2003, sec. A1 and A14.

35. "Iraqi Martyr Shamed Family (News)," *The Cincinnati Post*, Cincinnati, OH, May 31, 2003, *High Beam Research*, http://www.highbeam.com/doc/1G1=102664.380.html.

36. Alissa J. Rubin, "Despair Drives Suicide: Attacks by Iraqi Women," *New York Times*, July 5, 2008, http://www.nytimes.com/2008/07/05/world/middleeast/05diyala.html?scp=1&sq=&st=nyt.

37. Avi Issacharoff, "The Palestinian and Israeli Media on Female Suicide Terrorists," in *Female Suicide Bombers: Dying for Equality?* ed. Yoram Schweitzer, Memorandum no. 84 (Tel Aviv: Tel Aviv University Jaffee Center for Strategic Studies, August, 2006), 48.

38. Barbara Victor, *Army of Roses: Inside the World of Palestinian Women Suicide Bombers* (Emmaus, PA: Rodale Press, 2003), 33.

39. Pape, *Dying to Win*, 209.

40. "Palestinian Women Martyrs against the Israeli Occupation," 7/1/2008, 5, http://www.aztlan.net/women_martyrs.htm.

41. Pape, *Dying to Win*, 187.

42. Rosemarie Skaine, *Female Suicide Bombers* (Jefferson, NC: McFarland, 2006), 115–20; 140–49.

43. Marie-Louise von Franz, *The Passion of Perpetua* (Irving, TX: Spring Publications, 1980), 75.

44. Mary R. Lefkowitz, "The Motivations for St. Perpetua's Martyrdom," *JAAR* 44, no. 3 (1976): 412.

45. Lynne C. Boughton, "From Pious Legend to Feminist Fantasy: Distinguishing Hagiographical License from Apostolic Practice in the 'Acts of Paul/Acts of Thecla,'" *JR* 71, no. 3 (July 1991): 382.

46. Debra D. Zedalis, "Female Suicide Bombers," Strategic Studies Institute Publication, June 2004, http://www.strategicstudiesinstitute.army.mil/pdffiles/PUB408.pdf, 9.

47. Anne Speckhard and Khapta Akhmedova, "Black Widows: The Chechen Female Suicide Terrorists," in Schweitzer, *Female Suicide Bombers*, 63–80.

48. Ibid., 67–69.

49. Zedalis, "Female Suicide Bombers," 12.

50. Ibid., 11.

51. Mira Tzoreff, "The Palestinian *Shahida*: National Patriotism, Islamic Fundamentalism, or Social Crisis," in Schweitzer, *Female Suicide Bombers*, 14.

52. Victor, *Army of Roses*, 167; interview with Lisa Ling, "Female Suicide Bombers: Dying to Kill," *National Geographic Explorer*, "Lisa Ling Investigates," December 13, 2004.

53. Victor, *Army of Roses*, 168.

54. Tzoreff, "Palestinian *Shahida*," 18–19.

55. Ibid., 19.

56. Ahiya Raved, "Study: Female Suicide Bombers Seek Atonement," *Israel News, ynet news.com.* 1/10/06, 23:11. http://www.ynetnews.com/articles/0,7340,L-3198362,00.html.

57. Nawal al-Sa'adawi, *Kul al-'Arab*, December 24, 2004, Middle East Media Research Institute (MEMRI), *Special Dispatch Series* no. 876, March 10, 2005, quoted in Rivka Yadlin, "Female Martyrdom: The Ultimate Embodiment of Islamic Existence?" in Schweitzer, *Female Suicide Bombers*, 53 n. 8.

58. Ibid., 58.

59. Issacharoff, "Palestinian and Israeli Media," 48.

60. Schweitzer, *Female Suicide Bombers*, 34.

61. Skaine, *Female Suicide Bombers*, 51; Pape, *Dying to Win*, 227. According to all accounts, its first use was by Dhanu (Thenmuli Rajaratnam), the Tamil Tigress who assassinated Rajiv Gandhi in 1991.

62. Victor, *Army of Roses*, 106–7; 245–46.

63. Schweitzer, *Female Suicide Bombers*, 28.

64. Victor, *Army of Roses*, 106.

65. Bennet, "Scholar of English," sec. A1.

66. Issacharoff, "Palestinian and Israeli Media," 48.

67. Anne Marie Oliver, "Brides of Palestine," *Salon.com Life*, July 20, 2006, http://www.salon.com/mwt/feature/2006/07/20/suicide_bombers/print.html.

68. Reported in the blog, *Headlines and Deadlines: Canadian Media and the Middle East: Website of Honest Reporting, Canada*, Wednesday, November 29, 2006, posted at 12:16 p.m., http://blog.honestreporting.ca/my_weblog/2006/11/index.html.

69. Schweitzer, *Female Suicide Bombers*, 40.

70. Oliver, "Brides of Palestine," 3; Schweitzer, "Introduction" to Schweitzer, *Female Suicide Bombers*, 7.

71. Oliver, "Brides of Palestine," 3; Maria Alvanou, "Criminological Perspectives on Female Suicide Terrorism," in Schweitzer, *Female Suicide Bombers*, 105 n. 40.

72. Tzoreff, "Palestinian *Shahida*," 20.

73. Oliver, "Brides of Palestine," 2; Mahmood in Yadlin, "Female Martyrdom," 58.

74. Schweitzer, "Introduction," 11.

75. Castelli, *Martyrdom and Memory*, 201.

76. Ibid., 172.

77. Gail P. C. Streete, "Buying the Stairway to Heaven," in Levine, *A Feminist Companion to the New Testament Apocrypha*, 205.

List of Ancient Sources

Acta Pauli et Theclae. In *Acta Apostolorum Apocrypha*, edited, according to the edition of Constantine Tischendorff, by R. A. Lipsius and M. Bonnet. Vol. 1: 235–72. Leipzig: Hermann Mendelssohn, 1891.

"Acts of Paul and Theclae." ET, in *New Testament Apocrypha*. Edited by Edgar Hennecke and Wilhelm Schneemelcher. Philadelphia: Westminster Press, 1963–65. Vol. 2: 353–64.

Acts of Paul and Thecla. Translated by Jeremiah Jones. Saint Pachomius Orthodox Library, September/October 1995. http://www.fordham.edu/halsall/basis/thecla.html.

Amat, Jacqueline. *Passion de Perpétue et de Félicité suivi les Actes*. SC 417. Paris: Les Éditions du Cerf, 1996.

Ambrose. *On Virginity*. PL 16:197–243. ET, *NPNF²* 10:361–87.

Ante-Nicene Fathers. 10 vols. Edited by Alexander Roberts and James Donaldson. Revised by A. Cleveland Coxe. Reprint, Grand Rapids: Wm. B. Eerdmans Publishing Co., 1994–97. Christian Classics Ethereal Library. http://www.ccel.org/fathers.html.

Aristotle. *De anima* (*On the Soul*). Edited and annotated by W. D. Ross. OCT. Oxford: Clarendon Press, 1956.

———. *De anima. Books II and III* (*With Passages from Book I*). Translated with an introduction and notes by D. W. Hamlyn. Oxford: Oxford University Press, 1993.

———. *De generatione animalium* (*On the Generation of Animals*). Edited and annotated by H. J. Drossaart Lulofs. OCT. Oxford: Clarendon Press, 1965.

———. *Politica* (*Politics*). Edited and annotated by W. D. Ross. OCT. Oxford: Clarendon Press, 1957. Reprint, 1964.

Augustine. *The City of God*. PL 41:13–806. ET, *NPNF¹* 2:1–511.

———. *Expositions on the Psalms*, 120 and 137. PL 37:1605–18; 37:1774–84. ET, *NPNF¹* 8:532–683.

———. *On Sacred Virginity*. PL 40:395–428. ET, *NPNF¹* 3:417–38.

———. *On the Good of Marriage*. PL 40:373–96. ET, *NPNF¹* 3:397–413.

———. *On the Soul and Its Origin*. PL 44:475–548. ET, *NPNF¹* 5:315–71.

———. *Sermons*. PL 38 and 39.

Cyprian. *An Exhortation to Martyrdom*. PL 4:677–702. ET, *ANF* 5:347–50.

_____. *Letters.* PL 4:191–438. ET, *ANF* 5:275–409.

_____. *On the Dress of Virgins.* PL 4:451–78. ET, *ANF* 5:430–36.

_____. *On the Glory of Martyrdom.* PL 4:817–34. ET, *ANF* 5:579–87.

Dagron, Gilbert. *Vie et miracles de sainte Thècle: Texte grec, traduction et commentaire.* Subsidia Hagiographica 62. Brussels: Société des Bollandistes, 1978.

Egeria. *Siluiae aut potius Aetheriae peregrinatio.* Edited by W. Heraeus. Heidelberg, 1908. In *Bibliotheca Augustana, Itinerarium Egeriae, ca. 380.* http://www.hs-augsburg.de/~harsch/Chronological/Lpost04/Egeria/ege_it23.html.

Epictetus. *Enchiridion.* In Classics Archive. Edited by Elizabeth Carter. http://classics.mit.edu/Epictetus/epicench.html.

Eusebius of Caesarea. *History of the Church* (*Historia ecclesiastica*). PG 20:45–906. ET, *NPNF* [2] 1:1–387.

————. *History of the Church from Christ to Constantine.* Translated and with an introduction by G. A. Williamson. New York: New York University Press, 1966.

Gregory of Nazianzus. *Concerning His Own Life* (*De vita sua*). PG 37:1029–165.

————. *Concerning His Own Life.* In *Saint Gregory of Nazianzus: Three Poems.* Translated by Denis Molaise Meehan, 75–130. Fathers of the Church 75. Washington, DC: Catholic University of America Press, 1986.

Gregory of Nyssa. *Homilies on the Song of Songs, Homily 14.* PG 44:1062–88.

————. *Life of Macrina.* PG 46:462–998. Translated by W. K. Lowther Clarke. London: SPCK, 1916. In *Internet Medieval Sourcebook*, edited by Paul Halsall. http://www.fordham.edu/halsall/basis/macrina.html.

————. *On the Soul and the Resurrection.* PG 46:11–160. ET, *NPNF* [2] 5:430–68.

Hanson, K. C. *Collection of Latin Documents.* http://www.kchanson.com/ANCDOCS/latin/latin.html.

Ignatius of Antioch. *To the Romans.* PG 5:685–96. ET, *ANF* 1:73–78; *Early Christian Writings.* http://www.ccel.org/ccel/schaff/anf01.v.v.html.

Jacopo da Voragine. *Golden Legend.* Translated by William Caxton. Temple Classics. Edited by F. S. Ellis. In *Internet Medieval Sourcebook*, edited by Paul Halsall. http:www.fordham.edu/halsall/basis/goldenlegend.

Jerome. *Chronicle.* (*Chronici Canones.*) PL 27:675–702. ET, in *Selected Fathers of the Church.* Edited by Roger Pearse. Christian Classics Ethereal Library. http://www.ccel.org/ccel/pearse/morefathers.html.

————. *Letters.* PL 30:13–307. ET, *NPNF* [2] 6:1–295.

————. *On Famous Men.* PL 23:631–760. ET, *NPNF* [2] 3:359–84.

Libanius. *Selected Letters of Libanius: From the Age of Constantius and Julian.* Translated with an introduction by Scott Bradbury. Liverpool: Liverpool University Press, 2004.

Methodius of Olympus. *Symposium* (*Banquet of the Ten Virgins*). PG 18:27–240. ET, *ANF* 6:309–55.

Musurillo, Herbert R., introduction, text, and translation. *Acts of the Christian Martyrs.* Oxford: Oxford University Press, 1972.

————. *Acts of the Pagan Martyrs* (*Acta Alexandrinum*). Oxford: Clarendon Press, 1954.

Nicene and Post-Nicene Fathers. 1st series. 14 vols. Edited by Alexander Roberts, James Donaldson, and Philip Schaff. 2nd series. 14 vols. Edited by Alexander Roberts, James Donaldson, Philip Schaff, and Henry Wace. Reprint, Grand Rapids: Wm. B. Eerdmans Publishing Co., 1994–97. Christian Classics Ethereal Library. http://www.ccel.org/fathers.html.

Origen. *Contra Celsum* (*Against Celsus*). PG 11:641–1632. ET, *ANF* 4:395–669.

————. *Contra Celsum.* Translated with an introduction by Henry Chadwick. Cambridge: Cambridge University Press, 1953.

Palladius. *Lausiac History.* PG 34:995–1262.

————. *Lausiac History.* Translated by W. K. L. Clarke. London: SPCK, 1918. In *Internet Medieval Sourcebook*, edited by Paul Halsall. http://www/fordham.edu/halsall/basis/palladius-lausiac.html.

Passio sanctarum martyrum Perpetuae et Felicitatis. PL 3:13–62. ET, *ANF* 3:697–706.

Patterson, Stephen, and Marvin Meyer. *The Gospel of Thomas.* In *The Complete Gospels: Annotated Scholars Version.* Edited by Robert J. Miller. Santa Rosa, CA: Polebridge Press, 1992. Rev. and exp. ed., 1994.

Plato. *Complete Works.* Translated by John Cooper. Indianapolis: Hackett, 1997.

————. *Platonis Opera.* Edited and annotated by John Burnet. 5 vols. Oxford Classical Texts. Oxford: Clarendon Press, 1900–1907. Reprint, 1967.

Pliny the Younger. *Fifty Letters of Pliny.* Selected and edited by A. N. Sherwin-White. 2nd ed. Oxford: Oxford University Press, 2000.

————. *Letters of Pliny the Younger.* With an introduction by John Firth. Public domain ET, http://ancienthistory.about.com/library/bl/bl_text_plinyltrs3.htm.

Pontius the Deacon. *The Life and Passion of Cyprian, Bishop and Martyr.* PL 3:1541–58. ET, *ANF* 5:267–74.

Pseudo-Basil of Seleucia. *Life and Miracles of Saint Thecla, Virgin and Martyr of Iconium.* PG 85:477–618.

Quodvultdeus (Pseudo-Augustine). *On the Time of the Barbarians.* PL 40:699–708.

Seneca. *Ad Lucilium Epistulae Morales.* Translated by Richard Gummere. London: William Heinemann, 1918.

Tacitus. *Annalum libri.* Edited and annotated by C. D. Fisher. OCT. Oxford: Clarendon Press, 1906. Reprint, 1953.

————. *Annales.* Translated by Alfred John Church and William Jackson Broadribb. *Internet Ancient History Sourcebook*, edited by Paul Halsall. http://www.fordham.edu/halsall/ancient/tacitus-ann15a.html.

Tertullian. *Apologetic.* PL 1:305–604. ET, *ANF* 3:17–55.

————. *Exhortation to Chastity.* PL 2:913–30. ET, *ANF* 4:50–58.

————. *On Baptism.* PL 1:1305–34. ET, *ANF* 3:181–235.

————. *On the Soul*. PL 2:641–752. ET, *ANF* 3:181–235.

————. *On the Veiling of Virgins*. PL 2:887–914. ET, *ANF* 4:27–37.

————. *On Women's Apparel*. PL 1:1417–48. ET, *ANF* 4:14–25.

————. *To His Wife*. PL 1:1385–1418. ET, *ANF* 4:39–49.

————. *To Scapula*. PL 1:773–84. ET, *ANF* 3:105–8.

————. *To the Martyrs*. PL 1:691–702. ET, *ANF* 3:693–96.

————. *To the Nations*. PL 1:629–80. ET, *ANF* 3:109–47.

van Beek, C. J. M. J. [Cornelius Johannes Maria Joseph], editor. *Passio Sanctarum Perpetuae et Felicitatis*. Vol. 1. Nijmegen: Dekker & Van de Vegt, 1936. Vol. 2. Bonn: [Peter Hanstein?], 1938.

Bibliography

The Apocryphal Acts of the Apostles. Guest editor, Dennis R. MacDonald. *Semeia* 38. Atlanta: Scholars Press, 1986.

"As Christians Vanish from Their Cradle." *Zenda* 4, no. 19 (July 27, 1998). Reprinted with permission from *The Economist*, July 18, 1998. http://www.zindamagazine.com/html/archives/1998/july27_1998.htm.

Aymer, Margaret P. "Hailstorms and Fireballs: Redaction, World Creation and Resistance in the *Acts of Paul and Thecla*." *Semeia* 79 (1997): 45–62.

Barnes, Timothy. *Tertullian: A Historical and Literary Study*. Oxford: Clarendon Press, 1971.

Barnett, Sarah. "Death and the Maidens: Women Martyrs and Their Sexual Identity in the Early Christian Period." *culture@home*. http://www.sydneyanglicans.net/culture/thinking/369a.

Barton, Carlin A. "Savage Miracles: The Redemption of Lost Honor in Roman Society and the Sacrament of the Gladiator and the Martyr." *Representations*, no. 45 (Winter 1994): 41–71.

Bennet, James. "A Scholar of English Who Clung to the Veil." *New York Times*, May 30, 2003, sec. A1 and A14.

Bernall, Misty. *She Said Yes: The Unlikely Martyrdom of Cassie Bernall*. With an introduction by Madeleine L'Engle. Farmington, PA: Plough Publishing House, 1999.

Bomgardner, David L. "The Carthage Amphitheater: A Reappraisal." *AJA* 93, no. 1 (1989): 85–103.

Boughton, Lynne C. "From Pious Legend to Feminist Fantasy." *JR* 71, no. 3 (July 1991): 362–83.

Bowersock, G. W. *Martyrdom and Rome*. Wiles Lectures, Queen's University, Belfast. Cambridge: Cambridge University Press, 1998.

Boyarin, Daniel. "Body Politic among the Brides of Christ: Paul and the Origins of Christian Sexual Renunciation." In *Asceticism*, edited by Vincent L. Wimbush and Richard R. Valantasis, with the assistance of Gay Byron and William S. Love, 458–78. Oxford: Oxford University Press, 1995.

———. *Dying for God: Martyrdom and the Making of Christianity and Judaism*. Stanford, CA: Stanford University Press, 1999.

Bremmer, Jan N., ed. *The Apocryphal Acts of Paul and Thecla*. Louvain: Peeters Publishers, 1996.

———. "Drusiana, Cleopatra, and Some Other Women in the *Acts of John*." In *A Feminist Companion to the New Testament Apocrypha*, edited by Amy-Jill Levine with Maria Mayo Robbins, 77–87. London: T&T Clark, 2006.

———. "Magic, Martyrdom and Women's Liberation in the *Acts of Paul and Thecla*." In *The Apocryphal Acts of Paul and Thecla*, edited by Jan N. Bremmer, 36–59. Kampen, Netherlands: Kok Pharos, 1996.

———. "The Motivation of Martyrs: Perpetua and the Palestinians." In *Religion im kulturellen Diskurs*, edited by B. Luchesi and K. Von Stuckrad, 535–54. Berlin: Walter de Gruyter, 2004.

———."Perpetua and Her Diary." *Märtyrer und Märtyrakten*. Edited by Walter Ameling, 77–120. Stuttgart: Steiner, 2002.

Brock, Sebastian, and Susan Ashbrook Harvey, intro. and trans. *Holy Women of the Syrian Orient*. 2nd ed. Berkeley: University of California Press, 1998.

Brooten, Bernadette. *Love between Women: Early Christian Responses to Female Homoeroticism*. Chicago: University of Chicago Press, 1996.

Brown, Peter. *The Body and Society: Men, Women, and Sexual Renunciation in Early Christianity*. New York: Columbia University Press, 1988.

———. *The Cult of the Saints: Its Rise and Function in Late Antiquity*. Chicago: University of Chicago Press, 1981.

———. *Society and the Holy in Late Antiquity*. Berkeley: University of California Press, 1981.

Burkert, Walter. *Greek Religion*. Translated by John Raffan. Cambridge, MA: Harvard University Press, 1985.

Burns, J. Patout. "Authority and Power: The Role of the Martyrs in the African Church in the Fifth Century." In "Devotion and Dissent: The Practice of Christianity in Roman North Africa," Interdisciplinary Working Group for the Study of Christianity in North Africa during the Second through the Seventh Centuries, Vanderbilt University, Version: June 12, 1998. http://people.vanderbilt.edu/~james.p.burns/chroma/saints/martburn.html.

Burris, Catherine, and Lucas Van Rompay. "Some Further Notes on Thecla in Syriac Christianity." *Hugoye: Journal of Syriac Studies* 6, no.2 (July 2003). http://syrcom.cua.edu/syrcom/Hugoye/Vol6No2/HV6N2BurrisVanRompay.html.

———. "Thecla in Syriac Christianity: Preliminary Observations." *Hugoye: Journal of Syriac Studies* 5, no. 2 (July 2002). http://syrcom.cua.edu/surcom/Hugoye/Vol5No2/HV5NBurrisVanRompay.html.

Burrus, Virginia. *Chastity as Autonomy: Women in the Stories of the Apocryphal Acts*. Studies in Women and Religion 23. Lewiston, NY: Edwin Mellen Press, 1987.

———. "Macrina's Tattoo." *Journal of Medieval and Early Modern Studies* 33, no. 3 (2003): 403–17.

Cameron, Averil. *Christianity and the Rhetoric of Empire*. Sather Classical Lectures 55. Berkeley: University of California Press, 1991.

Cardman, Francine. "Acts of the Women Martyrs." *AThR* 70, no. 2 (1988): 144–50.

————. "Whose Life Is It? The *Vita Macrinae* of Gregory of Nyssa." In *Papers Presented at the 13th International Conference on Patristic Studies, Held in Oxford, 1999: Cappadocian Writers; Other Greek Writers,* edited by M. L. Wiles and E. J. Yarnold, with the assistance of P. M. Parvis, 33–50. St Patr 37. Louvain: Peeters, 2001.

————. "Women, Ministry and Church Order in Early Christianity." In *Women and Christian Origins,* edited by Ross S. Kraemer and Mary Rose D'Angelo, 300–29. New York: Oxford University Press, 1999.

Castelli, Elizabeth. *Martyrdom and Memory: Early Christian Culture Making.* New York: Columbia University Press, 2005.

Changing Bodies, Changing Meanings: Studies on the Human Body in Antiquity. Edited by Dominic Montserrat. London: Routledge, 1998.

Church, F. F. "Sex and Seduction in Tertullian." *HTR* 68 (1975): 83–101.

Clark, Elizabeth A. "Ascetic Renunciation and Feminine Advancement: A Paradox of Late Ancient Christianity." *AThR* 63 (1981): 240–57.

————. "The Celibate Bridegroom and His Virginal Brides: Metaphor and the Marriage of Jesus in Early Christian Ascetic Exegesis." *CH* 77, no. 19 (March 2008): 1–25.

————."Holy Women, Holy Words: Early Christian Women, Social History, and the 'Linguistic Turn,'" *JECS* 6, no. 3 (1998): 413–30.

————. "Ideology, History, and the Construction of 'Woman' in Late Antique Christianity." *JECS* 2, no. 2 (1994): 155–84.

————. *Women in the Early Church.* Message of the Fathers of the Church 13. Wilmington, DE: Michael Glazier, 1983.

Clark, Gillian. "Bodies and Blood: Late Antique Debate on Martyrdom, Virginity and Resurrection." In *Changing Bodies, Changing Meanings,* edited by Dominic Montserrat, 99–115. London: Routledge, 1998.

————. *Women in Late Antiquity: Pagan and Christian Lifestyles.* Oxford: Clarendon Press, 1993.

Cloke, Gillian. *This Female Man of God: Women and Spiritual Power in the Patristic Age AD 350–450.* London: Routledge, 1995.

Coffman, Elesha. "A Cave of One's Own." *Christianity Today,* February 4, 2000. http://www.christianitytoday.com/history/newsletter/2000/feb04.html.

"Columbine Families Mourn Virginia Tech." *CBS News.com,* April 20, 2007. http://www.cbsnews.com/stories/2007/04/20/columbine/main2709495 .shtml.

Cooper, Kate. "Insinuations of Womanly Influence: An Aspect of the Christianization of the Roman Aristocracy." *JRelS* 82 (1992): 150–64.

————. "A Saint in Exile: The Early Medieval Thecla at Rome and Meriamlik." *Hagiographica* 2 (1995): 1–23.

———. *The Virgin and the Bride: Idealized Womanhood in Late Antiquity*. Cambridge, MA: Harvard University Press, 1996.

Crossan, John Dominic, and Jonathan L. Reed. *In Search of Paul: How Jesus's Apostle Opposed Rome's Empire with God's Kingdom: A New Vision of Paul's Words and World*. San Francisco: HarperCollins, 2004.

Crump, J. J. "Syllabus on Medieval Women." University of Washington History Department, HSTAM 340 (Winter Quarter, 2003). http://home.myuw.net/jjcrump/courses/medWomen/aonwomen.html.

Cullen, Dave. "Who Said 'Yes'?" *Salon.com News*, September 30, 1999. http://www.salon.com/news/feature/1999/09/30/bernall.

D'Angelo, Mary Rose. "*Eusebeia:* Roman Imperial Family Values and the Sexual Politics of 4 Maccabees and the Pastorals." *BibInt* 11, no. 2 (2003): 139–265.

Davies, Stevan L. *The Revolt of the Widows: The Social World of the Apocryphal Acts*. Carbondale: Southern Illinois University Press, 1980.

———. "Women, Tertullian, and the *Acts of Paul*." *Semeia* 38 (1986): 139–49.

Davis, Stephen J. "Crossed Texts, Crossed Sex: Intertextuality and Gender in Early Christian Legends of Holy Women Disguised as Men." *JECS* 10, no.1 (2002): 1–36.

———. *The Cult of Saint Thecla: A Tradition of Women's Piety in Late Antiquity*. Oxford: Oxford University Press, 2001.

———. "A Pauline Defense of Women's Right to Baptize? Intertextuality and Apostolic Authority in the *Acts of Paul*." *JECS* 8, no. 2 (2000): 453–59.

Dearn, Alan. "Voluntary Martyrdom and the Donatist Schism." In *Papers Presented at the 14th International Conference on Patristic Studies Held in Oxford 2003: History, Biblical et Hagiographica*, edited by F. Young, M. Edwards, and P. Parvis, 27–32. St Patr 39. Louvain: Peeters, 2003.

Doran, Robert. "The Martyr: A Synoptic of the Mother and Her Seven Sons." In *Ideal Figures in Ancient Judaism*, edited by John J. Collins and G. W. E. Nickelsburg, 183–221. SBLSCS 12. Chico, CA: Scholars Press, 1980.

Droge, Arthur, and James D. Tabor. *A Noble Death: Suicide and Martyrdom among Christians and Jews in Antiquity*. San Francisco: HarperCollins, 1992.

Dronke, Peter. *Women Writers of the Middle Ages: A Critical Study of Tests from Perpetua (†203) to Marguerite Porete (†1310)*. Cambridge: Cambridge University Press, 1984.

Du Bois, Page. *Sappho Is Burning*. Chicago: University of Chicago Press, 1995.

———. *Sowing the Body: Psychoanalysis and Ancient Representations of Women*. Chicago: University of Chicago Press, 1987.

Ehrman, Bart D. *The New Testament and Other Early Christian Writings: A Reader*. New York: Oxford University Press, 1998.

Elliott, Allison Goddard. *Roads to Paradise: Reading the Lives of the Early Saints*. Hanover, NH: New England Press for Brown University, 1987.

Elliott, John K. Review of *A Feminist Companion to the New Testament Apocrypha*. Edited by Amy-Jill Levine, with Maria Mayo Robbins. *RBL* 2 (2008). http:// www.bookreviews.org/pdf/5408_5702.pdf.

Elm, Susannah. *"Virgins of God": The Making of Asceticism in Late Antiquity*. Oxford: Clarendon Press, 1994.

Erskine, Mark. "Is Martyrdom the Answer?" Unpublished paper, Humanities 102. Rhodes College, 1999.

Ferwerda, R. "The Meaning of the Word σῶμα (Body) in the Axial Age: An Interpretation of Plato's *Cratylus* 400C." In *The Origins and Diversity of Axial Age Civilizations*, edited by Shmuel Noah Eisenstadt, 11–126. Albany, NY: SUNY Press, 1986.

Festugière, A.-J. *Sainte Thècle, saints Côme et Damien, saints Cyr et Jean (extraits), saint George*. Paris: Éditions A. et J. Picard, 1971.

Frend, W. H. C. "Blandina and Perpetua: Two Early Christian Heroines." In *Les Martyres de Lyon (177)*. Colloques Internationaux du Centre National de la Recherche Scientifique, no. 575, 167–77. Paris: Éditions de Centre National de la Recherche Scientifique, 1978.

———. *Martyrdom and Persecution in the Early Church: Study of a Conflict from the Maccabees to Donatus*. Garden City, NY: Doubleday/Anchor, 1967.

Fridh, Åke. *Le problème de la passion des Saintes Perpétue et Félicité*. Stockholm: Almqvist & Wiksell, 1968.

Gilligan, Carol. *In a Different Voice: Psychological Theory and Women's Development*. Cambridge, MA: Harvard University Press, 1982. Reprint, 1994.

Godfrey, Mark. Review of *The Rising*, by Bruce Springsteen. http://cluas.com/music/albums/bruce-springsteen.htm.

Goodine, Elizabeth A., and Matthew W. Mitchell. "The Persuasiveness of a Woman: The Mistranslation and Misinterpretation of Eusebius' *HE* 5.1.41." *JECS* 13, no. 1 (2005): 1–19.

Gwynne, S. C. "An Act of God?" *Time Magazine*, December 20, 1999, 58.

Harrison, Verna E. F. "Gender, Generation, and Virginity in Cappadocian Theology." *JTS* 47, no.1 (1996): 38–68.

Hasan-Rokem, Galit. *Web of Life: Folklore and Midrash in Rabbinic Literature*. Translated by Batya Stein. Stanford, CA: Stanford University Press, 2000.

Hasofferett, Corinna. "The Woman and Her Seven Sons." "Time in Tel Aviv." December 15, 2004. http://timeintelaviv.blogspot.com/2004_12_01_timeintelaviv_archives.html.

Hayne, Léonie. "Thecla and the Church Fathers." *VC* 48 (1994): 209–18.

Heffernan, Thomas. *Sacred Biography: Saints and Their Biographers in the Middle Ages*. New York: Oxford University Press, 1988.

Honey, Linda. Review of *The Life and Miracles of Thekla: A Literary Study*, by Scott Fitzgerald Johnson. *Bryn Mawr Classical Review*, August 19, 2006. http://ccat.sas.upenn.edu/bmcr/2006/2006-08-19.html.

Ide, A. F. *Martyrdom of Women: A Study of Death Psychology in the Early Christian Church to 301 CE.* Garland, TX: Tangelwüld Press, 1985.

"Iraqi Martyr Shamed Family (News)." *The Cincinnati Post,* Cincinnati, OH, May 31, 2003. *High Beam Research.* http://www.highbeam.com/doc/1G1-102664380.html.

Irwin, M. Eleanor. "Gender, Status and Identity in a North African Martyrdom, 203 CE." In *Gli imperatori Severi: storia, archaeologia, religione,* edited by Enrico Dal Covolo and Giancarlo Rinaldi, 251–60. Rome: LAS, 1999. http://nemiship.multiservers.com/severi/perpetua.htm.

Issacharoff, Avi. "The Palestinian and Israeli Media on Female Suicide Terrorists." In *Female Suicide Bombers: Dying for Equality?* edited by Yoram Schweitzer, 43–50. Memorandum no. 84. Tel Aviv University: Jaffee Center for Strategic Studies, August 2006.

Jacobs, Andrew S. "'Her Own Proper Kinship': Marriage, Class and Women in the Apocryphal Acts of the Apostles." In *A Feminist Companion to the New Testament Apocrypha,* edited by Amy-Jill Levine, with Maria Mayo Robbins, 18–46. London: T&T Clark, 2006. Previously published as "A Family Affair: Marriage, Class, and Ethics in the Apocryphal Acts of the Apostles," *JECS* 7, no. 1 (1999): 105–38.

Jensen, Anne. *God's Self-Confident Daughters: Early Christianity and the Liberation of Women.* Translated by O. C. Dean. Louisville, KY: Westminster John Knox Press, 1996.

Johnson, Gregory. "The Martyrdom of Perpetua and Felicitas: An Analysis of Some Pertinent Issues." http://gregscouch.homestead.com/files/Perpetua.html.

Johnson, Scott Fitzgerald. *The Life and Miracles of Thekla: A Literary Study.* Hellenic Studies 13. Washington DC: Center for Hellenic Studies, 2006.

King, Helen. *Hippocrates' "Woman": Reading the Female Body in Ancient Greece.* New York: Routledge, 1998.

Klawiter, Frederick C. "The Role of Martyrdom and Persecution in Developing the Priestly Authority of Women in Early Christianity: A Case Study in Montanism." *CH* 49, no. 3 (September 1980): 251–61.

Kloppenborg, R., and W. J. Hanegraaff, eds. *Female Stereotypes in Religious Traditions.* Leiden: E. J. Brill, 1995.

Kraemer, Ross S. "The Conversion of Women to Ascetic Forms of Christianity." *Signs* 6 (1980): 298–307.

———, ed. *Maenads, Martyrs, Matrons, Monastics: A Sourcebook on Women's Religions in the Greco-Roman World.* Philadelphia: Fortress Press, 1988.

———. *When Joseph Met Aseneth: A Late Antique Tale of the Biblical Patriarch and His Egyptian Wife.* New York: Oxford University Press, 1998.

Lefkowitz, Mary R. "The Motivations for St. Perpetua's Martyrdom." *JAAR* 44, no. 3 (1976): 417–21.

Lefkowitz, Mary R., and Maureen B. Fant, eds. *Women's Life in Greece and Rome.* 2nd ed. Baltimore: Johns Hopkins University Press, 1992.

Levine, Amy-Jill. *The Misunderstood Jew: The Church and the Scandal of the Jewish Jesus.* New York: HarperOne, 2007.

Lifshitz, Felice. "The Martyr, the Tomb, and the Matron: Gendering the Past, 313–794." *Medieval Feminist Newsletter* 21 (Spring 1996): 30–32.

Loraux, Nicole. *Tragic Ways of Killing a Woman.* Translated by Anthony Forster. Cambridge, MA: Harvard University Press, 1987.

Luce, Stephen B. "Archaeological News and Discussions: Early Christian and Byzantine." *AJA* 47, no. 1 (January–March 1943): 120–24.

MacDonald, Dennis R. *The Legend and the Apostle: The Battle for Paul in Story and Canon.* Philadelphia: Westminster Press, 1983.

———. *There Is No Male and Female: The Fate of a Dominical Saying in Paul and Gnosticism.* HDR 20. Philadelphia: Fortress Press, 1987.

MacDonald, Dennis R., and Andrew D. Scrimgeour. "Pseudo-Chrysostom's Panegyric to Thecla: The Heroine of the *Acts of Paul* in Homily and Art." *Semeia* 38 (1986): 151–59.

MacDonald, Margaret Y. *Early Christian Women and Pagan Opinion: The Power of the Hysterical Woman.* Cambridge: Cambridge University Press, 1996.

Matthews, Shelly. "Thinking of Thecla: Issues in Feminist Historiography." *JFSR* 17, no. 2 (Fall 2001): 39–55.

McGinn, Sheila E. "The Acts of Thecla." In *Searching the Scriptures,* vol. 2, *A Feminist Commentary,* edited by Elisabeth Schüssler Fiorenza, 800–28. New York: Crossroad, 1994.

McGuckin, John A. *St. Gregory of Nazianzus: An Intellectual Biography.* Crestwood, NY: St. Vladimir's Seminary Press, 2001.

McLaughlin, Eleanor. "The Christian Past: Does It Hold a Future for Women?" *AThR* 57 (1975): 36–56.

Meadow, James B. "Teens 'Radiant,' Forever Young." *Rocky Mountain News .com,* April 26, 1999. http://denver.rockymountainnews.com/shooting/0426 doub5.shtml.

Meskell, Lynn. "The Irresistible Body and the Seduction of Archaeology." In *Changing Bodies, Changing Meanings,* edited by Dominic Montserrat, 139–61. London: Routledge, 1998.

Meyers, Carol. "Where the Girls Are: Archaeology and Women's Lives in Ancient Israel." In *Between Text and Artifact: Integrating Archaeology in Biblical Studies Teaching,* edited by Milton Moreland, 31–51. Atlanta: SBL, 2003.

Miles, Margaret R. *Carnal Knowing: Female Nakedness and Religious Meaning in the Christian West.* Boston: Beacon Press, 1989.

———. *Image as Insight: Visual Understanding in Western Christianity and Secular Culture.* Boston: Beacon Press, 1985.

———. "Patriarchy as Political Theology: The Establishment of North African Christianity." In *Civil Religion and Political Theology,* edited by Leroy S. Rouner, 169–86. Notre Dame, IN: Notre Dame University Press, 1986.

Miller, Patricia Cox. *Dreams in Late Antiquity: Studies in the Imagination of a Culture.* Princeton, NJ: Princeton University Press, 1994.

————. "Is There a Harlot in This Text? Hagiography and the Grotesque." *Journal of Medieval and Early Modern Studies* 33, no. 3 (Fall 2003): 419–35.

————. *Women in Early Christianity: Translations from Greek Texts.* Washington, DC: Catholic University of America Press, 2005.

Misset-van de Weg, Magda. "Answers to the Plights of an Ascetic Woman Named Thecla." In *A Feminist Companion to the New Testament Apocrypha,* edited by Amy-Jill Levine, with Maria Mayo Robbins, 146–62. London: T&T Clark, 2006.

Molinari, Andrea Lorenzo. *Climbing the Dragon's Ladder: The Martyrdom of Perpetua and Felicitas.* Illustrations by Tyler J. Walpole. Eugene, OR: Wipf & Stock, 2006.

————. "Climbing the Dragon's Ladder: Perpetua, Felicitas, Graphic Novels, and the Possibility of Writing Modern Hagiography." *SBL Forum* 1/30/2007–3/8/2007. http://www.sbl-site.org/publications/article.aspx?articleId=624.

Nauerth, Claudia, and Rüdiger Warns. *Thekla: Ihre Bilder in der frühchristlichen Kunst.* Wiesbaden: Harrassowitz, 1981.

Ng, Esther Yue L. "*Acts of Paul and Thecla*: Women's Studies and Precedent?" *JTS,* NS, vol. 55, no. 1 (April 2004): 1–29.

Nimmo, Beth. "Rachel's Legacy." *Rachel Joy Scott.com.* http://www.racheljoyscott.com/rachelslegacy.htm.

Nimmo, Beth, and Darrell Scott, with Scott Rabey. *Rachel's Tears: The Spiritual Journey of Columbine Martyr Rachel Scott.* Nashville: Thomas Nelson, 2000.

Oden, Amy, ed. *In Her Words: Women's Writings in the History of Christian Thought.* Nashville: Abingdon, 1994.

Oliver, Anne Marie. "Brides of Palestine." *Salon.com Life,* July 20, 2006. http://www.salon.com/mwt/feature/2006/07/20/suicide_bombers/print.html.

Osiek, Carolyn. "The Family in Early Christianity: 'Family Values' Revisited." *CBQ* 58, no. 1 (1996): 1–24.

————. "Perpetua's Husband." *JECS* 10, no. 1 (2002): 287–91.

"Palestinian Women Martyrs against the Israeli Occupation." http://www.aztlan.net/women_martyrs.htm.

Papathopoulos, Katharene. "Christian Asceticism." Unpublished paper, Religious Studies 301. Rhodes College, 2007.

Pape, Robert A. *Dying to Win: The Strategic Logic of Suicide Terrorism.* New York: Random House, 2005.

Perkins, Judith B. "The Apocryphal Acts of the Apostles and Early Christian Martyrdom." *Arethusa* 18 (1985): 211–30.

————. *The Suffering Self: Pain and Narrative Representation in the Early Christian Era.* London: Routledge, 1995.

Pesthy, Monika. "Thecla among the Fathers." In *The Apocryphal Acts of Paul and Thecla*, edited by Jan N. Bremmer, 164–78. Kampen, Netherlands: Kok Pharos, 1996.

Peterson, Amy Rachel. *In Perpetua: A Bride, a Martyr, a Passion.* Orlando, FL: Relevant Media Group, 2004.

Petterson, Alvyn. "Perpetua—Prisoner of Conscience." *VC* 41 (1987): 139–53.

Prinzivalli, Emanuela. "Perpetua the Martyr." In *Roman Women*, edited and with a new introduction by Augusto Fraschetti; translated by Linda Lappin, 118–40. Chicago: University of Chicago Press, 2001.

Rapp, Claudia. "Figures of Female Sanctity: Byzantine Edifying Manuscripts and Their Audience." *DOP* 50 (1996): 313–44.

Raved, Ahiya. "Study: Female Suicide Bombers Seek Atonement." *Israel News, ynet news.com* 1/10/06, 23:11. http://www.ynetnews.com/articles/0,7340,L-3198362,00.html.

Rhetorics of Resistance: A Colloquy on Early Christianity as Rhetorical Formation. Guest editor, Vincent Wimbush. *Semeia* 79. Atlanta: Scholars Press, 1997.

Ricci, Alessandra. "Interpreting Pilgrimage Centers: The Case of Ayatekla, Meriamlik." 16th Annual Byzantine Studies Conference, October 26–28, 1990. http://www.Tosana.net/conference/archives/1990/abstracts_1990.html.

Robeck, Cecil M. *Prophecy in Carthage: Perpetua, Tertullian and Cyprian.* Cleveland, OH: Pilgrim Press, 1992.

Ronsse, Erin. "Rhetoric of Martyrs: Listening to Saints Perpetua and Felicitas," *JECS* 14, no. 3 (2006): 283–327.

Rordorf, Willy. "Tradition and Composition in the Acts of Thecla: The State of the Question." *Semeia* 38 (1986): 43–52.

Rosin, Hanna. "Columbine Girl Who Really Said 'Yes' Shuns Fame." *Washington Post*, October 14, 1999, sec. C1.

Rossi, Mary Ann. "The Passion of Perpetua: Everywoman of Late Antiquity." *Pagan and Christian Anxiety: A Response to E. R. Dodds*, edited by Robert C. Smith and John Lounibos, 53–85. Lanham, MD: University Press of America, 1984.

Rubin, Alissa J. "Despair Drives Suicide: Attacks by Iraqi Women." *New York Times*, July 5, 2008. http://www.nytimes.com/2008/07/05/world/middleeast/05diyala.html?scp=1&sq=&st=nyt.

Russell, Jeffrey B. "Miracles and the Metanormal." http://www.veritas=ucsb.org/library/russell/Miracles.html.

Salisbury, Joyce E. *Perpetua's Passion: The Death and Memory of a Young Roman Woman.* New York: Routledge, 1997.

Scarry, Elaine. *The Body in Pain: The Making and Unmaking of the World.* New York: Oxford University Press, 1985.

Schlegel, Dom G. D. "The *Ad Martyras* of Tertullian and the Circumstances of Its Composition," *DRev* 61 (1943): 125–28.

Schüssler Fiorenza, Elisabeth. *In Memory of Her: A Feminist Reconstruction of Christian Origins*. New York: Crossroad, 1983.

Seaver, James Everett. *The Persecution of Jews in the Roman Empire (300–428)*. University of Kansas Publications, Humanistic Studies 30. Lawrence: University of Kansas Press, 1952.

Shaw, Brent D. "Body/Power/Identity: Passions of the Martyrs." *JECS* 4, no. 3 (1996): 269–312.

———. "The Passion of Perpetua—Christian Woman Martyred in Carthage in A.D. 203." *Past and Present* 56 (May 1993): 3–45.

Shaw, Teresa M. *The Burden of the Flesh: Fasting and Sexuality in Early Christianity*. Minneapolis: Fortress Press, 1998.

Shepard, Cyn. *A Columbine Site*. http://www.acolumbinesite.com.

Skaine, Rosemarie. *Female Suicide Bombers*. Jefferson, NC: McFarland, 2006.

Speckhard, Anne, and Kahpta Akhmedova. "Black Widows: The Chechen Female Suicide Terrorists." In *Female Suicide Bombers: Dying for Equality?* edited by Yoram Schweitzer, 63–80. Memorandum no. 84. Tel Aviv University: Jaffee Center for Strategic Studies, August 2006.

Springsteen, Bruce. "Paradise." *The Rising*. Columbia Audio compact disc CK 86600.

Steinhauser, Kenneth B. "Augustine's Reading of the *Passio sanctarum Perpetuae et Felicitatis*." In *Proceedings of the 12th Annual Conference on Patristic Studies, Held in Oxford, 1995: Augustine and His Opponents: Jerome, Other Latin Fathers after Nicea, Orientalia*, edited by Elizabeth A. Livingstone, 244–49. St Patr 33. Louvain: Peeters, 1997.

Streete, Gail P. C. (Gail Paterson Corrington, Gail Corrington Streete). "Authority and Authorship: *The Acts of Paul and Thecla* as a Disputed Pauline Text." *LTQ* 40, no. 4 (Winter 2005): 265–76.

———. "A Benefactor of Many and of Me Also." Unpublished paper delivered at the International SBL Annual Meeting, Vienna, Austria, June 22–26, 2007.

———. "Buying the Stairway to Heaven: Perpetua and Thecla as Early Christian Heroines." In *A Feminist Companion to the New Testament Apocrypha*, edited by Amy-Jill Levine, with Maria Mayo Robbins, 186–205. London: T&T Clark, 2006.

———. *The Divine Man: His Origin and Function in Hellenistic Popular Religion*. Berlin: Peter Lang, 1986.

———. "The 'Divine Woman'? Propaganda and the Power of Celibacy in the New Testament Apocrypha: A Reconsideration." *AThR* 80, no. 3 (July 1988): 207–23.

———. "The 'Divine Woman'? Propaganda and the Power of Chastity in the New Testament Apocrypha." In *Rescuing Creusa: New Methodological Approaches to the Study of Women in Antiquity*, edited by Marilyn B. Skinner, *Helios* 13, no. 2 (1986): 151–62.

———. "The 'Headless Woman': Paul and the Language of the Body in 1 Cor. 11:2–16." *PRSt* 18 (1991): 223–31.

———. "Of Martyrs and Men: Perpetua, Thecla, and the Ambiguity of Female Heroism in Early Christianity." In *The Subjective Eye: Essays in Culture, Religion, and Gender in Honor of Margaret R. Miles,* edited by Richard Valantasis, in collaboration with Deborah J. Haynes, James D. Smith III, and Janet F. Carlson, 254–64. Princeton Theological Monograph Series 59. Eugene, OR: Pickwick Publications, 2006.

———. "Perpetua's Passion: The Ethics of Martyrdom." Unpublished paper delivered at the ACTC (Association for Core Texts and Courses) Annual Conference, Dallas, TX, April 15–18, 2004.

———. "Sex, Spirit and Control: The Corinthian Women and Paul." In *Ritual, Power, and the Body: Historical Perspectives on the Representation of Greek Women,* edited by C. Nadia Seremetakis, 95–117. New York: Pella Press, 1993.

———. "Speaking and Silencing: The Female Martyr's 'Voice.'" Unpublished paper delivered at the AAR/SBL Annual Meeting, Toronto, Ontario, November 23–26, 2002.

———. *The Strange Woman: Power and Sex in the Bible.* Louisville, KY: Westminster John Knox Press, 1998.

———. "Women as Sources of Redemption and Knowledge in Early Christian Traditions." In *Women and Christian Origins,* edited by Ross Kraemer and Mary Rose D'Angelo, 330–54. New York: Oxford University Press, 1999.

Sullivan, Lisa M. "I Responded, 'I Will Not': Christianity as Catalyst for Resistance in the *Passio Perpetuae et Felicitatis.*" *Semeia* 79 (1997): 63–74.

Swan, Laura. *The Forgotten Desert Mothers.* New York: Paulist Press, 2001.

Tavard, George H. "Seeking the Kingdom." In *Woman in Christian Tradition,* 48–71. Notre Dame, IN: University of Notre Dame Press, 1973. http://www.womenpriests.org/classic2/tavard03.asp.

Tilley, Maureen A. "The Ascetic Body and the (Un)Making of the World of the Martyr." *JAAR* 59, no. 3 (Autumn 1991): 467–79.

———. *Donatist Martyr Stories: The Church in Conflict in North Africa.* Liverpool: Liverpool University Press, 1996.

———. "The Family of Faith: Relationships across the Boundary of Death." "The Practice of Christianity in North Africa: Death and Burial." Interdisciplinary Working Group for the Study of Christianity in North Africa during the Second through the Seventh Centuries, Vanderbilt University. http://people.vanderbilt.edu/~james.p.burns/chroma/burial/Tilleyburial.html.

———. "Harnessing the Martyrs: Social Control of Hagiography in Roman North Africa." Paper presented at North American Patristics Society, Chicago, May 30, 1998. http://www.people.vanderbilt.edu/~james.p.burns/chroma/saints/martilley.html.

———. "Managing the Rejection of Marriage: North African Asceticism." Interdisciplinary Working Group for the Study of Christianity in North

Africa during the Second through the Seventh Centuries, Vanderbilt University. http://people.vanderbilt.edu/~james.p.burns/chroma/marriage/tilleymar.htm.

———. "The Passion of Perpetua and Felicity." In *Searching the Scriptures,* vol. 2, *A Feminist Commentary,* edited by Elisabeth Schüssler Fiorenza, 829–58. New York: Crossroad, 1994.

Torjesen, Karen Jo. *When Women Were Priests: Women's Leadership in the Early Church and the Scandal of Their Subordination in the Rise of Christianity.* San Francisco: HarperSan Francisco, 1993.

Turcan, Marie. "Être femme selon Tertullien." *Vita Latina* 119 (September 1990): 15–21.

Tzoreff, Mira. "The Palestinian *Shahida*: National Patriotism, Islamic Fundamentalism, or Social Crisis." In *Female Suicide Bombers: Dying for Equality?* edited by Yoram Schweitzer, 13–23. Memorandum no. 84. Tel Aviv University: Jaffee Center for Strategic Studies, August 2006.

Valantasis, Richard R. "A Theory of the Social Function of Asceticism." In *Asceticism,* edited by Vincent L. Wimbush and Richard R. Valantasis, with the assistance of Gay Byron and William S. Love., 554–52. Oxford: Oxford University Press, 1995.

Van Henten, Jan Willem. *The Maccabean Martyrs as Saviours of the Jewish People: A Study of 2 and 4 Maccabees.* Supplements to the Journal for the Study of Judaism 57. Leiden: E. J. Brill, 1997.

Van Henten, Jan Willem, and Friedrich Avemarie. *Martyrdom and Noble Death: Selected Texts from Graeco-Roman, Jewish and Christian Antiquity.* London: Routledge, 2002.

Veenker, Jody. "Retailers: Marketing Martyrdom to Teens." *Christianity Today* 43, no. 14 (December 6, 1999). http://www.christianitytoday.com/ct/9te/9te22a.html.

Victor, Barbara. *Army of Roses: Inside the World of Palestinian Women Suicide Bombers.* Emmaus, PA: Rodale Press, 2003.

Vogt, Kari. "Becoming Male." Translated by Ruth Murphy. In *Women—Invisible in Church and Society,* edited by Elisabeth Schüssler Fiorenza and Mary Collins, 72–83. *Concilium* 182, no. 6 (1985). Edinburgh: T&T Clark, 1985.

Von Franz, Marie-Louise. *The Passion of Perpetua.* Irving, TX: Spring Publications, 1980.

Watson, Justin. *The Martyrs of Columbine: Faith and the Politics of Tragedy.* New York: Palgrave Macmillan, 2002.

Wicker, Kathleen O'Brien. "*Mulierum Virtutes (Moralia* 242E–263C)." In *Plutarch: Theological Writings and Early Christian Literature,* edited by H. D. Betz, 106–34. Leiden: E. J. Brill, 1975.

Wilfong, Terry. "Reading the Disjointed Body in Coptic: From Physical Modification to Textual Fragmentation." In *Changing Bodies, Changing Meanings,* edited by Dominic Montserrat, 116–36. London: Routledge, 1998. Pp. 276–97 in 1997 ed.

Wilson-Kastner, Patricia, et al. *A Lost Tradition: Women Writers of the Early Church*. Lanham, MD: University Press of America, 1981.

Yadlin, Rivka. "Female Martyrdom: The Ultimate Embodiment of Islamic Existence?" In *Female Suicide Bombers: Dying for Equality?* edited by Yoram Schweitzer, 51–61. Memorandum no. 84. Tel Aviv University: Jaffee Center for Strategic Studies, August 2006.

Young, Robin Darling. "The Woman with the Soul of Abraham: Traditions about the Mother of the Maccabean Martyrs." In *"Women Like This": New Perspectives on Jewish Women in the Greco-Roman World*, edited by Amy-Jill Levine, 67–81. SBLEJL. Atlanta: Scholars Press, 1991.

Zedalis, Debra D. "Female Suicide Bombers." Strategic Studies Institute Publication, June 2004. http://www.strategicstudiesinstitute.army.mil/pdffiles/PUB408.pdf.

Index of Scripture and Ancient Sources

Index of Subjects

Abraham, 35–37
abstinence, 78, 80, 81, 106
Abu Aysheh, Dareen, 103, 118, 142n1
ad bestias, 6, 44, 53
Aegeates, 3
Aetheria, 95
Africa (province of), 56
afterlife, 115
Agathonice, 68, 83, 135n54, 139n53
Agnes, 2, 62–63, 73, 87
Agrippa, 3
Agrippina, 3
Akhmedova, Khapta, 116, 145
al-Akhbar, 118
Alexander (the Syriarch), 44, 45, 85–88, 99
al-Nazar, Fatima Omar Mahmud, 114, 119
al-Qaeda, 112–14
al-Quds, 119
al-Rayasha, Reem Salih (Rim Riashi), 114, 119, 120
al-Sa'adawi, Nawal, 117–18
"altruistic suicide," 115
Alypius, 100
Amat, Jacqueline, 51–52, 56, 57
Ambrose, 59, 74–75, 90, 95
Ananias and Sapphira, 100
andreia (courage), 30–32, 34, 85
Andrew, 3, 5
Annulinus, 63
Antioch, 3, 42–46, 74, 85, 86, 94
Antiochus, 34–35
"anti-romance" narratives, 80
Aquila (judge), 74
Arafat, Yasser, 112, 113
arenas
    animals/beasts used in, 87, 88

feminine modesty and, 39–41, 70–71
martyrs as "spectacles" in, 6, 13, 45, 54
women martyrs in, 16, 39–42, 44–45
Aretē, 94,
Arria, 20, 71
asceticism *(askesis),* 11, 12, 50–51, 53, 78, 91–94, 126n41
Aspasius, 39, 55
athletic imagery, 22
Augustine
    on feminine frailty, 60, 62, 63, 73
    sermons of on Perpetua/Felicia, 59–62, 134n39
    on women as examples, 54, 72, 90
    on women martyrs, 58–59, 95
Avemarie, Friedrich, 7, 8, 25, 26–30, 29, 33, 36
Aymer, Margaret P., 42, 47, 80, 85–87

Babylonian Talmud, 37
baptism
    of Felicitas, 40
    of martyrdom, 45–46
    Paul on, 77
    of Saturus56
    Tertullian on, 78, 90–91
    Thecla and, 3, 5, 21, 85, 88–89, 99
    women teaching on, 80–81, 91
Barnes, Timothy, 51
Barnett, Sarah, 73, 75
Barton, Carlin, 13
Basil, 93, 100
Basilica Maiorum, 52
Basilides, 74, 136n5
Basil of Caesarea, 91, 93
Basil of Seleucia, 80, 90
beasts, arena, 87, 88
beheading, 50, 57, 63